THE HISTORY OF
ENGLISH

THE HISTORY OF
ENGLISH

Ishtla Singh

HODDER
EDUCATION
PART OF HACHETTE UK

First published in Great Britain in 2005 by
Hodder Education, part of Hachette UK
338 Euston Road, London NW1 3BH

http://www.hoddereducation.com

The advice and information in this book are believed to be true and
accurate at the date of going to press, but neither the author nor the publisher
can accept any legal responsibility or liability for any errors or omissions.

British Library Cataloguing in Publication Data
A catalogue record for this book is available from the British Library

Library of Congress Cataloging-in-Publication Data
A catalog record for this book is available from the Library of Congress

ISBN 978 0 340 80695 1

4 5 6 7 8 9 10

Typeset in 11/12 pt. Goudy by Servis Filmsetting Ltd, Manchester
Printed and bound by Replika Press Pvt. Ltd., India

What do you think about this book? Or any other Hodder Education title?
Please send our comments at www.hoddereducation.com

Contents

List of Figures

List of Tables

International Phonetic Alphabet (IPA) Symbols

Examples of pronunciation are based on Received Pronunciation.

Consonants

	Voiceless	Voiced
Fricatives	f = fat, laugh	v = vat, drive
	θ = think, Hathaway	ð = those, scathing
	s = sand, bus	z = zen, haze
	ʃ = shop, hush	ʒ = measure, freesia
	h = hand, horrendous	
Plosives	p = pint, stipend	b = bottle, hubbub
	t = tantrum, hate	d = dentist, hard
	k = kind, coconut	g = guy, anger
Affricates	ʧ = cherry, catch	ʤ = jam, fudge
Nasals		m — mine, hum
		n = naughty, handsome
		ŋ = hang
Liquids		l = leak, light
		r = right, wrought
Glides		j = year, young
		w = well, where

Vowels

Monophthongs

i	= tree, heat	u =	hoot, blue
ɪ	= hit, sizzle	ʊ =	put, could
e	= rain, hate (sometimes a diphthong – see below)	o =	note, Fido (sometimes a diphthong – see below)
ɛ	= death, help	ɔ =	saw, law
æ	= bat, ash	ɒ =	hot, pot
ə (schwa)	= pizza, around	ʌ =	but, Hull
a	= hat (Northern English)	ɑ =	hot (American English)

Diphthongs

eɪ	= rain, hate	əʊ =	note, Fido
aɪ	= hind, mice	aʊ =	proud, plough
ɔɪ	= boil, joy	ɪə =	here, ear
ɛə	= bear, air		

Other symbols

x = as in German ach, Scots loch

ʁ = as in French croissant

ɣ = a fricative sound with the same place of articulation as [g]

ç = as in German ich

y = as in French cru

~ = over a vowel or consonant symbol indicates nasalization

: = after a symbol indicates length (as in [e:])

ē = over a graph indicates length (as in ē)

* = depending on context, denotes either a reconstructed form, or one which is ungrammatical

< = derives from

> = becomes

[ ] = phonetic brackets

/ / = phonemic brackets

Acknowledgements

As always, there are huge numbers of people to whom I owe equally huge thanks for their support and encouragement during the writing of this book: without them, I may well have been history. Thanks to Eva Martinez and Lucy Schiavone at Arnold for their unfailing good cheer and patience; and thanks especially to Eva for her constructive feedback on drafts of the material. Thanks also to Susan Dunsmore, the copy-editor and Alison Kelly, the proof-reader.

Thanks as always to April McMahon and to Barbara Lalla, with both of whom I had my first student encounters with historical linguistics and the history of English, and who will remain on their pedestals forever. Special thanks too to Jennifer Coates, with whom I first co-taught a history of English language course at the University of Surrey Roehampton. Our long, enjoyable hours of putting together the course have inevitably fed into the material and approaches in the following chapters. More special thanks are also due to current colleagues: Clare Lees and Janet Cowen for their very helpful feedback on my forays into Old English and Middle English, and also generally for their continued support, encouragement and friendship. Many thanks too to my students, whose enthusiasm for the subject is always inspiring and wonderful to see; thanks especially to the class who took the history of English course in 2003–04 at King's College London and happily submitted to road-testing material for this book. Particular thanks to Fiona Parsons and Kaleem Ashraf for reading parts of the manuscript and for constructive feedback; and also to Sarah Pace, Elizabeth Drew, Mark Lane and David Campbell, whose constant offers of help and coffee are much appreciated.

Last but never least, to the host of other friends whose support has been unwavering – Judith Broadbent, Pia Pichler, Mari Jones, Devyani Sharma, Michel de Graff, Mark Turner, Bob Mills, Kate Wenham, Wendy Russell Barter, Sarah Barrett Jones – thanks to you all. And of the last group, extremely, hugely special thanks to Devyani Sharma, and also to Andrew Pitman, both of whom did everything to ensure that my life was as easy as possible when I was lost in the book, and also made certain that I came out again.

Introduction

The story of English in a historical context or, to use the well-known phrase, *the history of the English language*, is perhaps one of the few topics of linguistic research which has come to have popular appeal. In Britain, for example, the BBC ran *The Story of English* in 1986, and published an accompanying book of the same name in the same year (second edition 1992); Radio Four broadcast *The Routes of English* between 1999 and 2001 with a derivative television series (and of course, book) following in 2003. Robert Claiborne's *English – Its Life and Times* (1990) continues to be a popular read in its anecdotal approach to linguistic change, and David Crystal's more recent *The Stories of English* (2004), although a more academic treatment of the subject, promises to engender at the very least a similar amount of interest. For many of us, then, *the history of the English language* has been narrated, acted and documentarized into somewhat familiar territory: there are few who do not have at least some inkling of the rags-to-riches story of the language with humble and savage beginnings which grew to become the medium of literary genius for Chaucer, Shakespeare and Milton and, eventually, to conquer the globe.

As every student of the language soon discovers, however, this particular narrative represents only one (romanticized) telling of one particular aspect of a constantly unfolding story that is so enormous in its scope that it is impossible to capture. Like every living language, English is far from being (and indeed, has never been) a monolithic entity changing through the centuries in exactly the same ways, and at the same times, for all of its speakers. In fact, it is only when we begin to deconstruct the notion of what a language actually *is*, that we see there can be no such thing as *the* one history. This becomes clearer, for instance, when we consider the fact that *the English language* is not the holistic entity the phrase implies but instead, a collection of lects which, despite sharing a linguistic ancestry and linguistic properties, vary regionally, socially and, ultimately, individually; which possess in themselves a significant range of registers and styles; which are each constantly undergoing processes of linguistic change and being affected by socio-cultural changes which impact on their users; and which in the past few centuries have significantly increased in number throughout the world.

Such an entity therefore has *histories*, strands of which are typically woven together to create the stories of English which have become well known. The same process has occurred within linguistics itself: texts dealing with the history of English actually construct and narrate *a* history of the language, intertwining various threads to produce a coherent and chronological picture of significant and interesting diachronic change. In case this seems like a patchwork job, we should note that it is in fact no bad thing: given the enormity of the subject matter, and the limited time and resources of researchers, such an approach is the only way in which *any* aspect of English language history can be told. However, as Trudgill and Watts (2002: 1) have pointed out (with particular reference to linguistics texts), an unfortunate consequence has been that histories of the language typically follow much the same pattern in presenting 'a system of self-perpetuating orthodox beliefs and approaches which is passed down from one generation of readers to the next' and are rarely ever questioned.

This is a valid, but not easily resolved criticism. Certain stories of, and approaches to, the historical study of English are now well established in academic curricula and, until this changes, are ignored at an author's peril. In addition, it is not often possible for authors to collate and research enough primary data to begin rewriting histories of the language, and many are therefore often dependent on the resources of their colleagues. However, Trudgill and Watts' point is an important one in that it opens up the issue of whether there are ways in which the re-thinking and/or re-presentation of material can usefully be undertaken to produce, at the very least, variation on the established pattern of English language history.

This seems an appropriate moment at which to point out that this book has no claim to having made significant changes in historical narratives of English: that is a task better left to much more expert authors and researchers. What I have tried to do, however, is consider areas in conventional histories where 'orthodox beliefs' and approaches could make room for updated and/or somewhat different perspectives. This particular aim, plus more practical considerations of word limits, has meant that certain topics which are typically treated in great detail in some texts receive either passing comment, or none at all, here. For example, I have not included discussion of English in America, which is covered in detail in texts such as Baugh and Cable (2002) and Fennell (2001), but have considered instead the establishment of English in other colonial territories. In addition, my inclusion of different perspectives and approaches has of course been necessarily selective, both in terms of the topic I have focused upon and the research which has been represented. Such selection has been partly a matter of personal preference and partly, again, of practicality – there is simply not enough room, or personal lifespan, available to cover every interesting paper on every topic in enough detail.

So to the following chapters. Chapter 1 ('English as a Changing Language') sets the general context for considering linguistic change by looking at some of the major processes and patterns that have affected English throughout the centuries, and continue to do so. Chapter 2 ('Language Families and the Pre-History of English') discusses the work of the nineteenth-century philologers and later linguistic palaeontologists on Proto-Indo-European language and culture and also looks at the current research by McMahon and McMahon into quantitative methods in language classification. Chapters 3 ('Old English, 500–1100'), 4 ('Middle English, 1100–1500') and 5 ('Modern English I: Early Modern English, 1500–1700') outline a social and literary history for each period, and discuss some of the characteristic features of, and changes in, English at each point. Chapter 3, however, contains a particular focus on an Old English feature that typically engenders little discussion in histories of the language; namely the system of gender marking. Following the work of Anglo-Saxon/cultural and literary theory scholars, we explore the notion here that two competing but co-extant systems – grammatical gender and 'natural' gender – could be used in the Old English cultural construction, and reinforcement, of gender roles: a line of enquiry which has clear overlaps with the work of modern feminist linguists. Chapter 4 picks up a well-established debate on Middle English creolization, but attempts to apply a fresh perspective by considering the original hypothesis, as well as its established criticisms, in the light of current theories of creolization. This chapter also looks at certain 'orthodox beliefs' about the use of French and English in England after the Norman Conquest, and presents alternative and more current views that have surfaced in medieval literary scholarship. Chapter 5, which begins our look at English in the modern era, does not focus exclusively (as many histories tend to do – see Trudgill and Watts, 2002: 1–3), on the emergence of standard English but instead, highlights another dimension of the language's life in this period, namely, its establishment in overseas colonies. We consider here the migration of Early Modern varieties of English to Barbados – one of the earliest colonies – and the changes they experienced through contact in this new environment. Chapter 6 ('Modern English II, 1700 onwards') deals with English at a time when, because of its explosive expansion into new territories as well as its burgeoning textual resources, it becomes difficult to establish a chronological and adequate history of all its significant changes and features. Histories of the language, therefore, often choose to devote consideration to changes in the standard form, and to the establishment of English in one important colony, America. While these are of course significant, the eighteenth and nineteenth centuries do see the continued establishment of English-speaking territories around the world: a factor that would establish the pre-conditions for English as a global language in the twentieth and twenty-first centuries. As Trudgill (2002: 44) states, 'after 1700, there is . . . no real excuse for histories of the language which confine themselves to England, or even to England and the United States'. Chapter 6, therefore, attempts to focus on this expansionist dimension of English language history in the modern period, and breaks with the pattern of the previous three by amalgamating three relevant 'snapshots' of English from the eighteenth, nineteenth and twentieth centuries. The first looks at the rise of the prescriptive tradition in the eighteenth century and in particular, at the arguments put forward in Swift's *Proposal* advocating the importance of a 'fixed' and stable form of English for a young and growing empire. The second considers the colonization of Singapore in the second 'imperialist wave' of the 1800s, as well as the linguistic outcome of such contact situations in a look at Singaporean English, in particular, Colloquial Singapore English. Finally, the third 'snapshot' considers some of the predictions made at the end of the twentieth century for the future use of English now that it has been established as a global language.

It is very likely that you will be familiar with some of the material in the following chapters but I hope that their combination – in particular that of established and less well-known perspectives in the field – will offer something new in your journey through the histories of English. What I also hope becomes and will remain clear, is that these histories are far from over, and that many of the changes we observe in early periods recur constantly through time in new environments with new speakers and, indeed, are ongoing now. Histories of the language – of any living language – are therefore constantly unfolding, and it remains to be seen where they may end.

A final word on the material in the following chapters: each contains a number of 'Study Questions' that can be explored either individually or as part of group and seminar discussions. Some questions pertain to areas that I have been unable to devote much or any time to in the main discussion of the relevant chapter, but which are useful for increasing knowledge of a particular topic. All the questions necessitate further research to varying degrees and, where possible, I have included readings which will be helpful in beginning that process. Finally, the discussion of features and changes throughout the book assumes some familiarity with certain linguistic conventions, such as phonetic transcription. A list of the commonly used phonetic and other symbols is given at the beginning of this book.

1 | English as a Changing Language

1.1 Introduction

Chapter 3 begins our historical narrative of English in earnest, looking at the language in a series of snapshots which reveal something of the significant linguistic changes, as well as important socio-historical issues, which have characterized its existence at various points in its history. This approach is neither untried nor untested: texts such as Baugh and Cable (2002), Fennell (2001), Barber (1993), Strang (1970), to name but a few, have shown that this kind of historical (re·)construction effectively conveys both a general sense of linguistic change *through* time and a more specific awareness of significant changes *at* particular times. It is arguable, however, that this framework, in its inevitable representation of a language's history as a chronological series of discrete, significant 'linguistic events', does not wholly capture the dynamic and ongoing nature of linguistic change. For instance, discussions of lexical change which focus on the importance of compounding in Old English (OE), but on borrowing in Middle English (ME) and Early Modern English (EModE), obscure somewhat the continuous importance of both processes throughout all three periods. Similarly, a focus on inflectional change in OE and ME potentially marginalizes its ongoing significance in other periods, as well as creating the impression that it is the only notable dimension of morphosyntactic change. We will therefore attempt here to complement the period-based framework of later chapters by outlining some of the more common changes that have been (and continue to be) significant for English. There are, however, a few provisos to bear in mind before we begin. First, the following sections do not offer a comprehensive discussion of language change. Research in this area covers a great deal of ground: it is approached not only within different theoretical frameworks but also with differing (but related) questions in mind. Studies of language change can (and do) therefore address issues such as the differentiation between internally and externally motivated change (that is, change that occurs and proceeds because of factors either intrinsic to the language system or present in the external social context), or focus on determining the factors that actuate change in the first instance, and facilitate the transmission and retention of some features and the discarding of others. Change can also be measured sociolinguistically, in terms of variables such as age, gender and ethnicity, as well as of attitudes to it. All of these (plus others we have not mentioned) constitute huge areas of research and debate in themselves,[1] and it is impossible to do them all justice in the space of this one chapter. We will therefore confine our discussion to major *processes* of linguistic change, and – given the constraints of space as well as the primary focus of this book – our database deals largely with historical and contemporary examples from English. We begin with processes of sound change.

1.2 Sound Change

As McMahon (1994: 14) points out, *sound change* can actually be viewed as an umbrella term for a wide variety of changes. Its processes may affect single sound segments (vowels or consonants), combinations of sounds such as consonant clusters and diphthongs, prosodic features such as rhythm, stress and intonation, as well as underlie large-scale sound shifts. This section, however, considers some of the more common segmental sound changes and sound shifts which have affected English and continue to do so.

Sound changes which affect segments can either be *conditioned*, meaning that they only occur in specific phonetic environments, or *unconditioned*, meaning that they can affect all occurrences of a particular sound. One regularly occurring type of conditioned change is *assimilation*, a process through which one sound becomes more like another in its environment. Assimilation can be complete, in that the sounds involved in the process become identical (as in Latin *septem* > Italian *sette*), or it can be partial, so that instead they come to share certain features. For example, texts indicate that medial [v] in OE *efen/efn* 'even' was sometimes replaced by nasal [m] through assimilation to final nasal [n], resulting in spellings such as *emn*. A more recent example of partial assimilation can be heard in the pronunciation [hambæg] (*handbag*), which results from the replacement of [n] by bilabial nasal [m], because of conditioning bilabial [b]. In all of these examples, assimilation is considered *anticipatory* or *regressive*, in that the affected sound precedes the conditioning one. In *peseverative* or *progressive* assimilation, however, that order is reversed, as can be seen in the derivation of OE *wull* 'wool' from ancestral Germanic **wulno*.[2] Finally, assimilation can also be distant, in that the conditioning and affected sounds are separated by intervening segments. In Chapter 3, we will look at a particular instance of such assimilation, namely *i-mutation*, which affected certain nouns in the Germanic ancestor of English. Words such as *feet* and *goose* are descended from forms which marked their respective plurals with a final inflectional *–i*, as in **fōt/*fōti* ('foot/feet') and **gōs/*gōsi* ('goose/geese'). Anticipatory but distant assimilation with final *–i* caused fronting of the stem vowel and by the late OE period, this long ō [o:] had been replaced by long front [e:]. Final conditioning *–i* had also been obliterated, hence OE spellings such as *fēt* and *gēs*. A much later shift from [e:] to [i:] (see Chapter 5) resulted in our modern pronunciations of these words.

Dissimilation, the opposite of assimilation, occurs only sporadically in individual words. Examples include the change in Latin *peregrīnus* to Old French *pelerin* (the source of English *pilgrim*), and Old French *purpre* to English *purpel* ('purple') (McMahon, 1994: 15). Another type of segmental sound change is *epenthesis*, a process by which segments are inserted into a phonetic sequence. Epenthetic vowels, for example, typically break up consonant clusters, as in pronunciations such as [fɪlɪm] (*film*) and [arʊm] (*arm*), which are characteristic of Irish English varieties.

Segments can also be sporadically deleted in pronunciation: through *aphaeresis*, an initial segment is lost (as in the loss of word-initial [k] and [g] in words such as *knee* and *gnome*); and in *apocope*, a final vowel (as in modern English *name* [neɪm] from ME [naːmə]). In *syncope*, medial vowels disappear (as in modern English *monks* from OE *munecas*) and in *haplology*, a whole syllable is deleted (as in OE *Englalond* > modern *England*). Finally, through *metathesis*, another sporadic change, adjacent segments are re-ordered, as in OE *brid* and *ācsian* > modern English *bird* and *ask*. Interestingly, a modern pronunciation *aks* (which echoes its OE predecessor) also exists and has come to acquire, in some areas and for some speakers, the status of a shibboleth. It is, for instance, taken to be one of the most characteristic, and most denigrated, features of Black English in America (see Lippi-Green, 1997, for a full discussion).

All the changes considered so far affect segments in the particular environments of individual words. Languages do, however, also experience sound change on a much larger scale, as is evidenced by (largely unconditioned) shifts in the pronunciation of sets of vowels or consonants. In general, such shifts involve segments which share qualities that link them in some way. Thus, the First Germanic Consonant Shift (discussed in Chapter 2) affected sets of voiceless and voiced aspirated and unaspirated plosives in the Germanic ancestor of English; and the Great Vowel Shift (discussed in Chapter 5) occurred with the long vowels of Middle English. The same situation obtains with the two modern shifts we will consider briefly here; namely the Southern Vowel Shift and the North California Vowel Shift in American English.

The Southern Vowel Shift[3] (represented in Figure 1.1), which occurs throughout the Southern States and South Midland areas, essentially involves

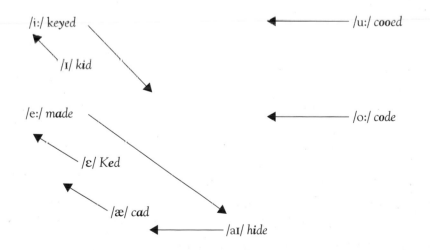

Figure 1.1 The Southern Vowel Shift

change in the pronunciation of short front vowels and of long front and back vowels. Labov (1996: 5) locates the beginning of the shift in the changing pronunciation of words with /aɪ/ such as *hide*, which becomes increasingly monophthongized and fronted. Words with long /e:/ (such as *made*) then move downwards to /aɪ/, and those with /i:/ (as in *keyed*) follow 'a parallel path towards mid-center position' (ibid.). Pronunciation of the short front vowels /ɪ/, /ɛ/ and /æ/ (as in *kid*, *Ked* and *cad*, respectively) shift forward and upward, taking on something of a glide quality so that a word like *bed* (/ɛ/), for example, becomes pronounced like *beyd* [bɛɪd] (Wolfram and Schilling-Estes, 1998: 139). In addition, the long back vowels /u:/ and /o:/ (*cooed* and *code*, respectively) are becoming increasingly fronted. Interestingly, the Southern Shift appears to be proceeding more rapidly in rural regions, possibly because 'Southern speakers in metropolitan areas are influenced by the speech of non-Southerners to a greater degree than are Southerners in rural locales' (ibid.).

The second shift we will illustrate here is the Northern California Vowel Shift, which largely involves the lowering and backing of the short front vowels and the fronting of back vowels. Since this shift has not been diagrammed by its primary researchers (most notably Eckert since the 1990s), I will not attempt to do so here. The description provided in Example 1.1, however, outlines its main movements (note that some changes are in fact conditioned):

Example 1.1 The Northern California Vowel Shift[4]

/ɪ/ think	> /i:/	before /ŋ/
/ɪ/ did	> /ɛ/	before other consonants
/ɛ/ friend	> /æ/	
/ʌ/ fun	> /ɛ/	
/æ/ Brad	> /a/	
/æ/ stand	> diphthong, the first element of which is shifting towards /i:/	before nasals
/u:/ dude	> /iw/	
/ʊ/ brook	>/ʌ/	
/o:/ goes	> diphthong, the first element of which is shifting towards /ɛ/	

Eckert (2002) argues that certain adolescent and pre-teen groups (primarily girls) construct social meaning through such pronunciation shifts, particularly in relation to heterosociability.[5] Eckert cites as an illustration the 'performance' of adolescence by two pre-teens, Trudy and Lillian. Both make use of Shift pronunciations, particularly when talking about defining issues in their developing adolescent persona. Trudy, for example, who appears to be constructing herself as tough Chicana (both behaviourally and linguistically), displays Shift pronunciations such as /ʌ/ > /ɛ/ in words such as *whassup* and *mud* in her narration of a fight for which she was suspended and which she clearly considers a reflection and reinforcement of her persona. Lillian also makes use of Shift pronunciations but this time as part of a construction of '(heterosexual) drama princess'. In a conversation with some male peers about her attending a school dance with Brad, Lillian's pronunciation of her supposed beau's name undergoes the /æ/ > /a/ shift. Eckert (2002: 3) states that 'along with a break in her voice, which highlights the fact there's a call for anger and emotion with Brad, this backed /æ/ draws attention to heightened adolescent style: "I'm **not** going with **Braːd**" '.

At the moment, the continued mapping of such shifts not only allows for the general observation of change in progress but also for speculation on how such changes in pronunciation spread and are retained in speech communities: difficult lines of enquiry in diachronic investigations. Work such as that of Labov and Eckert is therefore invaluable in creating a better understanding of how similar phenomena (such as the Great Vowel Shift) may have unfolded in the past.

1.3 Lexical Change

A colleague of mine was recently puzzling over a student's comment (after a lecture) that 'he was really fat'. He was confused, my colleague said – it seemed rude and inappropriate in the context but yet had been said as if complimentary. Being able to explain that the student had probably used the adjectival approbation *phat* left some of us feeling not too long in the tooth, but our smugness was temporary: the episode was also just one more reminder of how quickly words seem to change and of how difficult it is to keep track of them. Indeed, we are perhaps constantly aware of lexical change – we often see new words in journalistic reporting, for example; the inclusion of new words in dictionaries typically gets a mention in newspapers; and we can each probably remember roughly when certain words started to gain currency. I remember, for example, when loanwords like *glasnost* and *perestroika* began to occur frequently in the news and political debates, and also hearing words such as *minger* ('an unattractive person') and *bootylicious* for the first time.

In the following chapters, we will see that English has constantly undergone lexical change throughout its history; and in this section, we will consider some of the main ways in which this type of change occurs. We should note, however, that the major processes of change do not in fact affect the lexicon in its entirety. For instance, English has gained – and lost – countless nouns, verbs and adjectives over the centuries but prepositions and conjunctions, on the other hand, have remained largely unchanged. In addition, even within word classes open to change, there are many words which seem too well entrenched to be threatened by replacement or loss (cf. the notion of *core vocabulary* in Chapter 2). For example, while it is likely that adjectival terms of approbation (such as *cool, fab, wicked, phat*, and so on) will continue to undergo inter-generational change, or that a new penchant for different foods and lifestyles at any one time will introduce some new loanwords into general usage, it is unlikely that words such as *mother, father, boy, girl, thing, run, jump, have, be, old, nice, soft*, and so on will disappear. The phrase *lexical change* is therefore not as all-encompassing as it might appear.

Its processes, however, are numerous. One, for example, is *word loss*. We can never be sure of exactly how many words have been, and continue to be, dropped from a language but, in the case of English, texts from earlier periods, as well as word lists and dictionaries, indicate that it occurs relatively frequently. Thus, English has lost words such as *deodand* ('something devoted to God'), *blowen* ('prostitute'), *smicker* ('to look amorously or wantonly at someone') and *loitersacke* ('a lazy person'). It goes without saying that many of the words we use in modern English will very likely follow the same route of obsolescence in the future.

While some words fall completely out of use, others sometimes become resurrected and popularized by speakers who apply them to new domains, often with a change of meaning (see Section 1.4). Baugh and Cable (2002: 300, 307), for example, note that the First World War gave popular currency to words and phrases already extant in the language, such as *hand grenade* (first noted in 1661), *dugout* (1886), *machine gun* (1867), *periscope* (1822–34) and *no man's land* (1350).[6] Other examples include *broadcast* (1813), originally an agricultural term for the sowing of seed, and *radiator* (1836), once used as a generic label for anything (or anyone) which radiated heat, light or sound waves.

The revival of 'old' words is not, however, a major source of lexical augmentation in English. Much more productive processes, such as compounding, derivation, clipping, blending and borrowing which, among others, we will discuss below, have been used to great effect by speakers down the generations. Before we look at examples of these, however, it is important to note that once a new word, derived by any process, enters usage, it also comes to be treated like other words of its class. To take but one example, the loan *curry* (from Tamil *kari*), new to English in the late sixteenth century, is now treated like other English nouns: it can be pluralized (*curries*), take adjectival pre-modification (*Andy eats madly hot curries but I like a mild curry*) and be compounded (*are you going to the new curry-house?*). In addition, *curry* has gained an additional function as a verb (first recorded usage 1839), as in *are you going to curry the potatoes?* This process of *conversion*, whereby words come to function in more than one lexical category, is not only a relatively productive process of lexical augmentation for English (consider for example, the use of *drink* as both noun and verb, as in *drink your drink*, or *pretty* as adverb, adjective and noun, as in *that's pretty bad/a pretty picture/come here, my pretty*) but also, in the case of 'new' words, a good indication that the latter have become integrated into the 'native' wordstock.

One of the most productive sources of new words in English has been *compounding*, or the combination of two or more independent words to create a new one. The process can occur with various combinations, such as noun + noun (*bathroom*), adjective + adjective (*bittersweet*), verb + noun (*pickpocket*), adjective + noun (*blackboard*), preposition + noun (*overdose*), preposition + adjective (*ingrown*) and preposition + verb (*overdo*). In general, the final element of a compound functions as its head and determines its part-of-speech classification: thus, *sickroom* (adjective + noun) is a noun, and also denotes a type of room. In a few rare instances, compounds appear to either have equal heads, as in *tragicomic*, *Cadbury-Schweppes* or *Metro-Goldwyn-Mayer* (Trask, 1996: 32), or no explicit head at all. Formations such as *hatchback* or *bigwig* fall into this latter category of *exocentric* compounds, referring neither to specific types of backs nor to huge head-pieces.

As we will see in Chapter 3, compounding in Old English occurred primarily with words that were native to the language, as in *tungol-witega* ('star' + 'sage' = 'astrologer'), *werewulf* ('man' + 'wolf') and *wærloga* ('oath' + 'breaker'; now survives as *warlock*). Later, as English borrowed from other languages, compounding would take place with 'foreign' elements, creating formations that were completely 'non-native' and sometimes hybrid (in that they combined words from different languages). Examples of both types have been particularly prevalent in the domains of science and technology: English has created, for example, *dinosaur* (Greek *dino* 'terrible' + Greek *saur* 'lizard'), *submarine* (Latin *sub* 'under' + Latin *marin-* 'sea'), *telephone* (Greek *tele* 'far' + Greek *phone* 'voice'), *telescope* ('far' + Greek *scope* 'watcher'), *stethoscope* (Greek *stetho* 'breast/chest' + 'watcher') and *bronchoscope* (Greek *broncho* 'windpipe' + 'watcher'). Both *tele* and *scope* have become part of hybrid compounds such as *television* and *flouroscope*, which include words borrowed from Old French (*vision* ultimately from Latin) and Latin (*flouro* from Latin *fluere* 'to flow') respectively. Other, more everyday, hybrids include compounds such as *gentlewoman* and *gentleman*, where the first element ultimately derives from French *gentil* (first recorded as *gentle* in English in 1220), and the second (*man* and *woman* respectively) from the native English wordstock; *coffeehouse* (Arabic *qahwah* + English *house*) and *blue-green* (Old French *bleu* + English *green*).

Although English continues to take in loanwords, compounding has remained a productive source of new words – the twentieth and twenty-first centuries have seen creations such as *air raid*, *blackout*, *warbride* (first recorded during the First World War) and more recently, *software*, *hardware*, *network*, *playstation*, *e-mail*, *e-commerce* (in which the first element, *electronic*, has been shortened), *smartcard*, *bluetooth*, *dead presidents*, *eye candy* and *arm candy*, to name but a few. Some of these, you may have noticed, function as exocentric compounds: *firewall* used in the context of computers describes software which prevents unauthorized access to private data. Similarly, *bluetooth* refers not to an unfortunate result of poor dentistry but to a small radio chip that enables communication between hardware such as computers, printers and mobile phones, and *dead presidents* to an outmoded form of payment in this virtual age – paper currency. Finally, English also has compounds where an element already carries affixation, as in the compound adjectives *long-legged* and *green-eyed*, and the more recent compound nouns *dot-commer* and *ambulance-chaser*.

Derivation through *affixation* – using both native and 'foreign' elements from loanwords – is another major source of new words in English. As Trask (1996: 32–3) points out, however, not all affixes are equally productive. The suffix *–y* for example is used frequently, recently generating nouns such as *fitty* and *hotty*, whereas *–th* (as in *warmth* and *depth*) is not. Some affixes, while not constantly productive, appear to go through cycles of popularity. For instance, the *–wise* of words such as *clockwise* and *otherwise* was 'practically archaic' (Pyles and Algeo,

1982: 267) until about 1940 when it came back into frequent use, generating words such as *moneywise, healthwise, personalitywise* and *weatherwise*. Other affixes are used somewhat sporadically: the somewhat derogatory *–nik* of *beatnik* and *peacenik* (initially introduced via Yiddish words such as *nudnik* and reinforced by Russian *Sputnik*) made a reappearance in 2003 in *noisenik*. Similarly Mc, the prefix traditionally associated with Celtic surnames, has gained an additional and pervasive association with the *McDonald's* company. The latter has led to its limited use in coinages such as *McJob* and *McWorld* (for an example of the latter use, see Nettle and Romaine, 2000; quoted in Chapter 6).

Another source of new words in English is *clipping*, whereby a word is extracted from a longer one with the same meaning, as in *phone* from *telephone*, *photo* from *photograph*, *bra* from *brassiere*, *fridge* from *refrigerator*, *pram* from *perambulator* and *flu* from *influenza*. 'Extractions' such as these are treated as autonomous words and not abbreviations; in this case as fully functional nouns which take (as demonstrated earlier) plural markers and modification and participate in compounding (*loud phones, photo-frames, a very lacy bra, fridge-magnets, noisy prams, bird-flu*). English does also, however, compound clippings which typically do not stand on their own. Thus, we have *sitcom* (*situation* + *comedy*), the parallel *romcom* (*romantic* + *comedy*) and *satnav* (*satellite* + *navigation*), but not *rom or *nav. In addition, we also have instances where a clipped element has been combined with a full word, as in *zitcom* (sitcoms for an adolescent audience), and *frankenfood* (*Frankenstein* + *food*) which has been used as a derogatory term of reference for genetically modified victuals. Again, the clipped *com and *franken are not independent words.

Blending is another process which involves a 'sort of combination of clipping and compounding' (Trask, 1996: 34), as can be seen in *brunch* (*breakfast* + *lunch*), *smog* (*smoke* + *fog*), *motel* (*motor* + *hotel*), *electrocute* (*electricity* + *execute*) and the more recent *Bollywood* (*Bombay* + *Hollywood*). Advertising and certain types of journalistic writing (such as that in entertainment columns) provide fertile ground for blends but since many are often of the moment, they are also short-lived (hence their categorization as *nonce-formations*). Take, for example, the blend *Bennifer*, which was used extensively in 2003 to describe the relationship between Ben Affleck and Jennifer Lopez. *Bennifer*, however, has since gone the way of the actual union. Other possible nonce-formations include blends such as *stalkarazzi* (*stalker* + *paparazzi*) to describe photographers who capture images of celebrities in their private moments, *blobject*, to denote objects with curvilinear design, and the creations recently used by Nissan to advertise their Micra model in Britain, such as *spafe* (*spontaneous* + *safe*), *compacious* (*compact* + *spacious*) and *modtro* (*modern* + *retro*). According to the advertisements, the car was a perfect example of *simpology* (*simple* + *technology*).

New words can also result from *acronyms* and *initialisms*. Trask (1996: 36) draws a distinction between the two, stating that the former label applies to letter sequences which can be pronounced as a word, as in *AIDS* (*Acquired Immuno-Deficiency Syndrome, SARS* (*Severe Acute Respiratory Syndrome*), *yuppie* (possibly derived from <u>y</u>oung <u>u</u>rban <u>p</u>rofessional plus affix) and *snafu* (<u>s</u>ituation <u>n</u>ormal <u>a</u>ll <u>f</u>ucked <u>u</u>p). The sequences in initialisms have to be pronounced individually, as in *FBI* (*Federal Bureau of Investigation*), *FCUK* (*French Connection United Kingdom*), *CD* (*Compact Disc*), *DVD* (*Digital Versatile Disc*) and *USP* (*Unique Selling Point*). Although initialisms do not necessarily sound like words, they, and acronyms, do come to be treated like other lexical items. The examples here, for instance, all (apart from *snafu*) function as nouns: we say that *AIDS is a deadly virus*, we buy *bargain DVDs* and *CDs*, and can wonder about *yuppie-flu*, *FCUK's stock* and the *FBI's tactics*. In addition, many acronyms eventually come to be spelt like other words, possibly as a result of frequent use in writing: witness the representation of *snafu* and *yuppie* above, as well as of *laser* (*light amplification by stimulated emission of radiation*), *radar* (*radio detecting and ranging*), *scuba* (*self-contained underwater breathing apparatus*), *pilon* clauses (*payment in lieu of notice*) in legal documents, and *sinbad* (*single income no bird absolutely desperate*), a term used in nightclub marketing strategies to identify a certain sector of the male clientele.[7]

We also sometimes generate new words from trademark names. *Kleenex, hoover, scotch tape, escalator, aspirin, xerox* and *tipp-ex* are all examples of trade names which now function as common nouns (and in the case of *xerox* and *tipp-ex*, as verbs). *Teflon*, another trademark name, was famously applied adjectivally to Ronald Reagan (the *Teflon President*) in the 1980s to refer to the fact that none of the scandals which occurred during his term in the White House appeared to damage his reputation. More recently, the trademark name *Google* is also becoming used as a verb, with 'people now talk[ing] about "googling" and "being googled"' (*Global English Newsletter*, 25 July 2003). Its creators, however, would prefer that it did not follow the same route as *xerox* and *hoover*.[8]

Another means of deriving new words is through *back-formation*. Here, speakers remove what they think is an affix from a word to create a supposed 'base' form. English, for example, makes productive use of an agentive suffix *–er*, through which we derive nouns from verbs, as in *teach, write, sing, watch* → *teacher, writer, singer* and *watcher*. In its history, English has acquired nouns such as *pedlar* (adaptation of earlier English *pedder*), *editor, sculptor* (Latin loans), *burglar* and *lecher* (from Norman French), which all sound as though they carry final *–er*. Speakers have erroneously assumed, through analogy with the *teach~teacher* paradigm, that they must also derive from a 'base' verb form. We have therefore 'back-formed' the now very frequently used verbs *peddle, edit, sculpt, burgle* and *lech* (the latter of which, incidentally, also functions as a noun, as in *he is a complete lech*). More recent back-formations include the verbs *self-destruct* from *self-destruction* (note that *destruct does not exist as a verb in English), *televise* (< *television*), *baby-sit* (< *baby-sitter*) and *orientate* (< *orientation*) (Trask, 1996: 34–5).

Back-formation is a kind of re-analysis of a word's structure, but Trask (ibid.: 35) argues that *re-analysis* as a process is generally more complex, in that a word is interpreted as having a structure 'which is not historically valid' but which yields 'a new morpheme for use in coining other words'. For example, through analogy with words such as *bilateral, bilingual* and *bifocal*, which contain a prefix *bi*-meaning 'two', *bikini* has wrongly been thought to comprise *bi* + *kini*: an assumption strengthened by the fact that the word does indeed refer to a two-piece costume.

This re-analysis has resulted in the extraction of *kini* and its use in new formations such as *monokini* and more recently *tankini*. In this particular example of re-analysis, *kini* is not treated as an independent word (we have no costumes called **kinis*), and the same applies to morphemes such as *cran-*, *-licious* and *-tastic*, which appear to have been extracted from *cranberry*, *delicious* and *fantastic* and affixed in new creations such as *cranapple* and *cranorange*, *bootylicious* and *babelicious*, as well as *shagtastic* and *funtastic*. In some instances, however, speakers do re-analyse and extract a morpheme which comes to exist as an independent word. This has been the case with *burger* which originates in the word *hamburger*, the label for citizens (and later a type of steak) from Hamburg. Because the first syllable looks like English *ham*, the word has been re-analysed as a compound. *Burger* is therefore now used both autonomously (as in *let's get a burger*) and as the second element in food compounds such as *cheeseburger*, *chickenburger*, *vegeburger*, *fishburger* and even *beefburger*, which explicitly names the meat in the original *hamburger* steak.

Finally, we can also generate new words simply by making them up. Shakespeare, for example, invented *laughable* (1596) and *moonbeam* (1600), Gellet Burgess coined *blurb* (1907) and Lewis Carroll created *chortle* (1872). More recently, *bling* (and *bling bling*), denoting flashy jewellery and first used in the rap of the same name by Cash Money Millionaires, has come into frequent use in British English (and also entered the *Oxford English Dictionary* in 2003), and the success of the *Harry Potter* books has contributed *quidditch*, which now has an entry in the Collins Dictionary and has also been used to name an avenue in a new village – Cambourne – on the outskirts of Cambridge, England.

A major source of new words for English has been *borrowing* from other languages. You will notice in your general reading that quite a few texts comment on the inaccuracy of this label, since speakers of one language do not consent to 'loaning' elements, nor do those of the borrowing language give them back. However, as McMahon (1994: 200) points out, other metaphors such as 'stealing' or 'adoption' seem just as, if not more inappropriate, for this process of transfer. 'Borrowing' therefore continues to be the label of choice in denoting 'the attempted reproduction in one language of patterns previously found in another' (Haugen, 1950: 212; quoted in ibid.).

Borrowing happens in cases of language contact, and is dependent on a measure of bilingualism, which can range from the extremely restricted to the extremely fluent (McMahon, 1994: 200). The higher the number of active bilinguals (who are likely to attain good levels of fluency), the more likely it is that borrowing will take place. In addition, if the level of bilingual competence is high, then this is likely to impact on how borrowings are treated in the recipient language. We will look at this in more detail below.

Lexical borrowing can occur in various domains of usage, at varying levels of intensity and can enter a language through the medium of both speech and writing. Old English, for example, borrowed little from Latin (and mostly in the areas of trade and religion), but Early Modern English took in significantly larger numbers of loans from this language in subjects such as medicine and anatomy. Many of the Old English trade loans are likely to have been initially borrowed in spoken contexts, while those of a theological and scholarly nature may have been first introduced to English audiences through their inclusion in texts. Yet all borrowing appears to have one thing in common, namely the ideal of 'projected gain'. In other words, the borrower must stand to benefit in some way from the transfer of linguistic material (McMahon, 1994: 201). This gain can be both social (users of Language A may perceive Language B as having more social prestige and may thus see the use of B items as improving their own social standing) and practical (users of Language A may have taken on unfamiliar concepts or objects from B's culture and also need the terminology to accompany them). In many cases, both types of gain are intertwined. For example, English today carries a great deal of social prestige in communities around the world, partly because it is the main language of domains with global currency such as science and technology. But the fact that it is the dominant language in such areas also facilitates (and in some perspectives, necessitates) borrowing of relevant English terminology into other languages. In a historically earlier example, a significant proportion of French vocabulary entered Middle English after the Conquest of 1066 in domains such as religion, law, government and administration, warfare, the arts, fashion and even domestic life: areas where French speakers wielded the greatest influence. While some of these borrowings could be classed as having been necessary, in that they named concepts, trends and objects then unfamiliar to the English, they also undoubtedly carried an element of prestige, coming as they did from a language favoured by the upper classes (see Chapter 4 for a more detailed discussion). Similarly, the borrowings from Latin and Greek in the Early Modern period reflect this blend of necessity and prestige – many were argued to fill lexical gaps in English, which did not natively possess appropriate terminology in certain subject areas, but the fact that they were taken from languages with a revered classical tradition could not have been an insignificant consideration.

The last two examples in particular illustrate a common direction of borrowing in unequal relationships of social prestige (as we will see in Chapters 4 and 5, English has had, at different times in its history, less kudos than French and Latin). 'Common', however, does not mean inevitable, and languages do borrow from the less prestigious partner in a contact situation. This is sometimes the case in instances of cultural borrowing (McMahon, 1994: 201), where speakers of a language encounter unfamiliar commodities, concepts or objects which nonetheless become socially salient. Here, the names of such new entities or concepts are incorporated into the borrowing language, even if the donor culture (and language) is not considered 'equal'. Thus, when Germanic tribes first began settling in England in the fifth century, they took place names as well as terms for topographical features from the earlier Celtic inhabitants that they had (somewhat violently) displaced: a pattern that was repeated much later in British history with the colonization of places such as Australia and America where once more, words for local places, flora and fauna were borrowed from the indigenous aboriginal languages that became dispossessed.

In none of these contact situations is there evidence for a high level of fluent bilingualism: the new English-speaking settlers simply and economically took on the designations already in place without necessarily learning the languages of the groups they marginalized. Today, that flow of borrowings from less prestigious to more prestigious languages through restricted bilingualism can be observed in a somewhat different guise; namely, the incorporation of loans (in certain domains) from the languages of certain migrant minority groups to those of established majorities. For example, in the twentieth century, Britain became home to significant numbers of Indian and Pakistani settlers, many of whom successfully established themselves in the restaurant trade. Indian food, as it is generically called, has become a staple of British life and practically every 'Brit' (monolingual English speakers included) knows a *balti* from a *korma* from a *jalfrezi*, or a *samosa* from a *bhaji*. Similarly in American English, the Spanish of migrant Mexican settlers (also in the food trade) has bestowed words such as *enchilada*, *nachos*, *tortilla*, *tostada*, *quesadilla*, *fajita*, *jalapeño* and *taco*, as well as others such as *guacamole* and *tamale*, originally borrowed from Nahuatl (Baugh and Cable, 2002: 303).

Borrowing from less prestigious to more prestigious languages has also historically occurred in situations involving trade. The European trading giants of the fifteenth to the seventeenth centuries such as the Spanish and Portuguese, for example, exchanged goods with the indigenous peoples of areas such as Mexico, the Caribbean and Africa; and given the historical record, are generally unlikely to have viewed the latter as cultural equals. It is therefore possible that for some traders at the very least, bilingualism in the less prestigious tongue was restricted simply to the trading context. In addition, the level of bilingualism may have been extremely low, but this would not have been to the detriment of borrowing: as McMahon (1994: 204) states, for example, in such a context, 'we only need imagine a puzzled Spanish speaker pointing to the object in question with an enquiring look, and receiving the one-word answer *banana* from a co-operative Wolof speaker'. Ultimately, the most important issue in the borrowing context is that 'the borrowing speaker must understand, or believe he understands, the meaning of the items he is learning' (ibid.).

Cultural borrowing, however, does not always have to involve a marked imbalance of social power, and can simply occur as a reflection of the fact that concepts or objects from one culture are being absorbed into another. In this vein, English has taken words such as *déjà vu*, *limousine* and *rotisserie* from French, *yoga*, *mantra*, *tantra* and *chakra* from Sanskrit, *al dente*, *lasagne*, *linguine*, *pizza*, *paparazzi*, and *dolce vita* from Italian, *gestalt*, *abseil*, *zeitgeist*, *quartz*, *nickel*, *seltzer*, *delicatessen*, *pretzel*, *lager*, *poltergeist* and *Bundesbanke* from German, *bonsai*, *kamikaze*, *karaoke*, *karate*, *hibachi*, *sushi*, *samurai* and *sumo* from Japanese, and *chow mein*, *gung-ho*, *dim sum*, *wok*, *t'ai chi* and *feng shui* from Chinese.

It is also worth noting that borrowing between languages can occur because of close and continued cultural and linguistic proximity. For example, many speakers of Colloquial Singaporean English (CSE) are bi- or multi-lingual in other languages such as Hokkien, Mandarin and Malay. Thus, CSE speakers make use of Chinese loans such as *samseng* ('ruffian/gangster'), *ang moh* ('a Caucasian') and *hongbao* (a red packet typically containing money which is distributed at Chinese New Year), as well as of Malay loans such as *hantam* ('to make a wild guess'), *kampong* ('a Malay village, usually of wooden houses on stilts') and *tahan* ('to endure') (Wee, 1998: 181; see Chapter 6). In a similar and earlier parallel, English speakers in the late tenth–early eleventh centuries borrowed a significant number of words from Norse, spoken by Scandinavian settlers in the north and east of England. Close contact, plus the fact that English and Norse appear to have shared a high level of mutual intelligibility, is likely to have facilitated bi-directional borrowing and, as a consequence, many 'everyday' Norse words, such as *sky, skin, husband, egg, ugly, window, scorch*, as well as pronoun forms such as *they, them, their*, became part of 'everyday' English vocabulary. Interestingly, these loans appear to have brought no real social or practical gain: it is likely that neither language was perceived as being more prestigious than the other; and it is unlikely that husbands, ugliness and windows, for example, were new and unfamiliar concepts to the English. This particular process of borrowing did not therefore provide 'elevated' alternatives or fill lexical gaps but instead, provided a number of synonyms at a 'basic' level of English vocabulary which eventually became preferred in usage (see Chapter 3 for more detail).

Another aspect of borrowing we should consider is the question of how speakers go about integrating loanwords into the recipient language. The differences between the phonological and grammatical systems of individual languages can mean that loanwords from one language do not necessarily always 'fit' easily into the patterns of another. Borrowing speakers therefore have a choice in how they treat a loanword: they can either adopt it, keeping its form as close to the original as possible (despite its explicit 'foreignness' to the recipient language), or they can adapt (or nativize) it, making it conform to the patterns of their language. One of the interesting things about these processes is that they are not applied uniformly by speakers. For example, if a loanword is used by speakers fluent in the donor language, they may be more likely to adopt than adapt it. However, speakers who do not have such competence are more likely to resort to adaptation. McMahon (1994: 204–5) provides a neat illustration of this with the pronunciation of the French loan *croissant*. Many English speakers with competence in French will adopt and reproduce the pronunciation of that language, making use of the distinctive uvular trill and final nasalized vowel not characteristic of English pronunciation. However, English speakers unfamiliar with French adapt its pronunciation by substituting native sounds and patterns, producing pronunciations such as [krasɔn] or [kwasɒŋ] and on one occasion that I overheard in a coffee-shop [krɔɪzant], which seems to have been based solely on spelling.

Individual speakers will also shift between adoption and adaptation in pronunciation. This is sometimes dependent on context and self-presentation. For example, if we are trying to impress someone with our knowledge of another culture, or even of another language, we might pepper what we say with adoptions: a friend of mine, for instance, often invites her guests at formal dinner parties to partake of *pain de campagne*, but in more casual circumstances with people she knows well, passes round *bread*.

Speakers will also move between adoption and adaptation if they have knowledge of the patterns of the donor language but are unsure of the preferred option in the recipient language. For example, I first encountered the London station *Theydon Bois* on a London Underground map. Recognizing *bois* as the French word for 'wood/forest', I began to pronounce it [bwã]. Funny looks made me quickly realize that English speakers have actually adapted it, pronouncing it [bɔɪz], and I have since mended my ways. Another current and more widespread example of uncertainty concerns the pronunciation of phrases such as *pain au raisin*. Many English speakers approximate or reproduce the French pronunciation of *pain*, but are not quite sure what to do with *raisin*, which has long been adapted into English. The result is sometimes a rushed hybrid of French (*pain*) and English (*raisin*) pronunciations.

It is worth noting that adaptation is not just phonological, but can also be grammatical, depending on the structure of the recipient language. If the latter grammatically genders its nouns as masculine, feminine or neuter, for example, then borrowed nouns from a non-gendered language have to be accordingly assigned. In such cases, one gender category typically becomes the default option for the borrowing language: French, which today borrows heavily from English, typically treats such loans as masculine (*le weekend, le hamburger*), whereas Australian German (Heath, 1984; cited in McMahon, 1994: 208) tends to assign feminine gender to its borrowings.

Adaptation can sometimes result in grammatical re-analysis. Arabic, for example, contains the singular~plural pair *hashshāsh/hashshāshīn*, –*īn* being the plural suffix. English has borrowed the plural noun and in adapting it, has re-analysed the suffix as part of the stem. Hence Arabic plural *hashshāshīn* has become English singular *assassin*, which is now of course pluralized by the addition of –*s*. Similarly, Hindi plural *chints* has been adapted into English as singular *chintz*, again through the assumption that the plural suffix is in fact part of the stem.

Adaptation can also result in a process known as *calquing*, or loan translation. One of the best-known examples of this process is the translation of English *skyscraper* into different languages, as in French *gratte-ciel*, Spanish *rascacielos* and German *Wolkenkratzer*. Words and phrases in English such as *beergarden* (from German *Biergarten*), *academic freedom* (from German *akademische Freiheit*), *refried beans* (from Spanish *frijoles refritos*), *marriage of convenience* (from French *mariage de convenance*) and *that goes without saying* (from French *ça va sans dire*) are all similar examples.

In cases of contact where there is a high level of fluent bilingualism, speakers may be more likely to adopt rather than adapt loans. If a significant amount of such borrowing takes place, it is highly likely that its impact will extend beyond the lexicon and affect other language components, such as phonology and morphology. Thus, as we will see in Chapter 4, the influx of French loans into Middle English catalysed the emergence of phonemic /v/ in English ([v] had previously been a conditioned allophone of /f/, see Chapter 3) and also introduced new derivational affixes such as –*ese* (from Latin –*ēnsis*) which are still used productively today.

Finally, it is probably worth reiterating that loanwords (in particular adaptations) will be made to conform to certain patterns in the borrowing language. Thus, if English borrows a word which is a verb, or wants to turn a loanword into a verb, then it will be made to fit the language's productive verb paradigms. Such a loan will therefore be prefixed with *to* in the infinitive (as in *to exacerbate*), will take *–s* in the third person singular (*he/she/it exacerbates*) and will take the productive past tense suffix *–ed* (*they exacerbated the situation*). Similarly, nouns borrowed and adapted into English will be treated like other nouns, taking (as we have seen earlier in this section) the regular plural affix *–s* (*rubies*) and the possessive affix *–'s* (*ruby's gleam*), being modified by determiners and adjectives (*the gorgeous ruby*) and partaking in compounding (*ruby-red*).

1.4 Semantic Change

Speakers are very aware of change not only at the lexical level, but also at the level of meaning. The latter, also known as semantic change, can occur relatively quickly and easily, sometimes within a speaker's lifetime. It is therefore one of the types of change which often generates complaint, as some speakers may feel that younger users of a language are moving a word away from its 'true' meaning. You have probably, for example, heard complaints about words such as *gay*, which is remembered by a certain generation of English speakers as being used to mean (before the 1960s) 'bright' or 'cheerful'. I was recently lectured at length about change in the use of *aggravate*, which many speakers now use to mean 'to irritate', or 'to annoy'. This annoyed (aggravated?) my complainant because the word was not being used 'properly' any more: in her view, the 'real' meaning, namely, 'to make worse', was being eroded.

Such changes, however, are not at all unusual and interestingly, nor is the perception that they are somehow 'wrong'. Complaints such as those cited here are typically based on an assumption that each word has only one 'true', inherent meaning (embodied in the word's etymology) and any change is therefore a 'deviation' or 'corruption'. It is, however, arguable that the very nature of meaning itself, and the ways in which speakers work with it, actually create an environment conducive to change. Within this perspective, for example, many modern linguists subscribe to the Saussurean notion that the relationship between a word (or in Saussurean terms, the *signifier*) and the concept it stands for (the *signified*) is ultimately arbitrary and based solely on convention.[9] In other words, there is no 'natural' or intrinsic reason why the word *bag*, for instance, should refer to the entity it does and not to a couch or a type of food. It therefore follows that the signifier and the signified are ultimately independent entities, which implies not only that words generally do not possess inherent 'true' meanings, but also that meaning itself is open to change.

In addition, a signifier can actually be linked to more than one signified. We have so far assumed a one-to-one relationship between a word and a meaning for explanatory convenience (and complainants seem to do the same in assuming that one proper meaning is replaced by one 'wrong' one). The reality, however, is a bit more complex. Words actually tend to be polysemic, which means that they individually carry different meanings or, at the very least, 'a whole range of shades of meaning' (McMahon, 1994: 176). This implies that meaning is a somewhat dynamic and fluid property: words not only gain and lose meanings with relative ease, they also accumulate them. Thus, the relatively new usages of *aggravate* and *gay* have not meant complete loss of their older senses (we still use *aggravate* to mean 'to make worse', as in *if you scratch that rash, you'll aggravate it*; and we still understand the 'cheerful' meaning of phrases such as *with gay abandon*), and they may well go on to gain new ones. Overall, arbitrariness and polysemy appear to be pre-conditions for change in meaning: speakers can make any one or more meanings dominant in usage, and the independence of the signifier and the signified from each other does not essentially restrict such movement.

Other factors that open the way to semantic change include re-interpretation of data in the inter-generational transmission of a native language, changes in the material culture in which a language exists (since meaning appears to be inextricably intertwined with culture), changes in communities of users and the unfolding of processes of change in other components of the language with which meaning is closely linked. With regard to the first point, since carers do not actually transmit a clearly delineated and defined language to children, the latter may sometimes interpret linguistic data in different ways from adult speakers. In some instances, this may lead to semantic change. McMahon (1994: 177) cites as an example the change from Old English *(ge)bēd* 'prayer' > modern *bead*:

> if an adult using a rosary explains to a child that she is *counting her beads*, we have an ambiguous context: the adult intends to convey that she is saying her prayers, but the child sees only the accompanying concrete action involving the movement of the little spheres which make up the rosary. *Bead* consequently alters its sense.

Changes in the material culture can also lead to semantic change in particular words. The word *car* (from Latin *carrus* 'four-wheeled vehicle, chariot') has had a long history in English, initially being used to denote wagons drawn by animals and now, due to technological innovation, vehicles that run on a more metaphorical type of horsepower. The fact that words are adopted into use by various (and numerous) social groups also facilitates meaning change: the use of words such as *mouse, virus, infection, cookie, avatar, windows* and *firewall* in the domain of computers (and presumably, initially by the computer-literate), for example, has given these words additional meanings, many of which have now passed back into general usage. Similarly, words once exclusively used in particular domains are now used with somewhat different meanings by the wider community. *Lure*, for example, which now carries the meaning 'to attract', originated in falconry, where it was used to describe the feathery object a falconer would use to attract a hawk. *Trauma* began as a medical term describing muscular damage, but in general usage now refers to a mental state of upset: we talk of *emotional* and *mental trauma*, and can be *traumatized* by events that do not directly and physically impact on us.

Changes in a language's morphosyntax and lexicon can also be conducive to semantic change. Thus, a change such as *grammaticalization*, in which a 'full' word loses its autonomous status and comes to fulfil a grammatical function (see Section 1.5) typically involves change in meaning, as can be seen in the shift from Latin *passus* 'step' to the French negative adverb *pas*. Similarly, the introduction of loanwords into a language may also catalyze semantic change. If a loan comes to take over the principal meaning of a native word, then speakers may retain the latter and make one of its other meanings more central. The principal meanings of modern *womb*, *stool* and *worm*, for example, were once marginal in their OE antecedents *wambe*, *stōl* and *wyrm*, which carried the central meanings now part of the loans *stomach* (< Old French *estomac*), *throne* (< Old French *trone*) and *dragon* (< Old French *dragon*). Finally, psychological factors may be involved in semantic change (Ullmann, 1962). McMahon (1994: 181) notes that these may underlie both cases of re-interpretation (such as that proposed for *bead*) and instances where taboo topics come to be referred to by euphemistic expressions (see discussion below). As we will see, terms which are introduced as euphemisms often undergo change in meaning: *sleep*, for example, has acquired a particular meaning through its use as a euphemism for a sexual relationship (as in *he's sleeping with Ella*).

We now turn to some of the more common patterns of semantic change. One such is *restriction* (also known as *narrowing* or *specialization*), in which a meaning becomes more specific and thus narrows the application of the word to which it is attached. Thus, Old English *dēor* was once used as a general term of reference for all animals. However, this function was eventually taken over by the Latin loan *animal* and modern *deer* now applies to a specific type of beast. Other cases include OE *mēte*, which was used to refer generally to food, unlike its modern descendant *meat*; OE *hūnd*, once used to denote all canine types but now, in its modern form *hound*, typically applied to the hunting dog; and *liquor* (ME *licour* from French *licur/licour*), at one time a generic term for fluid but now mainly used as a label for a potent brew (examples from Pyles and Algeo, 1982: 244).

Another common change (but less frequent than restriction) is *extension*, also known as *generalization* or *broadening*. Here, a meaning becomes less specific, thus allowing for a broader use of the relevant word. The principal meaning of the word *mill*, for example, used to be contained in its reference to a place for grinding meal (the words *meal* and *mill* are in fact derived from the same source). However, the element of grinding meal appears to have been eroded, and a *mill* is now a place where practically anything can be made – witness *steel mill*, *cotton mill*, *woollen mill* and interestingly *flour mill*, the original product of mill grinding. Similarly, *barn* was once used to denote a storehouse specifically for barley but today can shelter anything from hay to animals to old biplanes; and our word *arrive*, which can now be used to mean 'to come to a place', once had the specific meaning of coming to a shore (the word derives from Vulgar Latin *arripare* (*ad* 'to' + *rīpa* 'shore') (McMahon, 1994: 179)).

Another common process of semantic change is *metaphorization*, through which words take on metaphorical dimensions of meaning in instances where speakers want to establish a link between two concepts. Good examples of this process can be seen in the metaphorical use of body parts in English: we talk about the *foot* of a mountain, the *eye* of a needle, the *mouth* of a river, the *head* of a company and the final *leg* of a race. We also use animal labels metaphorically when we apply them to humans: we call someone who we think is conniving and malicious *catty*, a timid person *mousy* and someone who whizzes from occasion to occasion a social *butterfly*. An apparently sexually predatory male is a *wolf*, while his female counterpart is a *vixen* or *minx*. A deceitful person can be a *worm*, an alluring female a *fox*, and an unlikeable one a *cow*. Food also provides terms which are used metaphorically: we can say that someone is a *honey* or that they are *bananas*, or *a few sandwiches short of a picnic*. In British colloquial usage, *tart* is used to describe (mainly) women thought to have multiple sexual partners, an attractive woman may be termed a bit of *crumpet*, and an extremely good-looking escort (male or female) is eye- or arm- *candy*. In general, metaphorical use tends to give words an additional abstract meaning: a quality evident not only in the examples above but also in the use of words such as *grasp*, which can refer to both a physical and mental hold (as in *she grasped the window frame/I find it hard to grasp what she's saying*), *see* which refers to both a visual and mental process (*he saw them coming up the drive/can you see what he means?*) and *come* and *go*, both of which denote physical movement as well as more mental developments (as in *he is coming here/can you see where I'm coming from?* and *he's going to Newcastle tomorrow/my life is going nowhere*). There is no shortage of such examples in English since, as Trask (1996: 44) notes, 'almost any sort of resemblance, real or imagined, may cause a word to be pressed into service as a metaphor'.

Semantic change may also occur through the metonymic use of words, which is based on a 'real rather than imagined link between concepts' (McMahon, 1994: 183). The most common type of *metonymy* is that in which a term that labels part of an entity comes to represent the whole. For example, an additional (and metonymic) meaning of words such as *crown* and *throne* is 'sovereign' (as in *James Bond is in the service of the Crown* and *who is the power behind the throne?*). Similarly, the places where centres of power are located come to stand for an entire office: a statement from the *White House*, *Downing Street* and *Buckingham Palace* is ultimately, and respectively, from the President of the United States, the British Prime Minister and the British monarch.

Synecdoche is the opposite of part-for-whole metonymy. Here, a term which describes an entity comes to be used to refer to a part. Thus, when we say things like *Rumania and China are finalists in the gymnastics competition*, we are in fact using the names of countries to mean their respective athletes. Similar examples can be seen in Shakespeare plays such as *King Lear*, where titled individuals are referred to by the names of their territories. In Act I, Scene 1 of that play, for instance, the king calls his daughter Regan *wife of Cornwall* (meaning wife of the duke of Cornwall, line 68), rebukes the earl of Kent with *Kent, on thy life, no more!* (line 155) and gives his daughter Cordelia in marriage to the king of France (*Thou hast her, France; let her be thine* (line 262)).

Words and their meanings can also undergo *amelioration* and *pejoration*. In both cases, a meaning change involves a measure of evaluation from speakers, who come to rate the word either positively or negatively. The effects of amelioration, a process through which words gain positive, or better, connotations, can be seen in the change of meaning in *knight*, whose principal meaning has an aristocratic flavour quite distinct from its humble OE ancestor *cniht* 'boy', 'servant'; *praise* 'to value highly', which descends from *appraise* meaning simply 'to put a value on'; and *nice*, which although regarded by many speakers as a 'tired' and 'overused' word, is actually derived from Latin *nescius* meaning 'ignorant' (examples from Pyles and Algeo, 1982: 248). Amelioration can sometimes lead to the weakening of a previously strong negative meaning: words such as *terribly* and *awfully*, for example, can now be used as alternatives to *very*, and in such contexts, carry no hint of negativity (as in *he's terribly good*; *she's awfully pretty*).

Conversely, pejoration involves a downward shift in evaluative attitude, and has occurred in English with words such as *sælig* 'blessed', which is quite different from its modern counterpart *silly*, and *vulgar*, which today has negative associations not present in its earlier use as a term of reference for the commonality (the meaning implied in phrases such as *Vulgar Latin*). *Boor*, which once had the meaning 'peasant', has also undergone pejoration, as has *lewd*, which at one time described the laity (as opposed to the clergy) (examples from Pyles and Algeo, 1982: 247). A recent example of pejoration in Britain can also be seen in the word *asylum*. When the word was first borrowed in the fifteenth century (from French *asyle*), it was used principally to denote a place where religious protection was offered to those accused of crimes or bad debts. By the seventeenth century it was used in reference to any place of refuge, and later in the eighteenth and nineteenth centuries, this particular meaning became restricted to denoting homes for people with ailments. Further restriction made *asylum* the term for places in which people with mental illness were treated and consequently resulted in its pejoration. In fact, as Morrish (2001: 11) points out, the word was so negatively viewed that in the 1970s and 1980s, its use in this sense had become taboo. Interestingly, in a separate development, the seventeenth-century meaning of 'sanctuary' continued in political contexts, as is evident in phrases such as *political asylum*. This was not initially evaluated negatively: during the Cold War, many dissidents, deserters and spies were offered asylum by the West, since 'their own countries wanted them, and so did we' (ibid.). Today, however, many Britons hear the word (in its political sense) in the phrase *asylum seeker* which, given the concerns and fears about immigration frequently voiced in the popular press, has come to have many negative associations. *Asylum* has therefore undergone pejoration in this context as well.

You will notice in other readings that pejoration is often discussed in conjunction with taboo and euphemism. Societies often develop taboos about a range of subjects which are variously seen as unpleasant, embarrassing, dangerous or extremely and uncomfortably powerful, and so avoid naming or talking about them directly. In such cases, euphemistic expressions are used instead, often effecting a semantic change in those terms themselves. Thus, English *Lord*, French *Le Seigneur* and Old English *hælende* 'healer' all allow for indirect reference to God (and in the case of the Old English term, Jesus). Animals such as weasels, wolves and bears have historically been tabooed from direct reference in many Indo-European languages, presumably because of the danger they once presented to human communities. The English word *bear* is thus originally a euphemistic term once used to mean 'brown'. Similarly, many societies have long viewed death as an uncomfortable subject for direct discussion. Some English speakers therefore prefer instead euphemistic expressions such as *passed away* or *gone to sleep*, giving a new meaning to such phrases. Indeed, even the word *undertaker* was originally a euphemistic term with a very different range of meanings from the principal one which it now carries: the word used to mean 'helper', 'contractor', 'publisher' and 'baptismal sponsor', among others (Pyles and Algeo, 1982: 249).

Sometimes euphemistic terms undergo pejoration if the social taboos remain strong, as can be seen in terms for subjects such as excretion. English speakers of particular generations (mine included) feel extremely uncomfortable saying *I'm going to the toilet* and if we have to make such an announcement, are much more likely to use terms such as *loo*, *restroom*, the American-influenced *bathroom*, or (depending on who we are talking to) jokingly childish alternatives such as *I'm going to have a wee/pee*. It is worth noting though that *toilet* is not pejorated for everyone – the majority of my students, who are in their late teens or early twenties, say they have no problem using the word, and typically find euphemisms used by much older generations, such as *little boys'/girls' rooms*, or *spending a penny*, laughable. To return to the cycle of pejoration that such terms can undergo, however, *toilet* was in fact a euphemism (deriving ultimately from French *toile* 'cloth') introduced to replace pejorated terms such as *privy*, *latrine* and *lavatory* – each of which was initially euphemistic (see Pyles and Algeo, 1982: 250).

The fact that people react negatively to certain issues and topics has led, in some instances, to an arguably deliberate use of euphemistic terms. An explicit, current example can be seen in the myriad expressions used by the nuclear industry to detract from the potentially horrific results of their weaponry. This *technostrategic language* (a term used by Cohn, 1987) includes terms such as *clean bombs*, *counter value attacks*, *collateral damage* and *surgically clean strikes*, which all obscure the actual scale of death and destruction. Weapons are also often given either innocuous names which 'domesticate' them, such as *daisy cutter* and *cookie cutter*, or romanticized labels which have connotations of godly (and therefore beneficent) power, such as *Titan* and *Polaris*. In another example of rendering the terrifying more familiar, *silos*, in which launch-ready missiles are kept, are referred to as *Christmas tree farms*. Such terms are not only used within the nuclear industry but have also entered the public consciousness via diffusion through the media. Their positive effect, however, remains questionable: during the 2003 furor over war in Iraq, for example, letters to newspapers such as the *London Metro* frequently complained that the use of euphemistic expressions allowed governments to hide from the grim consequences of war.

1.5 Morphological Change

Changes in morphology essentially means changes in word structure. However, since words are ultimately made up of sounds and in themselves make up utterances, a language's morphology is integrated with its phonology and syntax, and can be affected by changes they undergo. For instance, the process of *i*-mutation (see Section 1.2) for plural formation was a phonologically conditioned change, but the loss of conditioning –*i* (and hence of the process) has simply rendered words such as *feet* and *geese* morphologically 'irregular'. As an example of syntactic change influencing morphology, consider that a 'full' verb (that is, one which carries meaning and can be used as a main verb) can eventually become a verbal affix and hence, part of a language's morphology. Thus, the endings *–ás* and *–án* in Spanish verb forms, such as *tu comprarás* 'you will buy' and *ellos comprarán* 'they will buy', have actually developed from ancestral Latin *habēre* 'to have' (a full verb). We will revisit this process of grammaticalization in more detail in Section 1.6 but let us now turn our attention to some of the major ways in which morphological change can occur.

Re-analysis of a word's structure can result in changed morphological forms. We have already seen an example of this in Section 1.3 with the re-analysis of *bikini*. Re-analysis has also led to the development of *umpire* from *noumpere* and *apron* from *napron* (consider related *napkin*, *napery*): it seems that (Middle English) speakers analysed the initial nasal as part of a preceding indefinite article *a(n)*. The same kind of re-analysis, but with the opposite effect, gave English *nickname* from *(an) ekename* and *newt* from *(an) ewt*.

A great deal of morphological change appears to occur through the operation of *analogy*, a concept initially devised and explored in diachronic studies of sound change undertaken by the nineteenth-century scholars known as the Neogrammarians. A principle of the Neogrammarian approach was that certain sound changes operated with 'blind necessity' (McMahon, 1994: 20); that is, they occurred because they were inevitable and despite any consequences they might incur for the rest of the grammatical system. Thus, a sound change could result in the creation of opaque irregularities that left no trace of the fact that they were once the product of a regular process: witness again the example of *i*-mutated plurals. The Neogrammarians believed, however, that analogy would come into play after a sound change had operated, making irregular forms conform to a regular pattern. Thus, although other nouns, such as *book* (OE *bōc*) should have historically followed the *i* mutation pattern of *feet*, *geese* and others, they instead conformed to the more widespread one of forming plurals with *–s*, in this case giving modern English *books* and not, as might be expected, *beek*. We can see from this example, however, that the operation of analogy is in itself sporadic – if it were not, we would now have *foots* and *gooses*. This interaction between sound change and analogy is neatly summed up in Sturtevant's Paradox: sound change is regular but creates irregularity, whereas analogy is irregular but creates regularity. We will return to this below.

Analogy has also been invoked as a general explanatory principle in morphological change. One of its incarnations is *analogical extension*, which involves 'the generalisation of a morpheme or relation which already exists in the language into new situations or forms' (McMahon, 1994: 71). A typical example of this process lies in an area of English morphology that we have already mentioned a few times, namely the formation of the plural. As we will see in Chapter 3, Old English nouns, which were gendered, belonged to different inflectional paradigms which carried information on case and number. Thus, the plural form of a word like *stone* (OE *stān*; masculine gender) was *stānas* when used as a subject and *stānum* when an indirect object. On the other hand, the plural form of *ship* (OE *scip*; neuter gender) when in subject position was *scipu* but *scipa* when used in the possessive. Such inflectional declensions were substantially reduced by the end of the ME period (see Chapter 4). However, the *–as* ending of nouns such as *stānas* was retained, later becoming *–es/–s*. This inflection was initially re-interpreted as the only plural suffix for nouns belonging to the same class as *stān* and then, through analogical extension, was generalized (in the form *–es/–s*) to other noun classes which had originally made use of different inflectional paradigms (such as *scip*). It is now considered the characteristic, regular plural marker for nouns in English, and continues to be extended to most new additions, either made up or borrowed, as we saw in Section 1.3.

Cases of analogical extension are sometimes described in terms of *proportional analogy*, or *four-part analogy*, since speakers appear to invoke a kind of four-element equation in their analogical argument. If a child, for example, produces a plural such as *mouses* and is corrected, she will typically defend her choice with a proportional argument: if the plural of *house* is *houses*, then that of *mouse* must be *mouses*. If you need further convincing, think about what the plural of a word like *mongoose* might be (without looking at what a dictionary suggests!). You will probably initially focus on the second syllable and think that if the plural of *goose* is *geese*, then more than one *mongoose* has got to be a gaggle of *mongeese*. But the fact that *mongoose* is a different lexical (and physical) entity from *goose* may give you pause for thought, and your second suggestion will be based on comparison with other plural forms that you are familiar with in English: could it be *mongooses* in analogy with other *–s* plurals, or perhaps even an unmarked plural like *deer* or *sheep*? The point is that in each case, you will draw a proportional analogy with *singular : plural* forms that you already know and try out those patterns in coming to a decision. Incidentally, dictionaries appear to generally recommend *mongooses*, although two wits on the Wikipedia message board[10] individually suggest alternatives such as *polygoose* (re-analysing the first syllable of *mongoose* as *mono* 'one') and using phrases along the lines of 'a mongoose, and while you're at it, send me a second mongoose'.

Analogical extension has also occurred throughout English's history with verbs. The language has long had classes of strong verbs, which generate preterite and past participle forms through vowel change (as in *sing : sang : sung*) and weak verbs, which do so with an inflectional *–ed* suffix (as in *walk : walked : walked*) (see Chapter 3). The majority of verbs have historically belonged to the weak verb class, and throughout the centuries, some originally strong verbs (such as *help* and *creep*) have moved to using the *–ed* inflection (see Chapter 4). Just as analogical extension of plural *–s* for new nouns continues today, so too does the use of *–ed* for new verbs: witness *she texted me yesterday*; *I've e-mailed my CV*; *you know when you've been tangoed*!

As the *mongoose* example shows, analogical extension does not necessarily involve comparison with dominant, regular patterns. The analogy that generates *mongeese*, for example, is based on a method of plural formation that is no longer productive in English. Trask (1996: 106) gives a nice example of extension based on a small class of nouns in English derived from Latin and typically used with Latin plurals, such as *cactus : cacti, succubus : succubi, radius : radii*. English also has a singular noun *octopus*, which looks like a Latin derivative (given the *–us* ending) but which is in fact a Greek loanword. If we were to use the Greek plural, we would say *octopodes*, but (putting aside the occurrence of regular *octopuses*) many English speakers, through analogy with the Latin forms, actually produce *octopi*, making use of a generally unproductive pattern. Similarly, although the majority of verbs in English conform to the –*ed* past tense and past participle pattern, there have been cases where originally weak verbs have developed strong forms. A famous example is *dive*, originally a weak verb (*dive : dived*) but which, through analogy with the strong verb *drive* (*drive : drove*) developed a preterite form *dove* that is still in use. As a result of the same kind of analogy, English speakers sometimes use *brung* 'brought' (on the pattern of *sung*) and jokingly, *thunk* 'thought' (on the pattern of *sunk*).

Finally, in the context of our examples, we should again note the truism that analogy creates regularity, but is in fact irregular in its application. Despite the productivity of –*s* plurals and *ed* past forms, English still retains nouns and verbs which not only do not conform to this pattern, but also display no intention of doing so: we do not seem to be in any hurry to get rid of plural *teeth*, *oxen* and *sheep*, nor of preterite *broadcast, swam* and *bought*. It is difficult to say for certain, but it is possible that such 'fossilizations' remain because of literacy, which tends to inhibit analogical change. Written conventions of English preserve these as 'correct', which may well reinforce their use in spoken language, particularly from carers to children, who will correct analogical forms such as *tooths* and *buyed*.

Another type of analogical process is *analogical levelling*, which essentially affects paradigms of inflected words (such as the Old English nouns, verbs and adjectives we will look at in Chapter 3). In instances where sound changes affect paradigm forms, creating allomorphs (or morphological alternations in what is essentially the same word), analogical levelling may eventually 'level out' the resulting diversity. As an example, consider the Old English forms of the verb 'to choose' in Example 1.2 which, through the application of various sound changes, constitute an irregular paradigm. In modern English, the irregularity has been levelled out by the application of one alternant throughout, making the relationship between forms in the paradigm much more transparent.

Example 1.2 Verb paradigms for 'to choose' in Old English and Modern English

	Old English	Modern English
infinitive *to choose*	cēo[z]an	choo[z]e
past singular *I chose*	cēa[s]	cho[z]e
past plural *we chose*	cu[r]on	cho[z]e
past participle *you have chosen*	(ge-)co[r]en	cho[z]en

Both extension and levelling are considered systematic and regular types of analogy: they occur quite frequently, operate in the contexts of established patterns and paradigms, and can affect a fair number of forms. Analogy can, however, also be applied sporadically, as can be seen in instances of back-formation, *contamination* and *folk etymology*. As we noted in Section 1.3, back-formation is not a regularly productive process of word-formation, but it does occur on the basis of analogical patterns. Thus, we now have a verb *laze*, back-formed from the adjective *lazy*, in analogy with the English pattern *verb + –y = adjective* (as in *scare + –y = scary*). In cases of contamination, the form of a word is influenced by others, typically within the same semantic field. McMahon (1994: 75) notes that contamination occurs quite frequently in words which appear in lists, such as numerals. Thus, English *four* should historically have developed with an initial [k], but has been influenced by neighbouring *five*. In addition, contamination can sometimes occur bi-directionally: Old French *citeain* and *deinzein* ('inhabitant') influenced each other to become *citizein* and *denizein* in the French spoken in England during the Middle English period (see Chapter 4). Finally, in folk etymology, a word or phrase which seems 'opaque to the native speaker, often because it has a foreign origin, is reinterpreted, or has its morphological boundaries shifted so that its semantic and morphological structures coincide, making it transparent' (McMahon, 1994: 75–6). Thus, Italian *girasole* 'sunflower' has been re-interpreted as *Jerusalem artichoke* (Pyles and Algeo, 1982: 283) and French *asparagus* as English *sparrow grass*. In a personal example, my name was once re-interpreted into a more English-sounding alternative early in my first job, leading to messages being left for a mysterious *Esther Thing*.

Finally, we should consider change in the overall character of a language's morphology, or change in morphological type. Early nineteenth-century linguists such as Schlegel and Von Humboldt (see Chapter 2) proposed a classification of languages based on the intrinsic characteristics of their morphological systems, or the creation of morphological typologies. Three main morphological types of language were recognized: *isolating*, *agglutinating* and *inflecting*. In isolating, or *analytical*, languages such as Chinese and Vietnamese, each lexical or grammatical unit of information is carried by an individual morph, without affixation or modification, as in Example 1.3:

Example 1.3 Vietnamese

khi	tôi	dến	nhà	bạn	tôi,	chúng	tôi	bắt dầu	làm	bài
when	I	come	house	friend	I	plural	I	begin	do	lesson

'when I arrived at my friend's house, we began to do lessons'

(from Trask, 1996: 126)

In agglutinating languages like Turkish, Basque and Swahili, morphs are 'stuck' together to form words. Each morph has a particular function, but generally remains consistent in form, and although operating in conjunction with others, retains its transparency. Consider the morphemes from Turkish in Example 1.4:

Example 1.4 Turkish

Morpheme	{HOUSE}		{plural}		{possessive}	
Morph:	ev	+	ler			= evler 'houses'
:	ev			+	im	= evim 'my house'
:	ev	+	ler	+	im	= evlerim 'my houses'

(after Trask, 1996: 126)

In inflecting, or *synthetic*, languages like Latin, Greek and Old English, morphs may carry more than one unit of lexical/grammatical information. For example, in an Old English form such as *scipu*, final *–u* indicates that the noun (*scip*) has neuter gender, is plural and is functioning in either nominative or accusative case. Similarly, the *–eð* in OE *fereð* indicates that the verb form ('carry') is third person, singular and present indicative (see Chapter 3).

Not all languages actually fit easily into one of these three categories – for example, English has isolating/analytic characteristics (*I will see you tomorrow*), as well as those indicative of agglutinating (*tree* + *s* {plural} = *trees*) and inflectional/synthetic (*sleeps*= third person singular present indicative) natures. Nevertheless, it seems that many languages display a tendency towards one morphological type more than another, and can therefore be approximately classified as such.

Nineteenth-century linguists such as Schleicher assumed that languages naturally 'progressed' through these morphological types in a cyclic process of isolating to agglutinating to inflecting. In this perspective, the attainment of a synthetic state was the ultimate, ideal achievement. However, for some languages, the only movement possible from that high point was 'downward', and an inflecting language was likely to eventually find itself moving back to an analytic state: a process that was viewed as 'decline' and 'decay'. For Schleicher, the rate of decay was dependent on the extent to which speakers participated in 'historical life' or civilization. In essence, the more 'civilized' the people, the more advanced the linguistic 'decay'. Thus if a language did not consistently undergo inflectional decline, then it belonged to a people 'unfitted for historical life' who could only 'undergo retrogression, even extinction' (Schleicher, 1864, cited in McMahon, 1994: 322). Paradoxically, then, although a language may have attained synthetic perfection, its retention signalled its (and its speakers') impending demise.

Linguists such as Schleicher were right in assuming that typological change does happen, and that it could occur in particular directions, such as isolating to agglutinating. Trask (1996: 127) points out that classical Chinese appears to have been an isolating language but modern Chinese shows agglutinative tendencies by using morphs as affixes, such as the plural suffix *–men*, as in *wǒ* 'I', *wǒmen* 'we'; *tā* 'he', 'she', *tāmen* 'they'. However, such movement is neither inevitable nor uni-directional. 'The isolating languages of West Africa', for example, seem to have experienced the reverse movement, appearing to have descended from an agglutinating ancestor (ibid.). English shows signs of having descended from a highly inflecting language but, as we have seen, has increasingly developed both agglutinating and analytic tendencies. In addition, ideas of linguistic decay and perfection are no longer accepted in modern linguistics: such notions imply that certain characteristics, and by extension certain languages, are better than others, and no sensible, objective criteria for such evaluations exist. Finally, we now know that a language's morphological type – part of its basic system – signals neither its current vitality nor its impending demise. A language will not inevitably become extinct if it remains inflected; its potential for loss is instead directly linked to socio-political factors.

As McMahon (1994: 322) points out, it is true that speakers of an obsolescing language will indeed typically describe it as 'inferior' or as not as 'perfect' as the one replacing it, but these are the result of socio-political issues and are nothing to do with the structure of the language itself.

As a final point, we should note that change in morphological type can occur because of language contact or simply through the internal processes of intergenerational transmission. Thus, modern Armenian, descended from an earlier inflecting system, is mainly agglutinating, very possibly a result of centuries of contact with Turkish. On the other hand, as we will see in Chapter 3, the synthetic system of Old English appears to have been undergoing change without any outside help, and was well on its way to developing characteristics of other morphological types before significant periods of contact got underway.

1.6 Syntactic Change

McMahon (1994: 107–8) points out that work on diachronic syntactic change did not begin in earnest until the 1960s, with the establishment of the Generativist school. Since then, it has engendered a substantial field of research which we are unable to explore here. This section will therefore focus, like its preceding fellows, on processes and patterns of change which have affected English throughout its history.

Re-analysis, a process which we have already encountered as contributory to change in a language's wordstock as well as in its semantic and morphological systems, is also sometimes influential in syntactic change. An excellent example of this can be seen in one explanation of the development of English modals (cf. Lightfoot, 1979). Lightfoot argues that our modern modals (*may, might, can, could, will, would, will, should, must*) are descended from a set of Old English full verbs, or pre-modals. Between the Old English and end of the Middle English periods, however, these pre-modals became increasingly characterized by properties which set them apart from other verbs. For example, they could not be followed by an inflected infinitive (as in modern *I must to go*), and lost the ability to take a nominal object (*she could piano*). Pre-modal forms such as *sculde* and *wolde*, which had once signalled past-time reference, stopped doing so and all the pre-modal verbs retained an earlier OE characteristic of not carrying present-tense inflections.

The verbs that would eventually yield our modern modals therefore came to behave like an exceptional and distinct type by the sixteenth century. Lightfoot proposes that as a result, speakers re-analysed them as members of a new modal category. This re-classification is evidenced by certain structural properties: modals do not have infinitive (*to will*) nor non-finite forms (*they musted gone*); only modals (and auxiliary *be, have, do*) can invert with subjects in the formation of questions (*can she breathe?, is she breathing?* vs. *breathe she?*) and take a following negative marker (*he could not say that, I am not pleased* vs. *he speed not*).

Change in word order also constitutes syntactic change. Essentially, languages can be classified according to word-order types (or word-order typologies), which are partly based on the fundamental, unmarked (meaning typical and ideally, most frequently occurring) order of three constituents S(ubject), V(erb), O(bject). Thus, if a language frequently features unmarked structures such as *Jeannie* (S) *saw* (V) *a ghost* (O), then it will be categorized as SVO. On the other hand, if its typical sentence structure is more like *Jeannie a ghost saw*, then it will be termed SOV. We should note here that the three categories can actually serve as labels for much bigger constituents, as in Example 1.5:

Example 1.5 SVO constituents
that so-called sweet old lady   *tripped up*   *the girl who was walking past her house.*
S   V   O

In addition, a category such as O can include constituents that are not necessarily objects of the verb: consider sentences in English (an SVO language) such as *she is in the garden* (subject complement) or *she dances every night* (adverbial). In fact, because of this, some typological descriptions (such as those used in Fennell, 2001) replace O with X, but we will continue to use O here with the general understanding that S, V and O are a convenient shorthand for representing the order of constituents within a sentence.

The ordering of S, V and O are not the only salient characteristics of a word-order typology. The ordering of the three appears to be accompanied by certain structural properties – a proposal first made by Greenberg in 1963. Indeed, Greenberg found that languages in which V precedes O shared certain properties, as did those in which O precedes V – a finding which has been supported by later research. As a result, the six syntactic permutations (SVO, OVS, SOV, VSO, VOS, OSV) have been reduced to two general ones – VO and OV – with each carrying particular implicational properties (meaning that the presence of one property in a language implies the presence of another). The properties typically cited in word-order typologies are (1) the position of adjectives (A) relative to nouns (N); and (2) the position of genitives (G) relative to nouns (N). In VO languages, the noun tends to come first, yielding NA and NG orders, while the opposite holds in OV languages, which have AN and GN structures.

Some languages show a high degree of conformity to one of these patterns, and are thus said to exhibit *typological harmony*. However, there are quite a few that do not: English, for example, is VO but does not possess expected NA order (*a tortoiseshell cat*, not **a cat tortoiseshell*). Trask (1996: 148) also points out that Basque 'is a perfect OV language' except for the fact that its adjectives follow nouns rather than precede them, and Persian carries all the properties of a VO language apart from the fact that its objects precede verbs.

Through time, languages can move, or *drift* (see McMahon, 1994: Chapter 6) from one basic type to another, undergoing a series of interconnected changes in certain properties in the process. Indeed, it has been argued that languages which do not exhibit typological harmony are in a state of transition between the two types (see Lehmann, 1973, for instance). This process of drift has been postulated for the historical development of English from OV to VO. There is some textual evidence that the ancestor of English, North West Germanic, was essentially an

OV language: consider the data in Example 1.6 from Lass (1994: 219–20), taken from runic inscriptions of the third–seventh centuries:

Example 1.6 OV examples

(i) <u>ek Hlewagastiz Holtijaz</u>   <u>horna</u>   <u>tawido</u>

  S   O   V

'I, H.H. [this] horn made'

(ii) [me]z Woduride   <u>staina</u>   <u>þrijoz dohtriz</u>   <u>dalidum</u>

      O   S   V

'for me, W., [this stone] three daughters made

However, the evidence available for North West Germanic indicates a lack of typological harmony: nouns preceded adjectives and genitives could occur both before or after nouns, depending on the class of the latter. In addition, it seems that speakers of the language also made use of SVO order. All in all, the available evidence seems to provide a snapshot of a language undergoing typological change from OV to VO.

Although we do not have textual evidence from the early part of the period (see Chapter 3), this direction of change appears to have continued throughout Old English. Data from the eighth century (so far, the earliest available) indicate that the language was very similar to its Germanic ancestor, making frequent use of OV patterns (as in *Æðred me ah Eanred mec agrof* 'Æthred me owns; Eanred me carved'; inscription on a gold ring from Lancashire; in Trask (1996: 149)), but also of VO structures. By the later years of the period (which are much better documented), VO had become the norm, with OV becoming restricted to use in certain structures, such as when the main verb took an object pronoun (as in *hē hine geseah* 'he him saw' > 'he saw him'), or in subordinate clauses, as in *God geseah ðā þæt hit gōd wæs* ('God saw that it good was'). By the late twelfth century, VO had become established as the basic, unmarked word order for English. Today, English conforms in large part to the properties of VO languages, apart from adjective placement. Oddly enough, this was 'out of line in the earlier OV stage and is again out of line today' (ibid.: 150).

The final process of change we shall consider here is grammaticalization, a phenomenon first defined by Meillet (1912: 131) as 'le passage d'un mot autonome au rôle d'élément grammatical' ('the shift of an independent word to the status of a grammatical element'). Thus, 'full' nouns, verbs or adjectives can become part of grammatical categories such as auxiliaries, prepositions and adverbs and in turn, can be further grammaticalized into affixes. Such changes of category are typically accompanied by other developments, such as a change in phonological form as well as what is sometimes called 'semantic bleaching'. Grammaticalization is therefore, as McMahon (1994: 160) points out, 'the cross-componential change *par excellence*' in that it involves syntax, morphology, phonology and semantics. We will, however, follow McMahon in discussing it under syntactic change since it was first discovered through word-order typological surveys such as that of Greenberg.

Good examples of grammaticalization in English can be found in the latter's system of affixes, where a number of prefixes and suffixes have developed out of originally independent words which have since undergone both phonological reduction and semantic change. The prefix a–, for example, which is now opaquely fossilized in words such as *aside, alive* and *aboard* (and transparently in *a-hunting* and *a-shooting*), is derived from the preposition *on*. Perhaps one of the most famous examples of a grammaticalized English suffix is *–ly*, found today in adjectives such as *womanly* and *homely*, and adverbs such as *quickly* and *quietly*. The suffix ultimately derives from an OE noun *līc*, meaning 'body'. This noun began to be used in the formation of adjectives, initially becoming a comparatively unstressed *lic*, and in the process underwent a measure of semantic bleaching, coming to mean 'having the body or appearance of'. Thus OE *cræftlic* meant something like 'having the appearance of skill' (> 'skilful'). OE regularly derived adverbs from adjectives by the addition of *–e* (as in *riht* 'right' > *rihte* 'rightly'), and this pattern was also applied to *–lic* forms. Thus, the adverbial counterpart of an adjective such as *cræftlic* was *cræftlice* ('skilfully') (examples from Pyles and Algeo, 1982: 264). During the Middle English period, both forms of the suffix (spelt *lich* and *liche*, respectively) underwent further phonological reduction as a result of sound changes to unstressed syllables (see Chapter 4), and fell together as the *–li/–ly* inherited by modern English. This suffix, which is still productive in the derivation of adjectives and adverbs, has not only been extensively phonologically reduced but also fully semantically bleached: its only 'meaning' lies in its grammatical function. Its development from *līc* can therefore be considered a paradigm case of grammaticalization as defined by Meillet (1912). Interestingly, however, the grammaticalization of *–ly* has been accompanied by a parallel development of *līc* to modern *like* which, much like their OE predecessors using *lic*, modern English speakers affix to nouns to form adjectives, as in *human-like* and *god-like* (note that these are not identical in meaning to *humanly* and *godly*).

Like has also undergone a different direction of development, becoming used (primarily in speech) as a discourse marker (as in *there were* **like** *people blocking, you know?*) and a quotative complementizer (*Maya's* **like**, '*Kim come over here and be with me and Brett*'): changes that have been attributed to another distinct process of grammaticalization (examples and argument from Romaine and Lange, 1991: 240–77). As we will see, Romaine and Lange's explanation of grammaticalization in this instance does not conform to the paradigm case we have just outlined, but a brief discussion is included here to illustrate the fact that the process is not always viewed as a primarily syntactic one.

Discourse markers are 'particles which are used to focus on or organize discourse structure' (Romaine and Lange, 1991: 254). In American English usage, *like* tends to be placed before the part of a narrative that is intended to receive the most focus: thus, in the example above, and in utterances such as *she started to* **like** *really go for him* (from ibid.: 258), the speaker means to emphasize the respective issues of being blocked by people and genuinely falling for someone. The use of *like* as a quotative complementizer also has a focusing function, in that it typically introduces and frames *constructed speech* or *constructed dialogue*. The latter terms are used as more accurate descriptions of what is more familiarly known as *reported speech* which, in writing, is typically signalled by a framing clause followed by a statement in quotation marks, as in *John said, 'I'm going to kill him when I see him.'* As Romaine and Lange (ibid.: 243) point out, in such cases, the 'speech which is reported is someone's reconstruction of the speech event. It is a recollection which is more often accurate in general meaning than in precise wording.' In dialogue which contains constructed speech, the latter is typically 'the most focused part of the narrative', so that in utterances such as *I'm like, 'just how crazy are you?'*, *like* therefore directs our focus to the information the speaker wants to emphasize.

Romaine and Lange argue on the basis of their data that modern English speakers frame constructed dialogue in different ways, using verbs such as *said* (seen above), *go* (as in *she goes, 'Mom wants to talk to you'*) and *be* + *like* (as in *Maya's like, 'Kim, come over here . . .'*). Each appears to have particular functions, but the one which we will exemplify briefly here is *be* + *like*. Speakers in Romaine and Lange's database use this as a quotative complementizer when (re-)constructing their own speech or thoughts, as distinct from the speech of others, which is signalled by verbs such as *tell* or *go* (see Example 1.7).

Example 1.7 Like as a quotative complementizer
She **told** me that we put the story on the front page of the newspaper. I'm **like**, 'I know.'

(Romaine and Lange, 1991: 247)

The fact that *be* + *like* can be used to frame constructions of thought is particularly evident in speech such as that in Example 1.8:

Example 1.8 Like to frame constructions of thought
And Scott came up to the back door. He scared me half to death. He comes up and you know he looked pretty big. I was lying down on the couch, watching TV, and you know I could just see the outline of the body, and was **like** 'Waaaaaaaaaaa.'

(ibid.)

It is very unlikely that we would interpret this as meaning that the speaker actually made the noise represented by 'Waaaaaaaaaaa'. Instead, it seems more likely that this expresses his feeling of fear at the time. However, if he had framed it with *and I went . . .*, we would be more inclined to assume that he actually did scream. Another noteworthy aspect of the use of *be* + *like* as quotative complementizer is the fact that, in certain contexts, it allows the speaker reduced responsibility for the constructed dialogue that it introduces. Consider the excerpt in Example 1.9:

Example 1.9 Like and unspoken evaluation
She goes, 'Mom wants to talk to you'. It's **like**, 'hah, hah. You're about to get in trouble.'

(ibid.: 247)

Here, a son is recounting to his mother a conversation with his sister. He reconstructs what the latter has actually said (introduced by *she goes*), but also introduces an unspoken evaluation framed by *it's like*:

> It is as if the remark introduced by *it's like* is intended as a gloss of the sister's tone of voice, or what she might have liked to have said . . . Thus, the exchange might be interpreted as: 'I am reporting that my sister told me that you want to talk to me and she led me to believe that I was about to get in trouble.' However, the use of *like* does not commit him to the actual occurrence of what is reported . . . The son does not have the right to speak directly as and for his sister, in the presence of their mother, . . . particularly if this was not what she said or wanted the daughter to convey, but rather his own inference.

(ibid.: 248)

Romaine and Lange hypothesize that the use of *like* as a discourse marker and as quotative complementizer emerged from the grammaticalization of prepositional *like*, used in utterances such as *he looks like my father*. They framework their analysis, however, not in Meillet's definition of grammaticalization but in Traugott's (1982) semantic/pragmatic model of the process. In essence, the latter envisages the process in terms of movement from the propositional to textual to expressive components of the grammar. The propositional component comprises a language's basic resources (such as prepositions), the textual contains elements necessary for keeping discourse coherent (such as conjunctions and complementizers) and the expressive includes elements 'which express personal attitudes to the topic or to other participants' (McMahon, 1994: 169). Thus, in the case of *like*, Romaine and Lange hypothesize that prepositional *like* (propositional function) which can take nominal complements (as in *he looks like my father*) moves to being able to take sentential complements (as in *Winston tastes good like a cigarette should*) and is thus re-categorized as a conjunction or complementizer (textual function). This paves the way for its re-analysis as a discourse marker (as in *there were like people blocking*) or, if the clause/sentence is a 'quotation' of speech, as a complementizer that introduces such constructed dialogue (expressive function). Overall, Traugott's approach (in comparison with Meillet's emphasis on structural change) provides a much more effective and plausible explanatory framework for changes in the use of *like*.[11] It is not, however, wholly unproblematic; as the authors themselves admit, Traugott's model, like Meillet's definition, envisages grammaticalization as a uni-directional process, which makes it difficult to foreground the fact that the involved changes are much more messy. Thus, old and new functions of *like* will co-exist while grammaticalization is in progress, and the authors also hypothesize a two-way movement from textual to expressive functions (*like* functions as both discourse marker and quotative complementizer). Nevertheless, such work is complementary to more structure-based accounts of grammaticalization; together, they should achieve no less than increasing our understanding of such processes.

The explanations of the preceding sections have necessarily portrayed language change as an ordered and neat phenomenon. This is in fact not the case: change is, for want of a better phrase, quite 'messy' indeed. The processes we have considered may or may not occur, and if they do, do not affect the usage of all speakers, and certainly not at the same time. This means that change contributes to synchronic variation in a language system – old and new, and new and new, variants may co-exist at any one time in a speech community. It also has a diachronic effect – as some variants become dominant and are retained and as others are lost, the 'linguistic character' of the language (at least, of the language preserved in the textual record) also changes, as we will see in our narrative of English from Anglo-Saxon times to the present day (Chapters 3–6). But processes of change not only 'move' a language from one stage to another; they can also, given enough time and appropriate conditions, eventually result in the gradual emergence of a new language. Such lines of linguistic descent also constitute an integral part of a language's diachronic narrative, and it is to a discussion of research in this area that we turn in Chapter 2.

1.7 Study Questions

1. The following data illustrates a current vowel shift in American English – the Northern Cities Shift, which is taking place in the industrial inland North and is most strongly advanced in the largest cities including Syracuse, Buffalo, Cleveland, Toledo, Detroit, Chicago and Rockford:

The Northern Cities Shift

/ɪ/ kid	>	/ɛ/	/ɛ/ head	>	/ʌ/
/æ/ cad	>	/ɪ/	/a/ cod	>	/æ/
/ɔ/ cawed	>	/a/	/ʌ/ cud	>	/ɔ/

How does this compare to the Southern Vowel Shift (Section 1.2)? You may find it useful to represent these movements as in Figure 1.1.

Useful sources: Wolfram and Schilling-Estes (1998), the Phonological Atlas of North America (http://www.lingupenn.edu/phono_atlas).

2. Many brand-names make use of the word-formation patterns discussed in Section 1.3. Which patterns are evident in the following examples?: *Weetabix* (breakfast cereal), *Nescafé*, *Microsoft*, *Windolene* (window cleaner), *Ricicles* (breakfast cereal), *Lemsip* (cold and flu medicine), *Brightspace* (media sales company).

3. What patterns of semantic change have affected the following words? Note that more than one pattern may be in evidence: *hag, hacker, lame, glamour, crafty, harlot*. An unabridged dictionary will be useful.

4. Trace the grammaticalization pattern for English affixes *–hood* and *–less*. An unabridged dictionary will be useful.

5. Are the following affixes productive or unproductive? The fewer derivations you can come up with, the more unproductive they might be: *–ista* (*fashionista*), *–ism* (*hedonism*), *un–* (*unhappy*), *dis–* (*disallow*), *re–* (*redecorate*), *–ness* (*whiteness*). Can they each be used unequivocally with any member of the relevant word-class (for example, can *un–* be affixed to any adjective?), or do there seem to be limitations?

6. What languages do you think are currently major sources of borrowing for English? (Think about this in terms of your own variety, or one(s) with which you

are familiar.) List as many examples as you can and try to determine what category of loans they are (for example, cultural and/or prestigious borrowings).

7. Lightfoot (1979) stated that one of the distinguishing features of modals (Section 1.6) is that they cannot occur consecutively. This is not the case, however, in varieties such as Hawick Scots and Tyneside English, examples of which are given below. What functions are the modals serving in each data set?

(a) Hawick Scots
He *might can* do it, if he tried
He *must can* do it.
He *should can* do it
He *would could* do it, if he tried.
Note: I *would* like to *could* swim

(b) Tyneside English
I can't play on a Friday. I work late. I *might could* get it changed though.
The girls usually make me some (toasted sandwiches) but they *mustn't could* have made any today.
He *wouldn't could've* worked, even if you had asked him.
A good machine clipper *would could* do it in half a day.

Useful reading: Beal (1996), Brown (1991).

Notes

1. There are numerous works which an interested reader may consult. For an excellent overview of theoretical, primarily historical linguistic, approaches to language change (as well as a useful bibliography) see McMahon (1994). Coupland and Jaworski (1997) also provide a useful introduction and guide to sociolinguistic investigations of change.

2. The symbol '*' is used here to denote a form which is not historically attested but which is linguistically plausible. We will return to the question of postulated linguistic ancestors and language families in Chapter 2.

3. The online Phonological Atlas of North America provides current updates on the progress of this and other shifts at http://www.lingupenn.edu/phono_atlas.

4. Pronunciations can be heard at Eckert's webpage at http://www.stanford.edu/~eckert/vowels.html.

5. Not all adolescents participate in this shift. Bucholtz (1996) argues for example that non-use of the shifting vowel qualities is one of the linguistic ways in which 'nerd girls' in California distinguish themselves from other groups.

6. Dates of first occurrence are taken from the *Oxford English Dictionary*.

7. *Bird* is used in British English as a colloquial term of reference for females.

8. See 'This Year's New Words' (25 July 2003) at the *Global English Newsletter* site http://www.engcool.com/GEN/archive.php.

9. This is a highly simplified outline of Saussure's argument. For a more detailed discussion, see Harris (1988).

10. http://en.wikipedia.org/wiki/Talk:English_plural; accessed 1 April 2004.

11. See Buchstaller (2002), however, who does not agree that the development of the new functions of *like* is best explained by a grammaticalization model. The latter, she argues, cannot easily account for the word's synchronic multifunctionality. She therefore proposes instead a semantic field model, which essentially maps out the word's synchronic functions in a linked structure which radiates from a shared core.

2 | Language Families and the Pre-History of English

2.1 Introduction

In February 2002, the *Daily Telegraph* (a British newspaper) reported that space agencies such as NASA are contemplating the possibility of human interstellar travel and colonization in the not-too-distant future. Pioneer crews will be multi-national, multi-lingual, and on a one-way ticket: the journey to the nearest habitable star will take about one hundred years.

Imagine that you are one of these pioneer astronauts. You will spend the rest of your life on your spaceship and will never again be part of a community on Earth. You will have to adapt to life in outer space, and you will experience the world in ways in which those left behind could only begin to imagine. Some aspects of your life will of course unfold along familiar lines – you will make friends, fall in love, and possibly have children and grandchildren. But overall, your new home, your new life, as well as that of any offspring you have, will be forged in a new environment and with a new community.

Now think about your language situation. You and the crew have to be able to communicate effectively from the start, or your trip will be in serious trouble. You and some of the other members may speak only English; others may have Russian, or Swahili or Spanish as their native tongues. What language will unite you all? When you eventually set up home with your native Russian-speaking partner, what language will you use with each other and with your children? What will the latter speak with the other children on board?

If such a scenario ever came to pass, Sarah Thomason (*Daily Telegraph* 16 February 2002) predicts that, given its modern global status, English would play a primary role for pioneer crews and their offspring. Not only would it be a likely lingua franca for an Earth-launched crew but also, consequentially, a possible native language for the subsequent generations born on the journey. So, in theory, if after about two hundred years, descendants of the original crews returned to Earth, they would be able to converse easily with any remaining English speakers here. Or would they?

As long as English continued to have thriving communities of speakers on Earth and elsewhere, it would undergo processes of change such as those described in Chapter 1. In its migratory journey into outer space, which might eventually lead to total isolation from contemporaneous Earth-based English speakers, the language would very likely change significantly. In the first instance, an original multi-national crew might have varying levels of competence in different 'Englishes' (such as Russian English, or Indian English), and the contact among these could produce a *koiné* distinct from the English varieties on Earth. Within the space of a few generations, especially if contact with Earth was broken, sounds could be lost or added, grammatical inflections disappear, 'new words . . . coined and some familiar words fall by the wayside' (ibid.). Words retained from terran Englishes could also undergo semantic change in adaptation to the new environment. In addition, and in the best tradition of sci-fi drama, if any of our generations of space crew made and sustained contact with an extra-terrestrial culture and language, then 'Space Crew English' might very well come to incorporate linguistic influences from that interaction. Overall, if our Earth-bound and Earth-free 'English' descendants ever came into contact in the distant future, they might, unsurprisingly, regard each other's usage as quite alien indeed. In addition, this linguistic gulf could be exacerbated by SCE speakers' perceptions of themselves as a separate group: Thomason points out that they might come to identify themselves as a culturally and linguistically distinct community, separate from their Earthling kin.

You probably find yourself wondering at this point about the feasibility of such predictions of language change. After all, the existence of Space Crew English is only a distant possibility at the moment, and we have no way of forecasting exactly what English will be like in say, 50 years time, let alone two hundred. However, the assumptions about change and native speaker attitudes that linguists such as Thomason make for the development of English in an extra-terrestrial setting are firmly based on what we have managed to observe right here on Earth. As mentioned earlier in this chapter (and in Chapter 1), linguistic change through inter-generational transmission seems to be a sure and steady process. We therefore have no reason to believe that this would not continue with SCE speakers. In terms of contact, we know, from the evidence of historical records and modern occurrences, that it is a phenomenon that speech communities frequently undergo, and that it can have various linguistic impacts. For example, the current widespread adoption of English as a second language (L2) around the world has led to the emergence of new Englishes such as Indian English and Nigerian English.[1] As their names imply, these are currently perceived as *varieties* of English influenced by the native tongues of each particular region. Alternatively, there have been cases where the adoption of one language by a non-native speech community has eventually resulted in a new language altogether. French and Spanish, for instance, may have had their beginnings in the contact between the Vulgar (or common) Latin spoken by garrisoned soldiers of the Roman Empire and the Germanic languages of the subjugated Franks and Visigoths, respectively. In addition, contact can result in language states that are difficult to classify: Thomason and Kaufman (1988), for example, cite the case of Ma'a, spoken in Tanzania, which now shows such extensive structural influence from Bantu (with which it has been in sustained contact), that its status as an 'independent' language has become a matter of extensive debate. Finally, in relation to speaker perceptions about language use, we again know from current and historical evidence that socio-political considerations often influence linguistic classifications. For example, Scots, which is spoken in Lowland Scotland, is defined as a variety of English by some, and as a separate language by others who maintain cultural, political and linguistic autonomy from

England. Bokmål and Nyorsk, spoken in Norway, are considered separate languages even though they are, at the grammatical level, virtually identical (Wardaugh, 1992: 26). On the other hand, Cantonese and Mandarin, two Chinese 'dialects', are in fact so mutually unintelligible in speech that they could be considered separate languages (ibid.: 28).[2]

Thus, on the basis of such examples, we can hypothesize that SCE, if it ever materialized, would develop into either a variety of English or a new language with English ancestry, and depending on the predilections of its speakers, would be classified as one or the other. You may have noticed, however, that regardless of what its eventual categorization might be, it seems difficult to escape talking about SCE in terms of some kind of genealogical link with English. This intuitively makes sense on more than just the linguistic level: the relatedness between the language forms mirrors the cultural, social and even genetic links between the SCE community and their Earth human ancestry. In the same way, historical linguistics has established, alongside other disciplines such as anthropology and archaeology and now to some extent, genetics, certain connections between our linguistic present and past. The rest of this chapter discusses some of the better-known work in the establishment of linguistic relatedness, and also looks at some new developments in this particular field.

2.2 The Roots of English and Proto-Indo-European

As mentioned in Section 2.1, if Space Crew English ever became a reality, as well as an object of study or even curiosity, people would very likely have intuitions about its 'linguistic place'. So if, for example, it used words and pronunciations different from those on Earth, but still retained certain similarities (such as words like *and*, *the*, *a*, *man*, *woman*, *I*, *you*, or *one*, the use of *–s* to form plurals, *–ed* for past tenses), it would very likely seem sensible to include SCE in an 'English family unit'. Such intuitive groupings are shared by linguists and non-linguists alike: we do not have to be specialists to think that sentences such as those in Example 2.1 (1–3) reflect a level of similarity that may be beyond coincidence. Similarly, if the comparison was extended to include the Welsh and English equivalents in (4)–(5), we would probably agree that the new additions have elements in common with the first three, such as the words for *mother* and *my*. As such, all five could potentially constitute a 'general unit' but within that, French, Spanish and Italian would form a much tighter sub-grouping. In this case, our intuitions would be right – all these languages are part of the same language family unit, but the three Romance tongues, as they are known, are particular descendants of Latin.

Example 2.1

1. French: *ma mère est belle*
2. Spanish: *mi madre es bella*
3. Italian: *mi mama e' bella*
4. Welsh: *mae fy mam yn bert*
5. English: *my mother is pretty*

The search for linguistic relatedness and language families is one which has long preoccupied scholarly and philosophical circles in Europe, and has been, at every stage, heavily influenced by the contemporary socio-political *Zeitgeist*. For example, many scholars up until the nineteenth century worked within the framework of biblical tradition, which held that a divinely original, perfect 'proto-language' spoken at the time of the Creation had later split into daughter languages. Either the story of the collapse of the tower of Babel, or that of the post-Flood dispersal of Noah's three sons, Shem, Ham and Japheth, was taken as an adequate explanation for the world's linguistic diversity, as well as its linguistic affiliations (Eco, 1995). In fact, the names of Noah's offspring were transmuted into those of three major language groupings, determined by the migratory paths they had taken after the Flood. Thus, the languages of the Levant were termed Semitic, spoken as they were by the offspring of Shem; Hamitic languages were those of Africa, since Ham had fathered the Egyptians and Cushites; and the Japhetic tongues included those of Europe, since the prolific Japheth was alleged to have sired much of the rest of the world.

In 1767, in a little-remembered work entitled *The Remains of Japhet, Being Historical Enquiries into the Affinity and Origins of the European Languages*, a physician named James Parsons wrote that he had been spending quite a lot of his spare time 'considering the striking affinity of the languages of Europe'.[3] He had found it so fascinating that he was 'led on to attempt following them to their source' (Mallory, 1989: 9). To these ends, Parsons undertook extensive and systematic linguistic comparisons of Asian and European languages. He demonstrated, for example, the close affinity between Irish and Welsh through a comparison of one thousand vocabulary items, and concluded that they had once been 'originally the same' (ibid.). On the (justifiable) reasoning that counting systems were a cultural essential, and that words for numbers were therefore 'most likely to continue nearly the same, even though other parts of languages might be liable to change and alteration' (quoted in Mallory, 1989: 10), he compared lexical items for basic numerals across a range of languages, including Irish, Welsh, Greek, Latin, Italian, Spanish, German, Dutch, Swedish, English, Polish, Russian, Bengali and Persian. He also considered the relevant equivalents in Turkish, Hebrew, Malay and Chinese which, in their lack of affinity with those from the other languages, as well as with each other, emphasized the correspondences among the languages of the first group (see examples in Table 2.1). His conclusion was that the languages of Europe, Iran and India had emerged from a common ancestor which, in keeping with the dominant beliefs of the time, he cited as the language of Japheth and his progeny.

Despite its merits as a pioneering study which made use of methodologies later integral to historical linguistics, Parsons' work is not typically credited as being the catalyst for serious academic investigation into linguistic relatedness. Mallory (1989: 10) states that this may have been due to the fact that some of Parsons' assumptions and conclusions proved to be erroneous. In addition, Parsons was not a figure of authority in the philological world – he was, as mentioned earlier, first and foremost a physician. The work that would instead '[fire] the imagination of European historical linguists' (Fennell, 2001: 21) would

Table 2.1 Examples of Parsons' numeral comparisons

	One	Two	Three	Four
Danish	en	to	tre	fire
Old English	an	twa	thrie	feowre
Polish	jeden	dwie	trzy	cztery
Russian	odin	dva	tri	chetyre
Bengali	ek	dvi	tri	car
Latin	unus	duo	tres	quattuor
Greek	hen	duo	treis	tettares
Irish	aon	do	tri	ceathair
Welsh	un	dau	tri	pedwar
Chinese	yi	er	san	si
Turkish	bir	iki	üc	dört
Malay	satu	dua	tiga	empat

Source: Examples from Mallory (1989: 12, 14)

be that of Sir William Jones, an eighteenth-century philologer, lawyer and founder of the Royal Asiatic Society.

In the late 1700s, Jones had become Chief Justice of India. During the course of his posting, he began to study and read ancient documents (from the fourth–sixth centuries AD) written in Sanskrit. Sanskrit, literally meaning 'the language of the cultured', had been used in India from approximately 3000 to 2000 BC, and was the language of the Vedas (scriptures) fundamental to Hindu philosophy and religion. Other, later religious texts, such as the Upanishads and the Bhagavad Gita (which emerged around 1000 BC), were also composed in Sanskrit. By about 500 BC, this long-standing association with religious and philosophical subjects had turned Sanskrit into a language of the elite, used in the royal courts for matters of law and state and in temple rituals by high-caste Brahmans. From the tenth century AD, India began to undergo a series of Muslim invasions, and use of Sanskrit in prestigious domains almost all but died out. Today, it is 'a dead "living" language . . . restricted almost exclusively to religious ritual and academic study . . . spoken by a negligible and dwindling minority and cherished by scholars' (Lal, 1964: xi–xii).

Whereas Parsons' work had primarily revealed striking similarities between word forms, Jones' analytical comparison of Sanskrit with European languages such as Latin and Greek also uncovered affinities in grammatical structure. In addition, it also indicated that certain sounds in the languages being compared varied systematically. As an illustration of the kind of correspondences Jones observed, consider the data in Example 2.2, which sets out the first and second person singular conjugations for the verb *to bear* in five languages (note that this is not Jones's comparative table).

The inflectional endings of each form, which indicate the grammatical conjugation of the verb, are strikingly similar. In addition, the correspondences

Example 2.2 Comparison of *to bear*

	Sanskrit	Latin	Greek	OHG	Old Slavonic
I bear	bharami	fero	phero	biru	bera
You (sing) bear	bharasi	fers	phereis	biris	berasi

Source: data from Renfrew (1987: 11)

between sounds are also consistent. For example, wherever Sanskrit has *bh*, Old High German and Old Slavonic have *b*, and Latin and Greek appear to have *f/ph*. As we will see, such correspondences in sound would become formalized in the nineteenth century.

In 1786, on the basis of such work, Jones famously stated to the Asiatic Society in Calcutta that:

> The Sanskrit language, whatever may be its antiquity, is of wonderful structure; more perfect than the Greek, more copious than the Latin, and more exquisitely refined than either; yet bearing to both of them a stronger affinity, both in the roots of verbs and in the forms of grammar, than could have been produced by accident; so strong that no philologer could examine all the three without believing them to have sprung from some common source which, perhaps, no longer exists. There is similar reason, though not quite so forcible, for supposing that both the Gothic and Celtic, though blended with a different idiom, has the same origin with the Sanskrit; and the old Persian might be added to the same family.
>
> (*Third Anniversary Discourse*)

Jones, like his obscure predecessor Parsons, also traced the 'common source' back to migrations from the Ark. But the Sanskrit scholar's more widely received theories of linguistic relatedness attracted much more serious attention from his contemporaries. This was not always favourable – Fennell (2001) points out that some detractors devoted a great deal of time to trying (unsuccessfully) to disprove his theory:

> The story is often told of a Scottish philosopher named Dugald Stewart, who suggested that Sanskrit and its literature were inventions of Brahman priests, who had used Latin and Greek as a base to deceive Europeans. As one might imagine, Stewart was not a scholar of Sanskrit.
>
> (ibid.: 21)

With contemporary hindsight, however, he certainly appears to have regarded himself as a scholar of human nature!

Despite the best efforts of the naysayers, academic scrutiny of what Thomas Young, in 1813, came to call the 'Indo-European' group of languages, gathered momentum. The nineteenth century also saw a movement towards establishing methodologies for systematic comparison of the linguistic data, as well as of the development of common-source theories rooted not in biblical tradition but instead, in political sensibilities. Eco (1995: 103) states that whereas previous investigation into linguistic relatedness had ultimately been geared towards uncovering the original 'Adamic' language, by the nineteenth century scholars had come to view it as irrecoverable: 'even had it existed, linguistic change and corruption would have rendered the primitive language irrecuperable'. Since the original Perfect Language of humankind could not be found, focus shifted to the next best thing: determining the roots of the descendant 'perfect' languages – and by extension, cultures or races – of the world. Some contemporary linguistic work on the Indo-European family therefore became entangled with notions of Indo-European racial superiority; and it is here that the myth of the Aryans, which was taken up and exploited in the twentieth century, was born.[4]

By the nineteenth century, the methodologies of comparative philology had become well established. Scholars undertook (as they still do now) comparative analyses of *cognates*; that is, data which displayed similarities in terms of form and meaning not because of borrowing or coincidence, but because of genetic relatedness. This is an important specification, because any other kind of data can lead to erroneous conclusions. For example, if we created a list of a thousand random words in everyday use by modern English speakers, we could end up with a significant proportion which had a Latin or French provenance. If the history of English had been poorly documented, and scholars were unaware that speakers had incorporated numerous loanwords from those two sources at various points in time, we could easily, and mistakenly, conclude that English had a much closer affiliation with the Romance languages than it actually does. A similar situation could potentially obtain if we depended only on a few striking correspondences for determining genetic relationships. Thus, the similarity between English and Korean *man*, or German *nass* and Zuni *nas* 'wet' for example, could lead to the conclusion that these respective language pairs were closely connected. However, deeper examination shows that these are merely chance similarities – no regular and systematic correspondences which could justify close genetic affiliation between these languages exist.

The use of cognate data therefore theoretically reduced the possibility of making such mistakes but was of course dependent on its accurate identification. The nineteenth-century philologers reasoned that all languages had a *core lexicon*, a set of words which, in their everyday ordinariness, remained impervious to processes such as borrowing or rapid and extensive change. Such words were those which labelled concepts ubiquitous to human existence, such as kinship and social terms (*mother, father, daughter, son, king, leader*), *sun* and *moon*, body parts, a deity and the basic numerals, as Parsons had assumed in his study. The core element of a language's vocabulary therefore allegedly preserved its ancestral 'essence', yielding reliable indicators of genetic affiliation. Cognate databases, then, were compiled from posited cores, a practice which continues today in modern comparative work. It is worth noting however, that establishing a reliable cognate database is not always a straightforward matter – a point we shall return to in Section 2.3.

Cognate comparison established the fact that systematic grammatical, semantic and phonological correspondences existed between languages assumed to be related (as indicated in examples given on p. 44). However, by the middle of the nineteenth century, it was also being used to map out the linguistic genealogies of the Indo-European family. It was obvious to scholars then, as now, that languages changed over time, sometimes into completely different ones. This was known to be the case with Latin, which had spawned the modern Romance languages, and with Sanskrit, which had been the forerunner of Hindi. It was also known, from archaeological records in particular, that different peoples had historically migrated and dispersed over Europe and Asia. It was therefore highly likely that the modern languages of these two continents which Jones had linked back to a common source, now called Proto-Indo-European (PIE), had evolved out of the splitting up of that language into smaller sub-families, which then in turn had gone through their own processes of division. Thus, the correspondences between cognates could establish degrees of relationship between language groups *within* the Indo-European family.

The inevitable question followed: was it possible to trace these sub-families, especially since in some cases, historical records for certain cognate languages were sparse? Would it even be possible to determine the reality of sub-familial *mother* languages for which no textual evidence existed? Scholars such as Rasmus Rask, Jacob Grimm and August Schleicher believed it was, on both counts. Their reasoning was based on the assumption that though language change is inevitable, it is also largely regular and rule-governed. In other words, certain significant changes in language follow predictable patterns which, once determined, made it possible to work 'backwards' and re-create earlier and unattested forms. If a wide cognate database for a group of possibly related languages were available, the patterns of systematic correspondence that held among them could aid in the reconstruction of an earlier proto-form (see Figure 2.1). And an even wider database, in terms of both number of languages and number of cognates, would facilitate the reconstruction of the ultimate proto-source, Proto-Indo-European.

This process of *comparative reconstruction* (or the *comparative method*, as it is often known) became widely employed but interestingly, has never operated under a

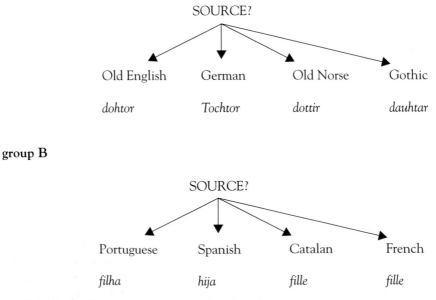

group A

SOURCE?

Old English	German	Old Norse	Gothic
dohtor	*Tochtor*	*dottir*	*dauhtar*

group B

SOURCE?

Portuguese	Spanish	Catalan	French
filha	*hija*	*fille*	*fille*

Figure 2.1 Indo-European cognates for *daughter*

system of set rules: it has remained largely dependent on a good database, an understanding of the kinds of routes of change languages seem to follow, and a healthy dose of common sense (a point we shall return to in Section 2.4). A great deal of reconstructive work has been done in relation to phonology, largely because sound change has long been accepted as an area where change does seem to occur with a high degree of predictability. As an example of this, consider the data in Table 2.2. You will notice that there are certain consistent correspondences among the bolded consonants that set Gothic, Old English and Old Norse apart from Sanskrit and Latin. Note that these correspondences hold across significant numbers of cognates in these and other Indo-European languages not exemplified here.

Table 2.2 Correspondence between consonants

	Sans.	Lat.	Goth.	OE	ON
full	purna-	plēnus	fulls	full	fullr
thunder	tan-	tonare	....	þunor	þórr
hound	cvon	canis	hunds	hund	hundr
hemp	....	cannabis	....	hænep	hampr
tooth	dant-	dens	tunþus	tōþ	tönn
corn	....	grānum	kaurn	corn	korn
brother	bhrātar	frāter	broþar	brōþor	bróðir
door	dhwar	fores	daur	duru	dyrr
guest	ghost-	hosti-s	gast-s	giest	gest-r

We can set out the correspondences (=) as in Example 2.3.

Example 2.3 Comparsion of correspondences

Sanskrit		Latin		Goth., OE, ON
p	=	p	=	f
t	—	t	=	θ
k	=	k	—	h
		b	=	p
d	—	d	=	t
		g	=	k
bh	=	f	=	b
dh	=	f	=	d
gh	=	h	=	g

This divergence in the latter three languages, which comprise part of the Germanic sub-family of Indo-European, was most famously elucidated by Jacob Grimm (one half of the storytelling Brothers Grimm) in 1822. The *First Germanic Consonant Shift*, or *Grimm's Law* as it is also known, theorized that these consonantal values had initially shifted in the ancestor of the Germanic languages, proto-Germanic, in prehistoric times (perhaps through contact; see

Baugh and Cable, 2002: 22). Other Indo-European languages, such as Sanskrit and Latin, however, were thought to have at least largely preserved the earlier consonantal values once present in PIE. Through systematic comparison of cognate data, Grimm reconstructed the relevant proto-segments for PIE, and established a line of transmission to proto-Germanic, as in the simplified schemata in Example 2.4:

Example 2.4 The First Germanic Consonant Shift

PIE		proto-Germanic
voiceless plosives *p, t, k	>	voiceless fricatives /f θ x/ (x > later h)
voiced plosives *b, d, g	>	voiceless plosives /p t k/
voiced aspirates *bh, dh, gh	>	voiced plosives /b d g/

Grimm's Law was later modified in 1875 by Verner's Law, which sought to explain apparent exceptions to the patterns in 2.4. For example, Grimm's Law leads us to expect that where Latin has /t/, for instance, a Germanic language like English should have /θ/. Instead, we have pairs such as *pater~father*, *mater~mother*, where the medial English consonant value is /ð/. This is also apparent in earlier stages of the language, as well as in historical cognates: witness Old English *fæder*, Old Norse *faðir*, Gothic *fadar*. Karl Verner theorized that the shift predicted by Grimm's Law had initially occurred in such words in proto-Germanic, but that a subsequent change to the voiced fricative had taken place when (1) it did not occur in word-initial position; (2) it occurred between voiced sounds; and (3) the preceding syllable had been unstressed. All three conditions had been present for words such as *father*: the consonant was word-medial, between two voiced vowel sounds, and the first syllable of the word was historically unstressed (subsequent changes to Germanic stress patterns, in which stress has come to be placed on primary syllables, have since obscured this feature).

Such work was significant in two ways. First, it established that certain types of sound change were so regular that clear patterns of predictable, rule-governed change could be established between values. Scholars could therefore work 'backwards and forwards', reconstructing plausible older, unrecorded values and then testing them to see whether their creations would actually yield the cognate data they had originally started with. It therefore lent tremendous weight to the assumption of the regularity of sound change, which would become the absolute doctrine of the nineteenth-century Neogrammarians. Though their work initially met with fierce opposition from the 'older grammarians', by the end of the 1800s, the Neogrammarian Hypothesis that 'every sound change takes place according to laws that admit no exception' (Karl Brugmann, quoted in Trask, 1996: 227) had become well and truly established.

Second, if proto-segments could reliably be reconstructed, then they could also be used to re-create proto-words. Thus, scholars could make use of cognate data such as that cited in Table 2.2 and reconstruct, segment by segment, the form for *daughter* in proto-Germanic (**dhuk'tᵉr*) and proto-Romance (**filla*) (see Figure 2.1). Reconstruction of PIE could also take place, again with an appropriate cognate database. Table 2.3 lists some samples of cognate data and reconstructed PIE forms.[5]

Table 2.3 Cognates and reconstructions

	father	widow	sky-father, God
Old English	fæder	widuwe	Tiw
Old Norse	faðir	....	Týr
Gothic	fadar	widuwo	....
Latin	pater	vidua	Iūppiter
Greek	patēr	....	Zeus
Russian	....	vdova	....
Lithuanian	....	widdewu	diēvas
Irish	athir	lan	dia
Sanksrit	pitar-	vidhava-	dyaus-pitar
PIE	*pətēr-	*widhēwo	*deiwos

It is important to keep in mind that plausible reconstructions have to be based on a much bigger set of data as well as likely rules of sound change. For example, on the basis of the data cited here, we could reasonably ask why *p, and not *f, is chosen as the initial proto-segment in the PIE word for 'father'. In fact, the choice has been made for two main reasons. First, a large number of the relevant Indo-European cognates (not cited here) have /p/ in this position, and it seems sensible to assume that this high level of occurrence is due to the fact that these languages retain a PIE value. Otherwise, we would have to stipulate that they all, perhaps independently, innovated an initial /p/ in this word, which seems counter-intuitive. Second, we know, through Grimm's Law, that the languages with initial /f/ belong to the Germanic sub-group, which preserves a general shift from *p > /f/. The fricative value is therefore a later one which takes place after proto-Germanic split from PIE, and is consequently unlikely to have been part of the latter language.

Another question we could reasonably ask at this point concerns the degree of validity for reconstructed forms. Since there are no records of PIE, for example, how do we know that such re-creations are right? Such a question is of course impossible to answer, although, according to Mallory (1989: 16), not impossible to debate:

> There have been those who would argue that the reconstructed forms are founded on reasonably substantiated linguistic observations and that a linguist, projected back into the past, could make him or herself understood among the earlier speakers of a language. Others prefer to view [them] as merely convenient formulas that express the linguistic histories of the various languages in the briefest possible manner. Their reality is not a subject of concern or interest.

Reconstructions are of course reasoned creations, but they are essentially that: creations. As such, their generation is highly dependent on the type of data that the researcher works with and also, to a certain extent, the nature of the prevailing climate in which the analysis is undertaken. For example, if twenty-fifth-century linguists, with sparse or non-existent historical records beyond the nineteenth century, were trying to reconstruct the common ancestor of twenty-third-century Space Crew English, Japanese English, Chinese English and American English, and the earliest texts available were nineteenth-century samples from the latter variety, then the reconstruction of, and beliefs about, 'proto-English' would inevitably be skewed in a particular direction. They would not necessarily be implausible, given the data, but they would also not necessarily be accurate.

In a real-life example of the somewhat subjective nature of reconstruction, Schleicher generated a PIE folk-tale, *Avis akvasas ka* 'The Sheep and the Horses' – a story that displays an overwhelming similarity to Sanskrit which, with the oldest textual database available at the time, was thought to be the closest relative to PIE. In addition, the early Sanskrit grammarians had compiled descriptive analyses of their language, detailing aspects of its morphology and phonology. Schleicher's narrative therefore reflects the heavy reliance he and his contemporaries placed on such linguistic and meta-linguistic sources for their theories of language change. By the twentieth century, scholars had revised and refined their theories of reconstruction as well as their databases, particularly in the light of discoveries of other extremely ancient IE languages such as Hittite. As such, 'The Sheep and the Horses' underwent striking metamorphoses, as can be seen in the one-line excerpt in Example 2.5. Note the changing databases and reconstructions for 'man':

Example 2.5 The Sheep and the Horses (excerpt)
'the sheep said to the horses: it hurts me seeing a man drive horses'

Schleicher's version (1868)
*Avis akvabhjams a vavakat: kard aghnutai mai viadnti *manum* akvams agantam.
(*manum 'man' – reconstructed from cognate Sanskrit *manus*, Gothic *manna*, English *man* and Russian *muz*)

Hirt's version (1939)
*Owis ek'womos ew^{e}wek^{w}et: kerd aghnutai moi widontei *gh'^{e}monm* ek'wons ag'ontm.
(*gh'^{e}monm 'man' – reconstructed from cognate Latin *homo*, Gothic *guma*, Tocharian B *saumo*, Lithuanian *zmuo*)

Lehmann and Zgusta's version (1979)
*Owis nu ekwobh(y)os ewewk^{w}et: Ker aghnutoi moi ekwons agontm *nerm* widntei
(*nerm 'man' – reconstructed from cognate Sanskrit *nar-*, Avestan *nar-*, Greek *aner*, Old Irish *nert*)

(after Mallory, 1989: 17)

Although Schleicher's attempt at PIE storytelling did not quite enchant, his other contributions to comparative philology were significant. Mallory (1989: 17), for example, credits him with pioneering the field of comparative reconstruction. What he is perhaps best remembered for, however, is his adoption of the biological model of the family tree to map linguistic relationships; versions of this are commonly found in historical linguistic texts today, and also applied to the more recent classification of other language families. In this model, illustrated in Figure 2.2, PIE sits at the head of the IE family tree, as the *Ursprache* (early or original language). It is *mother* to various *daughters*, or 'fundamentals', as Schleicher termed them. These *sisters* then 'produce' their own daughters.

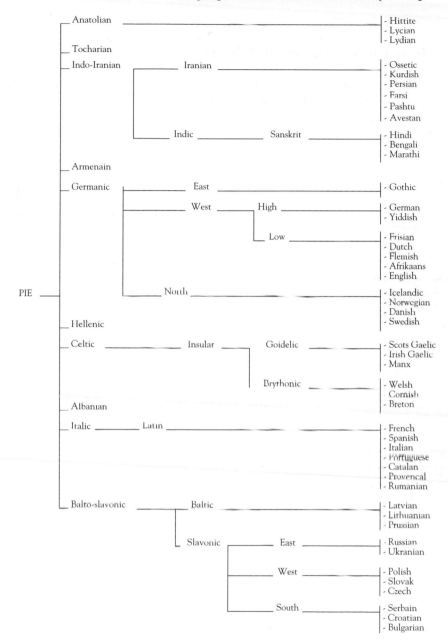

Figure 2.2 The Indo-European family

The family tree model has remained a constant in historical linguistics, but it has not escaped some (justifiable) criticism. Mühlhäusler (1986: 252), for example, stated that the tree is a 'cultural interpretation rather than an objective mirror of reality', a comment which has resonances with Eco's (1995) assertion that the nineteenth-century search for Indo-European roots was partly an exercise in the creation of particular national identities. Even Schleicher's contemporaries felt that the tree model did not adequately reflect certain known facts about the languages pinned on its branches. For example, the model predisposes an assumption that languages diverge suddenly and completely and then continue to develop in isolation from each other. Yet this is extremely unlikely. If we take the new Englishes as an example, even though they are sometimes named as and considered distinct entities (Singaporean English or South African Indian English) following different evolutionary paths in different linguistic environments, they are all also still defined as belonging to an English continuum of varieties (cf. Section 2.1). Modern technology ensures that contact between users of different Englishes can occur, and it is likely that they therefore maintain a high level of mutual intelligibility. It is possible that one day, if circumstances allow, some of these new Englishes could gradually evolve into completely separate and distinct languages (again, as we theorized in Section 2.1), but it certainly would not happen overnight. Similarly in the historical context, Trask (1996: 185) points out that languages like Latin spread across the Roman Empire and became a 'vast dialect continuum'. Thus, anyone travelling across the Empire in the seventh–eighth centuries would have 'found the language changing only very gradually in any direction . . . nowhere were there any sharp boundaries separating one emerging new Romance language from another'. It would be a long time before Latin's daughters would be recognized as distinct, national languages.

Despite the shortcomings of the genetic tree model, it quickly became established as (and has remained) the most popular mode of representation for language families.[6] Once it had become accepted, it was only a matter of time before discussion and investigation moved in focus from the 'language family' to the 'people family':

> The model constrained one to frame questions such as when did the Germanic languages separate from the Balto-Slavic? And this was easily translated into the questions: When did the Germanic *peoples* move off from the Balto-Slavic peoples? When did the Celts separate from the Italic peoples? The Indians from the Iranians? And such historical questions demand a specific type of answer, not far removed from chasing after the offspring of Noah.
>
> (Mallory, 1989: 18)

In the following section, we look briefly at some of the attempts that have been made to discover the PIE *Urheimat*, or homeland, and its people.

2.3 Meeting the Ancestors I

As indicated at the end of the last section, interest in reconstructing the linguistic affiliations of Europe and Asia spread to reconstructing the patterns of dispersal for their speakers. One of the primary concerns, therefore, was to discover the location of the original PIE homeland from which those paths of migration could be traced, not just through the linguistic record, but perhaps through the archaeological as well. After all, historical communities would very likely have left tangible traces of their existence beyond those suggested by language.

In this context, there were several factors to consider. If the hope was to equate the Proto-Indo-Europeans with archaeological evidence, how were scholars to know what to look for, given that the existence of these people was assumed rather than definitively proven? What time periods were to be investigated? And geographically, where was one supposed to look? Had the *Urheimat* been in somewhere in Asia, or somewhere in Europe?

A major consensus appears to have been to start looking for answers in the proto-lexicon. If terms for flora and fauna could be reconstructed, for example, they could provide an indication of geographical area. Similarly, PIE terms for animals and community life could also be used to build up a picture of their lifestyle, perhaps even providing some clue as to why dispersals would have begun in the first place. This area of research became known as *linguistic palaeontology*, a term coined by Adolphe Pictet (1859).

A database of reconstructions began to take shape: forms such as *aratrom* 'plough', *grno-* 'grain' and *yeug-* 'yoke' appeared. The Proto-Indo-Europeans appear to have kept *uksen* 'oxen', cows (*gwou-*) and other livestock, such as sheep (*awi-* > ewe), swine (*su-*) and goats (*ghaido*). A PIE *gen* 'family' (eventually in genetics and *kin*) may have lived in a *domo* 'house', furnished with *keromo-* 'pottery' (> 'ceramic') and would have drunk *melg-* 'milk' from the livestock and eaten dishes made with the *mel* 'meal' of their *grno-*. They may sometimes have had *pisk-* 'fish', wild *ghans-* 'goose' and when available, wild *abel-* 'apples'. They wore clothes made of woven (> *webh*) *wel-* 'wool' and possibly *lin-* 'flax' (> linen), and footwear made of *letrom* 'leather'. Much work would have been done with tools fashioned from *stoino-* 'stone', as well as wood and bone (all examples from Claiborne, 1990: 29 30).

In terms of environment, linguists were able to reconstruct words for snow *sneigw-* and freezing cold *gel-* (> congeal), but not for the more tropical *palm tree* or *coconut*, or even subtropical *olive* or *vine*. The Proto-Indo-Europeans also appear to have been familiar with animals such as the "*bher-* 'bear', *wlkwo-* 'wolf', *bhibru* 'beaver', and with the *as-* 'ash', *elmo-* 'elm', *bherag* 'birch' and *bhago* 'beech' trees (all examples from Claiborne, 1990: 30–1).

On the basis of such reconstructions (as well as an assumption that they were equivalent in meaning to their modern reflexes; a point we shall return to later), a range of possible homelands was suggested, most of which were situated in either Central Asia or Northern Europe. It was also popularly assumed that PIE culture, existing sometime between 4500 and 2500 BC, had been pastoral, rather than agricultural. In 1890, Otto Schrader postulated that the *Urheimat* had been situated in the South Russian steppe, stretching from Carpathia to Central Asia, where there was evidence of nomad pastoralism having been practised (Renfrew, 1987: 15). This theory would prove influential in twentieth-century debates on the 'Indo-European problem', as it came to be known.

Until the beginning of the twentieth century, theories such as Schrader's depended solely on the 'evidence' of linguistic reconstructions. However, developments in the field of prehistoric archaeology began to be taken into consideration with the publication of Gustav Kossina's work in 1902 ('The Indo European question answered archaeologically'). In brief, he identified the Proto-Indo-Europeans with a community which had developed a specific type of pottery – known as Corded Ware – and proposed a north German homeland. Renfrew (1987: 15) states that Kossina was the first to equate prehistoric peoples and their languages with pottery types: a correspondence that still carries weight in some current schools of thought, although others warn that 'pots do not equal people' (Mallory, 1989: 164).

Kossina's integrative approach to archaeological and linguistic data was later famously adopted by V. Gordon Childe (1926) who, like Schrader, placed the *Urheimat* in South Russia. In the latter part of the twentieth century, the archaeologist Marija Gimbutas carried on the argument for a homeland situated in the South Russian steppes. Gimbutas equated the original Proto-Indo-Europeans with a culture – the Kurgan – which appeared in this area in the fifth and early fourth millennia BC. In the spirit of linguistic palaeontology, she drew support from linguistic reconstructions (such as those cited above), stating that the environment of the Russian steppes well suited the world described by the proto-lexicon:

> in the fifth and fourth millennia the climate was warmer and damper . . . and what is now the steppe zone was more forested . . . including oak, birch, fir, beech, elder, elm, ash, aspen, apple, cherry and willow . . . [and] such forest animals as aurochs elk, boar, wild horse, wolf, fox, beaver, squirrel, badger, hare and roe deer.
>
> (Gimbutas, 1970: 159–60; quoted in Baugh and Cable, 2002: 40)

The archaeological evidence, largely available from the grave goods left in the distinctive burial mounds for which this culture was named, suggests that these early people were nomadic, warlike pastoralists who made use of horses and wheeled vehicles, had a patriarchal society and worshipped a pantheon of sky gods and the sun. Gimbutas argued that the booming population of Kurgans/Proto-Indo-Europeans dispersed from their steppe homeland in three successive waves of aggressive migration (4400–4200 BC, 3400–3200 BC, and 3000–2800 BC), moving eastwards into central Asia, Persia and India, westwards into central Europe and the Balkans and southwards eventually into Anatolia (Kortlandt, 1990: 6; Trask, 1996: 359). These invasions essentially destroyed peaceful, settled, agricultural and possibly matriarchal communities across Europe, where 'horses and wheeled vehicles [had been] unknown' and 'fine ceramics . . . and clay female figurines [had been] produced in thousands' (Trask, 1996: 359). Once the Kurgan aggressors had vanquished or absorbed those indigenous communities, the archaeological record changed, indicating instead abandoned settlements and the cessation of the production of delicate pottery and female figurines. In their place, fortified locations appeared, as did cruder pottery; and the horse and wheeled vehicles were introduced to everyday life as well as to iconography, as has been evidenced by stelae decorated with suns, horses, chariots and weapons. In addition, burial mounds like those of the Kurgans began to appear across the landscape, and in them, a 'new physical type . . . very different from the earlier European skeletons but identical to those found in the steppes' (ibid.: 360).

Gimbutas' theory, then, assumes that the languages of the Indo-European family resulted from these successive migrations: as each wave of Kurgans moved out into virgin territory, or conquered already extant communities, they took their original PIE with them. In these new environments, and in isolation from the 'motherland' and perhaps each other, these dialects of PIE would eventually evolve into distinct daughter languages. Gimbutas' assertion that there was no other culture than the Kurgan 'in the Neolithic and Chalcolithic periods which would correspond with the hypothetical mother culture of the Indo-European as reconstructed with the help of common words' (quoted in Renfrew, 1987: 17), as well as no other significant expansions which would satisfactorily explain the dispersal of the Indo-European languages, has had widespread linguistic (see Kortlandt, 1990; Mallory, 1989 for example) and archaeological support. Mallory (ibid.: Chapter 6), for example, provides a detailed accumulation of evidence and rationales for the Kurgan homeland theory. Among other things, he argues that since the IE family represents but one strand in the fabric of human speech (there are other prehistoric language families in Europe and Asia, let alone the world), the original Proto-Indo-Europeans must have had neighbours which they either had contact with, or were historically related to. If we can find such neighbours, then we arguably also find a plausible location for the PIE homeland. In this vein, he cites the languages of the non-Indo-European Finno-Ugric, or Uralic family, which have been argued to bear the traces of some kind of early relationship with PIE speakers. There is a general consensus that the proto-Uralic homeland was situated in the 'forest zone of Eastern Europe–western Siberia', and that its speakers may therefore have shared a border with those of PIE 'somewhere in the vicinity of the forest-steppe zone of south Russia' (ibid.: 149, 151). Mallory cites as evidence of this relationship two groups of lexical borrowing: (1) loanwords borrowed by proto-Uralic from Indo-European daughters; and (2) loanwords borrowed at an earlier date from PIE itself. In terms of the first class, the Uralic languages preserve lexical forms originally borrowed from PIE daughter Indo-Iranian, arguably the result of Gimbutas' first migratory wave of PIE speakers. For example, the Finnish and Votyak words for 'pig', porsas and pars, respectively, appear to have been derived from proto-Indo-Iranian *parsa- and not the earlier PIE *porcus. On the basis of a substantial number of similar loanwords, Mallory states that it is a safe assumption that:

> About 2000BC Indo-Iranians were providing a series of lexical items, pertaining particularly to agriculture (such as *pig, goat, grain, grass*) and technology (*hammer, awl, gold*) to Finno-Ugric peoples situated roughly between the middle Volga and the Ob. This would place the Indo-Iranians to their immediate south (lower Volga-Ural).
>
> (ibid.: 149)

However, such borrowings into the Finno-Ugric family could be argued to merely indicate that Uralic proto-speakers had had some (minimal) contact with speakers of an IE daughter language. It only offers some weight to the assumption that PIE and proto-Uralic were neighbours if we accept that the former's Indo-Iranian descendants had settled relatively near their ancestral doorstep. As such, loanwords such as those of group (2) would offer more compelling evidence of a close relationship. Mallory (ibid.) gives no examples of these early loans from PIE, but states that there are also striking correspondences between noun and verb inflectional endings in both PIE and proto-Uralic. The presence of such similarities has led, in some circles, to the postulation of a distant genetic affiliation between the two families, linked through a common source, Proto-Indo-Uralic. Others have maintained that the correspondences could equally be evidence of contact between 'unrelated' PIE and proto-Uralic speakers. Regardless of the truth of the matter, if we accept that affinities exist between these two language families, either through contact or genetic relatedness, then the physical proximity of the Uralic homeland to the South Russian steppe could make the latter a viable candidate for the *Urheimat* of PIE speakers.

The Kurgan/Russian steppe homeland theory has not been without its detractors as well. The archaeologist Colin Renfrew has been one of its most vigorous opponents, on a number of fronts. Renfrew finds the notion of aggressive warrior nomads problematic and untenable: pastoral economies have lower yields than agricultural ones, and are therefore less liable to the kinds of population explosions that can lead to significant migrations. In addition, if the Kurgans set out to simply find more land for subsistence, why were three waves of sustained aggression necessary? In his view, it is also unlikely that any prehistoric people had the kind of resources necessary for large-scale invasions and conquests of populated areas. Renfrew (1987) instead postulates a more peaceful linguistic dispersal, which goes hand in hand with a technological advance, namely, the spread of agriculture. He places the original PIE homeland in Anatolia and postulates that members of this community would have crossed over into Greece sometime in the seventh millennium BC. He states that there is sound evidence that the 'first farmers of Europe were settled in Greece (and Crete) before 6000BC' (ibid.:147), sowing wheat, peas and vetch, and herding sheep, goats, cattle and pigs. It is assumed that some of the neighbouring hunter–gatherer populations would have acculturated to farming techniques and in turn, would have 'spread' those to other similar nomadic communities. As Renfrew (ibid.: 128) states, 'the new economy of farming allowed the population in each area to rise', which could result in 'small, local movements of twenty or thirty kilometres'. Thus, farming communities spread in line with the 'wave of advance' model proposed by Ammerman and Cavalli-Sforza, which involves 'slow, continuous expansion with movements usually being over short distances' (Ammerman and Cavalli-Sforza, 1984; quoted in Renfrew, 1987: 128). Eventually, this would result in the 'peopling of the whole of Europe by a farming population, the descendants of the first European farmers' (1987: 150). As these farming communities spread into new environments, so did the original PIE, which would change, over the course of the centuries, into discrete daughter languages. In areas where earlier hunter–gatherer populations existed, the latter may have, especially if they were sparse in number, assimilated linguistically to the IE farmers. However, where those populations were denser and a sense of community stronger, as is thought to have been the case in

Brittany and areas of Portugal, the non-IE languages may have impacted on the development of the relevant IE daughters. Renfrew (ibid.: 151) also theorizes that if these stronger communities adopted farming techniques, then they too would have experienced an increase in population, which may have strengthened the chances of survival for their native languages. This, he says, may be the explanation for the survival of non-IE languages such as Etruscan and Basque in the geographical midst of IE tongues.

Renfrew's stance has attracted significant support. Gamkrelidze and Ivanov (1990) also place the PIE homeland somewhere in eastern Anatolia and Trask (1996: 361) states that Renfrew's hypothesis 'makes considerable sense to some archaeologists'. However, it also offers a few challenges for linguists. Mallory (1989: 179), for example, states that an Anatolian homeland ignores the strong likelihood of contact or genetic affiliation between PIE and the Uralic family. Renfrew's position instead has PIE emerging from among languages to which it is not related, such as Hattic and Hurrian, which may strike some as odd. The time-depth is also problematic: a seventh-millennium homeland in Anatolia and subsequent dispersal to Greece are incongruent with certain reconstructions in the proto-lexicon. For example, the horse, 'which is thoroughly embedded in the reconstructed vocabulary as well as in Indo European ritual' and should therefore figure prominently in Anatolian and Greek cultures between 6500 and 6000 BC if Renfrew is right, is not attested in either until the fourth and third millennia BC respectively. On the basis of such and similar points of departure, Mallory (1989: 179) concludes that Renfrew's solution is 'brave' but not convincing (see Mallory, 1989: Chapter 6 for a detailed critique of Renfrew's position).

It seems unlikely at the moment that such areas of debate will be definitively solved. Working back to periods for which there is often little material, linguistic and archaeological, means that it is incredibly difficult to fill such puzzles in neatly. It also means that while some of the methodologies devised to this end are plausible, they are also sometimes flawed. For example, on the surface, linguistic palaeontology makes a great deal of sense – find out how ancestral people labelled their world, and then find the world. Thus, we might assume that because we can find PIE cognates for mead (such as Germanic Met, Greek methu 'wine', Russian med, Lithuanian medus 'honey', Iranian mid, Sanskrit madhu 'liquor'), then it is highly likely that PIE speakers also drank a fermented, intoxicating beverage called *medhu-. However, this kind of reasoning ignores the fact that (as we saw in Chapter 1) semantic change occurs frequently and often rapidly; and in this particular case, it is quite common for a word meaning simply 'drink' to become specialized in denoting an alcoholic beverage: witness the change in English liquor (Chapter 1), and Slavonic pivo, which now means 'beer' instead of its original 'drink'. Similar issues have arisen with the actual designation of the PIE homeland. On the whole, the flora and fauna reconstructed for the proto-lexicon have a wide geographical distribution, but some are more restricted, thereby holding promises of physical delimitation. One of these reconstructions is that for 'beech' (*bhergo-). Many cognates exist across the IE daughters, implying that the word also existed in PIE. The common beech (to which this label was initially thought to apply) has a limited distribution, in that it is confined to central

Europe, and is not native east of Poland and the Ukraine. Claims were therefore made for a homeland within the 'beech tree line', but again a major obstacle lay in the fact that it was unclear whether the PIE word actually designated what modern scholars understood to be a beech tree. Some of the cognates on which the reconstruction was based actually refer to different entities: the Greek means 'oak', and those in other languages mean 'elder' and 'elm' (Baugh and Cable, 2002: 39). A similar situation arose with the reconstruction for 'salmon' (*loksos). Salmon is also restricted in distribution to northern Europe, which could place the PIE homeland in that area. However, subsequent re-examination indicated that the word may have labelled the more commonplace 'salmon trout'.[7] As a final case in point, Renfrew (1987: 82) points out that we do not actually know whether the reconstructed words for animals such as the horse and the cow actually refer to domesticated or wild animals – a significant issue when we consider that the presence of these animals has been used to support arguments for the existence of both warrior pastoral and peaceful agricultural economies.

In addition to the potential ambiguities of the proto-lexicon, we should also bear in mind that reconstruction of the latter is by no means complete. There are many words which scholars have been unable to reconstruct, and they are surprising in their ordinariness. For example, it has been possible to reconstruct 'eye' and 'eyebrow', but not 'eyelid' (Mallory, 1989: 161); or 'butter', 'snow' and 'feet', but not 'milk', 'rain' or 'hands' (Renfrew, 1987: 81). If the necessary cognates for such everyday words could disappear, then it is entirely possible that words which did designate, or at the very least delimit, the original homeland have also vanished from the daughter languages as their speakers' environments changed. The overall lesson seems to be that no matter how plausible the evidence may seem, we cannot blindly impose our perspectives and expectations on people who lived in a world we can only begin to imagine.

Expectations are important to mention here because debates about the PIE homeland have often included charges of subjectivity and selectiveness on the part of their supporters. For example, Trask (1996: 360) points out that many of Gimbutas' critics claim that her readings of the evidence fit the match she wanted to make: 'they argue that most of the physical evidence she adduces either has other explanations or is simply contradicted by further evidence which is silently ignored'. Mallory (1989) makes much the same statements about Renfrew's position. The fact of the matter is, as in any discipline, evidence can be interpreted to fit certain frameworks. In cases such as this, where evidence is drawn from different fields, in each of which uncertainties and gaps in knowledge exist, it is up to the researcher to pull the different strands together into a coherent pattern as best they can. Consequently, we end up with some ragtag theories, but with some decently put together ones as well. Indeed, the very fact that theories such as those of Gimbutas and Renfrew are still around, and are still being debated, is testimony to the fact that they each have a significant level of substance. Thus, we may never find the definitive answer to the question 'where is the Indo-European homeland?', but instead, will probably join Mallory in asking 'where have they put it *now*?' (paraphrase of Mallory, 1989: 143).

2.4 Meeting the Ancestors II

In the last section, we noted that as nineteenth-century work into linguistic (and genetic) relatedness progressed, scholars moved away from the search for the original Adamic language of humankind, and instead became increasingly focused on the provenance of particular language families, such as the Indo-European. Interestingly, as the twentieth and twenty-first centuries have unfolded, research has generally and increasingly moved back to seeking out the ultimate original source. Palaeo-anthropology and more recently, genetics, have sought to identify our original human ancestors, their *Urheimat* and subsequent patterns of dispersal. Certain linguists have also joined in this search, seeking to establish early links between the large, recognized language families, and in some cases even positing an original linguistic matriarch, known as Proto-World. Thus, proposals have been made for, among others, a genetic affiliation between IE and Semitic (Levin, 1971); IE and Sino-Tibetan (Pulleyblank, 1978); Sino-Tibetan and Austronesian (Wurm, 1982); Sino-Tibetan, North Caucasian and Yeniseian (Starostin, 1984), North Caucasian and Etruscan (Orël and Starostin, 1990) (cited in Trask, 1996: 380; see Chapter 13 for a detailed discussion).

There have also been proposals for super-families, one of the most famous being that for Nostratic (from Latin *nostros* 'our countrymen'), which links the IE, Uralic, Altaic, Afro-Asiatic and Kartvelian families. Although it was first proposed by Holger Pedersen in 1903, detailed work on Nostratic began to be carried out in the 1960s by the Russian linguists A. Dolgopolsky and V.M. Illich-Svitych, the latter of whom added Dravidian to the family. The Nostratic grouping has perhaps received the highest amount of detailed work done in the historical linguistic tradition: Illich-Svitych, for example, applied the comparative method to reconstructed data from the individual *Ursprache* of each language family (such as PIE, Proto-Italic, and so on) and recreated a detailed phonological system for Proto-Nostratic, as well as some seven hundred lexical items and a few grammatical processes.

Other well-known proposals for super-families have taken shape through the work of Joseph Greenberg, who used a much more controversial methodology for his groupings, namely *multilateral comparison*. This involves comparing huge numbers (hundreds or thousands) of words from the languages being investigated and determining whether there is a high frequency of resemblance between any of them. In cases where the number of resemblances is deemed to be significant, a genetic relationship between the relevant languages is declared. Greenberg used this technique throughout his career, establishing independent classifications for the Australian and African families of languages which have largely been accepted. For example, in relation to the latter, he classified the 1,500 or so African languages into four families; a categorization to which there is 'almost no serious opposition' (Trask, 1996: 386). Again with multilateral comparison, he proposed another super-family, termed Indo-Pacific, which links the Papuan languages of New Guinea and surrounding islands, the language of the Andaman Islands and also the now extinct languages of Tasmania. The Indo-Pacific grouping has remained controversial, but even more so has been Greenberg's classification of the languages of the Americas, of which there are approximately 650. He maintained the existence of two already established families, those of Eskimo-Aleut and Na-Déné, which comprise about 50 languages, but grouped the remaining 600, spanning North and South America as well as the Caribbean, into a single family which he named Amerind. The vituperation received by this hypothesis, and indeed by Greenberg, from fellow linguists was enormous: Trask (1996: 387) cites criticisms which label the work as 'worthless', 'crude and puerile', 'misguided and dangerous' and 'completely unscientific'. On the other hand, Greenberg's thesis has received support from areas of research outside linguistics, such as genetics. For example, the geneticist Cavalli-Sforza, researching gene maps for the native American population, has postulated the existence of three distinct population groups 'whose distribution corresponds remarkably well to the distribution of Greenberg's three language families, with the Eskimo-Aleut and Na-Déné speakers being genetically noticeably distinct from the comparatively homogenous remainder: Greenberg's Amerinds' (ibid.: 387–8). Before his death in 2001, Greenberg, undeterred by his critics, was working on yet another superfamily, Euroasiatic, which would include IE, Uralic-Yukaghir, Altaic, Korean, Japanese, Ainu, Gilyak, Chukchi-Kamchatkan and Eskimo-Aleut.

It perhaps goes without saying that all such work is always going to be controversial. The majority of historical linguists, while having a better than average grasp of the workings of various languages, have a less than superhuman knowledge of all of them. Knowledge of the various language families therefore tends to be specialized, and it is difficult, if not impossible, to wholly endorse or productively scrutinize groupings which include families with which the researcher is not familiar. It is possible too that certain groupings contradict researchers' perceptions about genetic affiliations, and their reactions are consequently negative: Trask (ibid.: 379), for example, states that racist perspectives once precluded the incorporation of Chadic, whose native speakers are predominantly Black, into the larger Afro-Asiatic family, which contains languages whose speakers are primarily White. There is also a very real issue of time-depth. We know that languages undergo continuous change and given enough time (say, a few thousand years) can evolve in mutually unintelligible forms, despite a genetic relationship. In addition, the written record is relatively sparse – many languages have never been written down, no known text is more than five thousand years old, and no language's entire history to date is represented by available texts. Consequently, as we have seen, proto-forms, both at the head of and within a language family, have typically had to be reconstructed. Because the comparative method is well established in reconstructive methodology and possibly also because such reconstructed forms have an anchor in actual data, we have come to accept that by and large, 'shape' can be given to languages spoken up to about eight thousand years ago (bearing in mind, of course, issues such as semantic change). However, when the reconstructions themselves become the database for further reconstructions, researchers may be forgiven for becoming somewhat nervous. Remember that reconstruction can depend heavily on the database used, as well as on what the researcher considers plausible avenues of change. Given this measure of subjectivity, the use of unattested forms as 'DNA' for hypothetical languages such as Proto-Nostratic, for example, which, if it had existed, would have been spoken 10,000–15,000 years ago, or for Proto-World (up to at least 100,000 years ago), leaves even the most supportive linguist feeling rather unsettled. We are left in the position of only being able to say whether such reconstructions, given the database used and the methodology employed, are plausible; but they bring us no closer to verifying or falsifying the existence of such early languages or their genetic affiliations. Therefore, what is typically presented as an exercise in rationality is very often an act of faith, which may go some way towards explaining the sometimes personal vehemence of the criticisms levelled against this kind of work.

This brings us to an important point: how rational, how scientific, are the methods used for grouping and reconstructing language families? One of the side effects of considering if, and how, we can discover languages and genetic affiliations with no recorded data, is the deeper scrutiny of what we do when we actually have data. Even though some of the results of Greenberg's multilateral comparison, for example, have become largely accepted (as in the case of the Australian and African classifications), the method itself has been criticized as unscientific and subjective. Thus, McMahon and McMahon state that, in terms of his Amerind classification, Greenberg fails to make explicit the criteria on which phonetic and semantic resemblances between the languages being compared are based, and so 'mass comparison could produce a whole range of results, depending on the linguist's personal judgement' (2003: 18). The short-comings of this methodology are often no doubt emphasized in contrast to its seemingly more sensible alternative, comparative reconstruction. But even this long accepted procedure has its limitations. We have already mentioned the fact that the method does not preclude a measure of subjectivity in terms of reconstructed forms, and that it cannot reliably work beyond a certain time-depth. There are, however, other issues. For example, as we have seen, regular and repeated correspondences between cognates are taken as symptomatic of genetic affiliation between languages. In addition, cognates are drawn from the 'stable' elements of a language's lexicon, in order to minimize the risk of contamination from chance similarities and loanwords. It is important to note, though, that this only works if the assumption of stable lexis is true. McMahon and McMahon point out that this has never been tested (nor is it clear how it might be); and there are also attested cases where borrowing across allegedly stable elements has occurred: witness, for example, the 'everyday' borrowings from Old Norse into Old English at the end of the Anglo-Saxon period (see Chapters 1 and 3). In cases where knowledge of the socio-historical context of a language's development is sparse or non-existent, we cannot always be certain of the validity of the cognate database. The result is, of course, that we could end up con-structing an inaccurate system of relationships. More generally, an overarching issue with the comparative method lies with the fact that it is not, ultimately, an objective and generalizable method for determining linguistic affiliations. McMahon and McMahon (ibid.: 13–14) quote a contribution on the HISTLING on-line discussion group which states that 'it is a mistake to assume that the

C[omparative] M[ethod] is a set of airtight procedures which, if followed faithfully, will produce the desired answers – genetic relationships will automatically emerge' (Bob Rankin, 2 May 2002). Indeed, the method is typically elucidated in the context of its application to families such as Indo-European (as in this chapter), which becomes its anchor in extrapolation to 'newer' cases. With no set procedures, the method is essentially heuristic in nature and therefore very open to erroneous conclusions and groupings, especially in cases where the linguist has little or no knowledge of the languages in question.

As such, no statistical, objective tests exist for the determination of genetic affiliation, as well as the degrees of that affiliation, between languages. This is perhaps because:

> There has been a strong tendency to see comparative linguistics as an art rather than a science, and as requiring sensitivity and depth of knowledge of one particular language group on the part of the individual scholar, rather than generalisable techniques which allow the processing of large quantities of data, regardless of the region or family from which they come.
> (McMahon and McMahon, 2003: 9)

Given this state of affairs, it is not surprising that language classifications and relationships remain an area of controversy. It is also not surprising that some researchers are now looking at ways in which the discipline can be made more disciplined. The benefits of this would be mainly twofold. First, the use of an objective, testable and generalizable methodology would allow the field itself to progress: researchers could apply a defined set of procedures to relevant data from any set of languages and statistically determine whether genetic affiliations existed or not. For those so inclined, this would have the potential for ultimately testing super-family groupings. Second, it would bring comparative work in line with methodologies employed by other disciplines such as genetics and archaeology which, with some similar aims in mind, are increasingly taking note of linguistic attempts to 'meet the ancestors'. At the moment, the lack of quantitative analysis and evaluation in comparative linguistics means that it is not producing data which is 'interpretable and usable by neighbouring disciplines' (ibid.: 20). The authors also point out that at the moment, hypotheses (and their methodologies) which are viewed as unreliable by linguists, such as those of Greenberg, often find sympathetic ears among practitioners in other fields, who may see them as bold and progressive ideas. In addition, given the lack of other options, such practitioners may take it upon themselves to develop those ideas and create their own approaches to quantification and evaluation of linguistic data. If linguists want to convincingly demonstrate their reservations about certain classifications, as well as retain control of the data, then they must also be able to provide viable alternatives.

McMahon and McMahon are currently spearheading a project geared towards developing quantitative methods for language classification. Detail on their work so far is available on their website,[8] and in McMahon and McMahon (2003), but I will outline the main points here. First, they are working within a framework proposed by Embleton (1986: 3; quoted in McMahon and McMahon, 2003: 21) for developing a quantitative methodology in linguistics. Embleton (ibid.) states that this is a three-stage process, involving (1) developing a procedure, based on either 'theoretical grounds . . . a particular model, or on past experience'; (2) verifying the procedure by applying it to data 'where there already exists a large body of opinion for comparison'; and (3) applying the procedure to cases where linguistic opinion has not yet been established or produced. Thus, the method, once devised, can be tested for reliability on data that is already categorized and if it succeeds, be generalized to new, untested cases.

McMahon and McMahon have decided to test their procedure on the established Indo-European family, using a cognate database of 200 lexical items. They emphasize, however, that their primary focus in determining cognacy is meaning rather than form; that is, if two words in two languages have the same meaning, then they are considered cognates. Their data is based on Dyen, Kruskal and Black's (1992) 200-word comparative lists for 95 IE languages and dialects[9] and includes items with meanings such as 'and', 'father', 'foot', 'snow', 'three', 'that', 'two', 'woman', and so on. Dyen *et al.* also provide numerical information, namely the percentages of both cognate and non-cognate material that holds between each pair of languages. The latter percentage (that of non-cognate material) yields a 'distance matrix', which indicates the level of distance between the two languages being compared. This data has been fed into programs from the PHYLIP package, which were developed for the reconstruction of evolutionary histories in biology. As the authors state, the programs treat the numerical encodings of genetic and linguistic data in exactly the same way, and run them through the same quantitative procedures. They also have an additional advantage: the programs do not just produce one tree of relationships but instead, generate a set of plausible models. They then select the tree which is most appropriate to the data that has been input; that is 'the tree where branch lengths and order of branching are most consistent with the distances in the data matrix' (McMahon and McMahon, 2003: 29–30). Thus, the effects of a linguist's preconceptions or judgements about linguistic relationships are minimized in the final result, which, as a product of a set of objective procedures, can also be reliably tested for statistical significance. It must be borne in mind, of course, that the programs are only as effective as the data they are given, and it is arguable that the initial determination of cognates, as well as of the degrees of relationship between them, is inevitably subject to human error. However, this is currently unavoidable, and the only solution would seem to be to retain an awareness that there must be a margin of error for all results.

The trees generated as most plausible by the three PHYLIP programs used (Neighbour, Fitch and Kitch) produced very similar patterns of grouping. In addition, they were not significantly dissimilar to the traditional IE tree. Repeated tests, involving re-sampling of the cognate data, demonstrated that the sub-family groupings, such as Germanic, Celtic, Slavic and Romance, were 'extremely robust' (ibid.: 36). In different runs, the languages within those sub-families do appear in slightly different permutations, but all languages consistently stay within their sub-group. The fact that the computer programs largely confirm the less scientific groupings of traditional comparative linguistics is no bad thing: it validates the years of careful research and thought that have gone into determining linguistic relationships, and it also adds some weight to certain assumptions and principles of the comparative method. In addition, the programs generate trees that have 'statistical robustness and assured viability' (McMahon and McMahon, 2003), and that is certainly a step in the right direction. When the authors are assured that they have developed a satisfactory set of procedures for quantitative analysis, they propose to apply them to non-Indo-European languages, in particular little-investigated tongues such as those of the Andean Quechua and Aymara families. Since these languages, which are primarily oral, are in danger of becoming obsolete in the near future, the McMahons' work will have the additional advantage of, at the very least, archiving material which would otherwise have been lost. Overall, research such as the McMahons' promises to move comparative linguistics out of a kind of historical navel-gazing and gives it the potential to both stand as a credible 'science' in its own right and to join forces with other well-established scientific disciplines (such as archaeology and genetics) which are also geared towards reconstructing human history. In the words of Cavalli-Sforza (2000: vii), productive synthesis of reliable results from such fields will ultimately converge towards 'a common story . . . behind [which] must lie a single history' which no-one can help but be fascinated by, since it is ultimately a history of ourselves.

2.5 Study Questions

1. What language families other than the Proto-Indo-European have been classified? Are there cases where classification of individual languages or of groups of languages has proved to be problematic? (Consider here the issue of linguistic isolates.) Useful readings: Trask (1996), Bright (1992), Asher (1994), Voegelin and Voegelin (1977), Baugh and Cable (2002).

2. In 1856, Johannes Schmidt proposed, as an alternative to the tree model, the use of a wave model to map language families. How does a wave model work, and what are its advantages and disadvantages in comparison with the established linguistic family tree? Useful reading: Trask (1996), Mallory (1989).

3. Reconstruction of past language stages makes use not only of the Comparative Method (Section 2.2) but also of another process known as internal reconstruction which analyses data from only one language. Using an example of such reconstruction, explain the method's aims and principles. Are there also, as in the case of the comparative method, limitations to what it can achieve? Useful reading: Trask (1996), Hock (1986), Lass (1975).

Notes

1. See Jenkins (2003: 22–3) for definitions of new Englishes.

2. The question of what constitutes a language as opposed to a dialect is not an easy one. Generally speaking, languages are considered mutually unintelligible, while dialects are mutually intelligible entities. However, as we have seen, a significant dimension of the definition is socio-political.

3. Parsons was not the first scholar to undertake such work. Investigation into 'striking linguistic affinities' had been done by, for example, Marcus Boxhorn (Fennell, 2001: 20) and Joseph

Scaliger (Mallory, 1989: 9) in the seventeenth century and by William Wooton in the early eighteenth (Fennell, 2001: 21).

4. Eco (1995), for example, quotes Adolphe Pictet's glorification of the Aryan race, 'destined by providence to one day rule the entire world . . . summoned from the very beginning to conquer'. He also states that the Aryans possessed a 'language . . . filled with images and intuitive ideas, which bore the seeds of all the future richness of a magnificent poetic expansion and of the most profound thought' (*Les origines indo-européenes ou les Aryad primitifs 1859–63*; cited in Eco, 1995: 106).

5. See Trask (1996: Chapter 8) for a detailed and accessible discussion of the Comparative Method.

6. See Mallory (1989: 19–21) for an illustration of other proposed models.

7. Mallory (1989: 160–1) points out that the PIE word for 'brook trout' has also been reconstructed, and the only area in which salmon *and* brook trout are historically attested is the Pontic-Caspian. Thus, for those so inclined, 'the fish that was once employed to dismiss the steppe region can be used to support it'.

8. *Quantitative Methods in Language Classification* at http://www.shef.ac.uk/english/language/quantling.

9. Dyen *et al.*'s (1992) data are available online at http://www.ldc.upenn.edu.

3 | Old English, 500–1100

3.1 Introduction

In 2003, a panellist on BBC Radio Four's *The News Quiz* (a light-hearted take on current events), in citing a particular study[1] on the speech of Queen Elizabeth II, commented on her increased use of 'simple and common Anglo-Saxon vocabulary' – as opposed to 'elevated' Latinate terminology – in public addresses (broadcast 14 June 2003). It was clear from the comedy sketch that followed, as well as from the reactions of the studio audience, that this assumption of discrete 'simple' and 'complex' – and by an unsurprising extension, 'vulgar' and 'refined' – elements in English is not at all uncommon. Ickowicz (undated), for example, in his guide to effective public speaking, typifies those who make use of Latin, French and Greek words instead of 'simpler Anglo-Saxon based terms' as articulate, since the loanwords 'communicate thoughts clearly, dynamically, succinctly'. Similarly, Marr (2002) wrote that English prose is the arena in which tensions between 'earthy, direct, sensual' Anglo-Saxon vocabulary and 'cerebral, abstract' Latin and French loans play out. Mo Mowlam, Britain's Secretary of State for Northern Ireland, was once reported to have used a 'strong Anglo-Saxon expletive', when she allegedly told another minister to 'eff-off' (*Daily Telegraph*, 13 May 2002). Thus 'simple' and 'common' Anglo-Saxon is often typified as the gut instinct of English – immediate and aggressive – while the classical languages and French provide the 'cerebral' and 'abstract' elements which give the language the veneer and polish of civilization. The alleged 'simple' nature of Anglo-Saxon is therefore perceived as dual: it is the basic, and base, level of English.

The reasons such assumptions persist are partly linguistic and partly socio-cultural. In terms of actual language use, a significant proportion of our modern 'everyday' words, such as *and, but, man, woman, child*, are in fact inheritances from an Anglo-Saxon past, whereas many of the words used in formal and specialized registers were once borrowed from Latin and French, often at times when they had much more social clout than English. For example, the establishment of Norman French rule in England after 1066 (see Chapter 4) began a process of elevating French to a level of social prestige that still continues to this day. Latin has long had a venerable tradition in European scholarship, as well as in cultural and religious life, and English has repeatedly borrowed from it throughout its history (see p. 91, and in particular Chapter 5). These languages therefore have an established association with social power, elevated social status and learning (a perspective that is still perpetuated in educational ideologies), hence the view that their contributions to English comprise the 'cerebral', 'dynamic' and 'succinct': qualities that are 'better' than the everyday Anglo-Saxon that laid the foundations of English.[2]

Other established ideologies also feed such perceptions. There is arguably, for example, a kind of cultural silence about Anglo-Saxon. The language is often positioned as that of marauding, barbarian Germanic hordes; and while many of us grow up knowing about Trojan horses and Hercules, and at the very least have heard of Julius Caesar and Cicero, all of whom are also popularized through television and cinema, the adventures of the Anglo-Saxon hero Beowulf and the song of a lonely seafarer (to mention only two of the many Anglo-Saxon poems we have) largely remain the preserve of a smaller, academic audience. However, anyone interested in Anglo-Saxon culture and language soon finds that all preconceptions of 'basic-ness' and 'baseness' have to be thrown out the window. Old English, as the language of this period is commonly known,[3] often comes to be labelled instead as difficult by those new to its study; and the cultural and literary artefacts which have increasingly been studied since the second half of the twentieth century have contributed to (in academic circles at the very least) an alternative narrative of a rich, vibrant and sophisticated culture. As Mitchell (1995: 99) states:

> What we know about the Anglo Saxons has increased so dramatically since 1950 that those of us who became interested in them before then can only blink with astonishment at the advances in our knowledge of their language, their literature, their history, their culture, their material circumstances, their way of life, and their attitudes to life and the mysteries which lie beyond it.

We will not be able to explore the Anglo-Saxon period in the depth it merits[4] but hopefully this chapter will give some indication of just how 'simple' things Anglo-Saxon aren't.

3.2 Social History

It is easy to forget, in the face of the current global and seemingly established presence of English, that it is in fact a relatively young language in the context of human linguistic history. Humans have probably been speaking to each other for tens of thousands of years (see Chapter 2), but we can really only begin to think of an 'English language' a few hundred years into the common era. In one of the main sources of information on this early period of English, *The Ecclesiastical History of the English Nation*, the seventh-century monk Bede (often given the honorific Venerable) cites *circa* 449 AD as the date of the first significant landings of the language's Germanic progenitors on what would become English soil. This date is therefore often cited in relation to the initial emergence of the English language. However, it is important to note that these initial migrants, known collectively but somewhat erroneously as the Anglo-Saxons, were not English speakers. They spoke instead the closely related Germanic dialects that would become the roots of English within a few generations of settlement and interaction in England. We will therefore, like Fennell (2001), take 500 AD as a more sensible birth-date for English.

It is also worth noting that England's (and indeed Britain's) history did not begin with English. It is thought that the island had been home to human populations some 50,000 years earlier, although some estimates put this as far back as 250,000 (Baugh and Cable, 2002: 43). Regardless of the accuracy of such time-depths, what is certain is the fact that the island was settled during the Stone Age (which lasted in England until approximately 2000 BC), initially by Palaeolithic (old Stone Age) and later Neolithic (new Stone Age), possibly migrant populations. While archaeological and palæontological traces of these peoples remain, no linguistic ones do – we have no idea what language(s) they spoke.[5]

The first settlers in Britain to leave a linguistic legacy were the Celts. This group, which comprised bands of tribes, were once a prolific and dynamic migratory force. By the beginning of the Christian era, they had settled in Gaul and Spain, Britain, western Germany, northern Italy, Greece and Asia Minor. They first began to reach Britain in approximately 600 BC and were probably the first speakers of an Indo-European language to settle there.

As we saw in Chapter 2, the PIE daughter Celtic eventually split into Brythonic and Goidelic. The Goidelic-speaking Celts ultimately settled in Ireland, Scotland and the Isle of Man, giving rise to Irish Gaelic, Scottish Gaelic and the now defunct Manx, while Brythonic speakers initially settled in England but later moved into what is now Wales, Cornwall and Brittany, spawning Welsh, Cornish and Breton. It is difficult, if not impossible, to ascertain exactly when the split between Brythonic and Goidelic occurred, or which band of speakers arrived in Britain first. What is certain, however, is that these new settlers displaced the older languages and cultures extant there – an obsolescing fate their own descendants would encounter much later in the face of English.

Certain unflattering stereotypes of these early Celts as savage warriors still have some currency (witness, for instance, characterizations in films such as *Braveheart*) but the archaeological record in fact points to the emergence of a 'sophisticated culture of warriors, druid-priests and artists' within Britain, which established and took advantage of successful trade zones from 'western Scotland and Wales south all the way to Brittany; south-eastern England with northern Gaul and the Low Countries' (Schama, 2000: 25). Celtic culture in Britain, therefore, appears to have developed not in isolation from, but instead in contact with, continental Europe.

In 55 BC, Britain was invaded by Julius Caesar, an event whose motivation is somewhat unclear, since a popular Roman view of Celtic Britain was not the modern historian's vision of a sophisticated culture but instead, to paraphrase Schama (2000: 25), of a land on the edge of the civilized world. It is possible that Caesar carried out his invasion by invitation: there was a great deal of in-fighting between various tribes, and some of the Celtic kings may well have wanted to demonstrate that they had a strong Roman alliance, which would curb their more aggressive and expansionist kinsmen. Whatever the thinking behind the invasion, it was in reality a disaster: Celts hostile to the Romans put up effective resistance to this and subsequent campaigns in 54 BC.

Nevertheless, working relations between the Celts and Romans continued – successful trading remained uninterrupted, and many sons and rivals of the British Celtic kings often ended up in Rome. A more successful attempt at invasion and colonization came in 43 AD under the Emperor Claudius, who employed a more successful combination of 'military ruthlessness and shrewd political pragmatism' (ibid.: 29). His troops (40,000 strong) managed to subjugate the tribes of the central and south-eastern regions within three years. They were helped immensely by the willingness of many of the tribal kings to capitulate, perhaps in the belief that a Roman alliance would 'strengthen rather than weaken their authority' (ibid.).

The Romans never penetrated far into Wales and Scotland, and eventually most of what is now England (bordered and protected in the north by Hadrian's Wall), and the Brythonic Celts settled there, came under Roman rule – a situation which obtained for about three hundred years. The co-operation of many of the tribal kings seems to have made this an easier transition than it would otherwise have been, but the peace between Roman overlords and subjugated Celts seems to have been initially uneasy. There were numerous revolts, the most famous of which was led by Boudicca in 60 AD, and which ultimately destroyed Colchester (the first Roman city established in England) and left approximately 70,000 Roman soldiers and Romanized citizens dead.

Despite such uprisings, the Romanization of the conquered areas and tribes was extensive – there is ample evidence today of Roman roads and villas in England, as well as of the adoption of Roman styles of dress, entertainment and even cooking utensils. Latin became the official language of public and government records (some remnants of which remain) and eventually of Christianity, which spread into some areas of England in the third century AD. More recently, fragments of Latin writing, from receipts, letters, invitations and bills, have been found in the soil around the forts on Hadrian's Wall, which would have housed garrisoned soldiers and their families (ibid.: 34).

By the late second-early third centuries AD, the Romans and the Brythonic-Celts seem to have settled into a largely peaceful co-existence, which even allowed for inter-marriage and the emergence of a hybrid Romano-Celtic culture in some areas. This cultural exchange also had linguistic consequences: by the third century, the sons of Celtic kings allied with Rome were growing up speaking and writing Latin. This home-grown elite consequently had access to high social positions in the governing of the province. It is difficult, if not impossible, to say exactly what role Latin played for this stratum of society – did some abandon their native Celtic, for example? Were some proficient bilinguals in Latin and Brythonic? Were others simply competent in using Latin in certain specialized domains? What does seem certain is the fact that the majority of the Brythonic Celts continued to use their native language during the Roman occupation. There was never a general shift to Latin, nor was there enough significant contact to engender the birth of new forms, as may have occurred on the continent (cf. French and Spanish; see Chapter 2).

In the fourth century, the Roman Empire began to be attacked by 'the Hun' along its continental boundaries, and troops were withdrawn from England to shore up numbers there. England itself also began to undergo raids from Saxon tribes, which led to the establishment of Saxon Shore forts along the eastern and southern coasts. However, the depleted numbers of Roman legions at all boundaries meant that invaders encountered significantly lessened resistance, and in 367 England felt the brunt of this. In three co-ordinated raids, Anglo-Saxons arriving from across the North Sea, Picts from Scotland and the Gaelic Dal Raita (also known as the Scoti) from Ireland unleashed severe destruction across the land. Rome subsequently sent reinforcements, but they were not sufficient to deter the invaders. Further pleas for assistance fell on ears more preoccupied with the collapse of the Roman Empire on the continent, and in 410 the last of the Roman legions were withdrawn from England, leaving the Brythonic Celts – 'tamed' after centuries of Romanization – on their own.

According to Bede, the native Britons, desperate for some respite from the continuous attacks by the Picts and Dal Riata, formed a pact with their other Germanic aggressors. The latter 'received of the Britons a place to inhabit, upon condition that they should wage war against their enemies for the peace and security of the country, whilst the Britons agreed to furnish them with pay' (Bede, Book I, Chapter XV, in Halsall (2000)). The Saxons easily succeeded in their task, but in what Bede describes as a sudden *volte-face* entered an alliance with the Picts and turned savagely on their Celtic 'hosts'. In 440, invasions began in earnest and in 446, the Celts made a last frantic appeal to Rome for help.[6] None came, and to paraphrase Caesar, the Germanic tribes came, saw and conquered. A new era in the island's history had begun.

One of the inevitable consequences of piecing together narratives of events that occurred such a long time ago (and with limited resources) is that in trying to get the sequence of events right, we end up thinking about them in a kind of linear timeline (a schematic that is in fact used in some texts, such as Fennell (2001); Burnley (1992)). Thus, many modern accounts of this time portray it as a 'tidy compartmentalization of British history', with a 'wholesale destruction of Roman Britain immediately followed by [a] violent reincarnation as Anglo-Saxon England' (Schama, 2000: 45). In fact, as Baugh and Cable (2002), Mitchell (1995), and Schama (2000) note, the transition was much slower and generally much less dramatic. This is not to say that there was no significant hostility between the *Saxons*, as the Celts generally called the invaders, and the *wealas* ('foreigners') as the invaders rather tellingly and cheekily called the Celts. Linguistic and cultural history attests to the fact that large numbers of the Brythonic Celts were forced to leave England, moving into Wales, Cornwall and Brittany. Quite a few must also have been killed in skirmishes with the newcomers. But it seems that a large number also stayed where they were and eventually assimilated with their Anglo-Saxon neighbours. Since the latter were looking to settle on 'already-worked land with *in situ* peasantry . . . and since the only interest the unfree country people had was in calculating which kind of overlord offered the more secure protection, there was an easy fit between the new and the old' (Schama, 2000: 46).

But who exactly were these Anglo-Saxons? As implied earlier, the name is somewhat misleading, since it labels only two of the invading tribes and leaves others, such as the so-called Jutes and the Frisians, invisible. These culturally and linguistically related Germanic tribes were Indo-European in origin, and had migrated out of the *Urheimat* to an area now known as the Great North German Plain. Once in England, however, these tribes tended to settle largely in different areas of the country. According to Bede, the Jutes initially settled in Kent (which still carries its Celtic name), the Saxons in Sussex (south Saxons), Wessex (west Saxons) – areas both south of the Thames (also Celtic) – and later in Essex and Middlesex (both north of the Thames). The Angles settled in the east coast (today, East Anglia), as well as north of the Humber (Northumbria). In each area, tribes would forge useful alliances, or would come together under a powerful leader, and so establish a small kingdom. Eventually, seven of these, known as the Anglo-Saxon Heptarchy, were established: Northumbria, Mercia, East Anglia, Essex, Sussex, Wessex and Kent. One of these kingdoms would gain political supremacy over others at different times: in the early part of the seventh century, Northumbria gained prominence, in the eighth century, Mercia and then in the ninth century, Wessex, under Ecgbert (802–839) and later, Alfred (871–889).

In the late sixth century,[7] Pope Gregory the Great sent missionaries to the kingdom of Kent, where the Jutish ruler, Æthelbert, had married a Frankish Christian princess, Bertha. This band of 'godspellers', led by St Augustine, eventually managed to convert Æthelbert, baptising him into the Christian faith within a few short months. Important monasteries such as those at Jarrow and Lindisfarne were soon established (one of their main purposes being the copying of sacred texts and histories of the early Church), and during the seventh century, most of England became Christianized.

Upon Æthelbert's conversion, Pope Gregory styled him *Rex Anglorum* 'King of the Angles', a title that would later be taken by the leader of any prominent kingdom. This is one of the earliest significant uses of a label (promoted by Bede), derived from the name of one of the Germanic tribes, as a general term of reference. As mentioned earlier, the Celts had initially referred to the invaders as *Saxons*, and early Latin writers had followed this trend, giving the tribes the generic name *Saxones*, and the land they settled on, *Saxonia*. However, the terms *Angli*, *Anglia* and *Angelcynn* ('Angle-kin') soon began to co-occur as general terms of reference. However, the Germanic dialects spoken by the tribes seem to have always been referred to collectively as *Englisc*, again derived from the name of the Angles, and from 1000 onwards it was the language of *Englalond* ('land of the Angles') (Baugh and Cable, 2002: 50–1).

The descendants of the Germanic invaders appear to have settled relatively quickly into their new home. However, in the late years of the eighth century, the sins of the fathers were visited upon the sons and daughters of the original invaders. A series of destructive Viking raids began, as the pressures of over-population in Norway and Denmark took hold (Schama, 2000: 54). The *Danes*, as the English called them, appear to have initially engaged in effective and profitable intimidation, wreaking havoc within a particular area until the relevant leader paid them off (ibid.), and so exploiting any animosity and feuding which existed among the settled communities. This state of affairs soon became intolerable – the Vikings destroyed centres of Christianity such as the monasteries at Lindisfarne and Jarrow, and the threat and actuality of violence, plus the demands for pay-offs, were unceasing. The result of this was not one the Vikings would have foreseen – alliances between previously warring and hostile factions were forged in an attempt to mount effective resistance. In Scotland, the Picts and Dal Riata buried their differences, uniting their kingdoms in 811 under the guidance of the Pictish king, Constantine I. In England, the Anglo-Saxon kingdoms too submitted to a single ruler, Alfred, the only English king ever formally titled 'the Great'.

Alfred became ruler of Wessex in 871, following the death of his brother Æthelred. In the years following, he waged a series of campaigns against the raiders, enjoying some small victories as well as lamenting quite a few defeats. In 878, however, he won a significant victory at Edington over one of the Viking chieftains, Guthrum. Indeed, this victory was military *and* spiritual: Guthrum was so impressed by the skills of Alfred's Christian soldiers that he also decided to convert. Alfred was godfather at his baptism in 878.

Alfred and Guthrum also signed the Treaty of Wedmore in this year, in which Guthrum agreed to stay in East Anglia (which he had seized before the battle at Edington) and to refrain from attacking Wessex, Mercia, Essex and Kent. The Treaty also allowed for Viking settlement in East Anglia, Mercia and Northumbria, east of a line of demarcation which ran roughly from London to Chester. This area, subject to Viking rule, became known as the Danelaw. And the settlers, following Guthrum's lead, largely became Christian. Thus, Alfred managed a '*modus vivendi* with a Christianized, and therefore, relatively peaceful Viking realm' (Schama, 2000: 61).

Attacks from other Viking bands nevertheless continued throughout the late ninth century but were successfully repulsed. In the latter years of the tenth century, however, a new and concerted wave of hostilities began, led in large part by Olaf Tryggvason (King of Norway in 995). The king of England at that time, another Æthelred who became known to posterity as 'the Unready' (although the Old English *unræd* meant 'ill-advised'), had lost a great deal of the support and allegiance Alfred had managed to build up, leaving the new wave of invaders, like their predecessors, able to exploit the resultant instability. They too exacted hefty tributes from English areas, 'thereby subsidising the long-term presence of further Viking fleets' (ibid.: 68) and were eventually joined by King Svein I of Denmark, whose successful campaign resulted in his acceptance as King of England in 1013. His personal triumph was short-lived, however – he died in 1014, and was succeeded by his son Cnut. In 1016, Æthelred and his son Edmund Ironside also died, and Cnut took Æthelred's widow, Emma of Normandy, as his wife. Her son by Æthelred, Edward the Confessor, would become embroiled in some of the intrigues that eventually led up to the events of 1066. To all intents and purposes, England became and remained a Danish colony ruled by Danish kings until 1042, when the line of Alfred was restored with the accession of the Confessor. However, as we will see in the following chapter, there was only a short period of respite before England passed into yet another set of continental hands.

While the physical and cultural effects of the Viking raids were both extensive and dramatic, the linguistic consequences appear to have been much more peaceful. Pyles and Algeo (1982: 103) state that the 'Scandinavian tongues' at that point were 'little differentiated from one another', and were also largely mutually intelligible with the English spoken by the descendants of the original Germanic invaders. Culturally, they also shared similar perspectives, legends and histories. Thus, the Danelaw and later settlements actually brought together peoples who ultimately had a great deal in common, which quickly facilitated inter-marriages and neighbourly living. The Vikings appear to have assimilated to their English-speaking neighbours, and the close and intimate contact between the two groups provided the opportunity for English to borrow quite a few, sometimes surprising, lexical items from Old Norse, as the language of the Vikings is often labelled. Indeed, some scholars argue that the contact between the two languages catalysed certain structural changes in English, a point to which we shall return in Section 3.4.

3.3 Anglo-Saxon Literature

Before we turn our attention to features of Old English usage in Section 3.4, we should take note of the sources from which our linguistic and cultural knowledge of the Anglo-Saxon period is largely derived. The available literature – poetry and prose dating mainly from the tenth and eleventh centuries – has been described collectively as 'one of the richest and most significant of any preserved among the early Germanic peoples' (Baugh and Cable, 2002: 69). Approximately 30,000 lines of Old English poetry survive in the written medium, remnants of a much larger body of material originally composed for oral delivery, as is evidenced by the consistent use of alliterative measure and of specific metrical stress patterns (such as strong weak strong weak): effective devices of oral performance and for aural reception. On the page, each line of poetry comprised two half-lines linked by alliteration and a particular pattern of stress (see Mitchell, 1995: 287ff. and Hamer, 1970: 16–18). The lines in Example 3.1 exemplify the general form of Old English verse (note the alliterating half-lines):

Example 3.1 OE verse

Wrætlic is þes wealstān;	wyrde gebræcon,
Burgstede burston,	brosnað enta geweorc.
Splendid this rampart is,	though fate destroyed it,
The city buildings fell apart,	the works of giants crumble.

(From *The Ruin*, verse and translation by Hamer, 1970: 26–7)

Towards the end of the Anglo-Saxon period, rhyme also came to be used as an 'additional ornament', but the composition of alliterative verse seems to have carried on until the fifteenth century (ibid.: 19).

Surviving Anglo-Saxon poetry ranges across the treatment of mythic, heroic and ecclesiastic subjects, sometimes merging themes of all three. Thus, poetry that nostalgically recounts a Germanic pre-history of heroic deeds and epic struggle is often 'overlaid with Christian sentiment', and that which treats 'purely Christian themes contain[s] every now and again traces of an earlier philosophy not forgotten' (Baugh and Cable, 2002: 69). Despite such thematic overlap, however, certain broad categorizations are possible (Mitchell, 1995: 74–5). There are, for instance, 'heroic' poems such as *Beowulf*, *Deor*, *The Fight at Finnsburh*, *Waldere* and *Widsith*. Historical, biographical poems such as *The Battle of Brunanburh* and *The Battle of Maldon* also exist, as do religious poems such as *The Dream of the Rood* ('Cross'), *Christ* and *Judith*, Christian allegorical compositions such as *The Phoenix*, *The Panther*, *The Whale* and biblical paraphrases such as *The Metrical Psalms*. Lives of the saints were also popular poetic material, as illustrated by *Andreas*, *Elene*, *Guthlac* and *Juliana*. Short elegies and lyrics are comprised by *The Wife's Lament*, *The Husband's Message*, *Wulf and Eadwacer*, *The Ruin*, *The Wanderer* and *The Seafarer*. There are also riddles, gnomic verses (which comprise general maxims), and finally, poems which do not fall into any particular category, such as the *Charms*, *The Runic Poem* and *The Riming Poem*. All of these are collated in the six volumes of the Anglo-Saxon Poetic Records (see Bradley, 1982).

Anglo-Saxon prose writing is characteristically associated with Alfred, the so-called 'father of Old English prose' and a keen patron of learning. On his ascension, Alfred made the revival of education a priority, seeking to provide texts which he deemed important to his subjects' welfare and interestingly, to their sense of self and nationhood. He learnt Latin so that he could undertake translations of important works, and established a 'circle' of translators to aid in this enterprise. The efforts of Alfred and his circle produced translations of Pope Gregory's *Cura Pastoralis* 'Pastoral Care' (which includes Alfred's educational policy in the *Preface* or *Letter*), translations of Boethius' *Consolation of Philosophy* and the *Soliloquies* of St Augustine. Alfred's circle is also associated with the translation of Bede's Latin *Ecclesisastical History* into Old English. Alfred himself, however, is probably most famously associated with the *Anglo-Saxon Chronicle*, a record of important events in English history. The *Chronicle* no doubt also served as a useful propaganda device, since it would inevitably pay particular attention to the successes of its patron, but the record it offers of life in England until approximately the thirteenth century is invaluable and fascinating.

Other prose writings include translations of Pope Gregory's *Dialogues*, and of the *Historia adversus Paganos* by the Spanish priest Orosius, both probably instigated by Alfred. There are also homilies written in the late tenth century, such as *The Blickling Homilies* (around 971), Ælfric's *The Catholic Homilies* (990/994), *Lives of the Saints* (993/999), and the *Homilies* of Wulfstan (who died in 1023). Portions of both the Old and New Testaments were also, translated into English, and prose fiction such as *Apollonius of Tyre*, *Alexander's Letter to Aristotle* and *The Wonders of the East* were also made available. There is also, of course, a body of prose writing in the domains of science and medicine, as well as legal documents such as laws, charters and wills (see Treharne and Pulsiano, 2001, for more detail).

Last but not least, it is noteworthy that Alfred's patronage of writing and translation meant that such works were composed in the dialect of English that prevailed in his home kingdom, that of Wessex. As a result, the West Saxon dialect of Old English was subsequently developed as a literary standard, and its prominent position might well have continued if the Norman Conquest, and ensuing events, had not unfolded. We will return to the development of a standard form of English in Chapters 5 and 6.

3.4 The Language of Old English

In this section, we will consider some of the typical features of Old English (OE) usage. There are, however, a few provisos we should bear in mind. First, and importantly, our knowledge of OE is based wholly on surviving textual material which, while providing a rich source of information (Baugh and Cable, 2002: 69), does not provide a comprehensive record of the language. Nor do we have complete copies of every text ever produced, nor do we know, with absolute certainty, what OE was actually like in the mouths of its everyday speakers – a not unimportant consideration when we consider the difference between everyday speech and formal writing. Thus, extant OE texts give us only an *indication* of contemporary, formal language use, specifically in the written medium, and not a full picture of the OE speech community.

In addition, as we have already mentioned, the OE database is heavily concentrated in one dialect area of Anglo-Saxon England, namely Wessex. Most textbooks (including this one) therefore describe linguistic features that pertain mainly to West Saxon. We should remember, however, that OE, like any other living language, was not uniform across the general speech community. There were, for example, regional dialectal divisions, initially established by the settlement of the various Germanic tribes in different areas of England, and continued by the varying rates and directions of change that each underwent in its particular environment. The available evidence has allowed scholars to distinguish four main dialects: Northumbrian, Mercian (sometimes collectively known as Anglian), West Saxon and Kentish. Northumbrian and Mercian were spoken in the areas of mainly Anglian settlement north of the Thames, while Kentish emerged in its namesake Kent, which became home to mainly Jutish communities. Textual material for these dialects is scant – a few charters, runic inscriptions, brief fragments of verse and of biblical translation have survived in Northumbrian and Mercian, but even less now exists in Kentish (Baugh and Cable, 2002: 53).

In addition, we should bear in mind that no single dialect would have been uniform in itself: it is reasonable to assume that there must have been variation influenced by extra-linguistic factors such as social position, age, and gender, much as there is now. There is no concrete evidence for such sociolinguistic variation, given the limited textual production of the time, but that should not give us licence to assume that it did not exist.

The last point of note about Old English before we start looking at features of the language is that even though it often looks frighteningly different to modern English, there are many ways in which it is quite similar. In essence, most of the differences we perceive are down to the use of archaic lexical items, grammatical features which we no longer use and OE spelling conventions, which not only make use of unfamiliar symbols and rules, but also in some cases reflect pronunciations that are long gone. Thus, if we look back at the two lines of *The Ruin* quoted in Example 3.1, we will very likely find *wrætlic* and *brosnað* unfamiliar, the use of *ge-* in *gebrǣcon* and *geweorc* opaque, and graphs such as *þ, ð* and *æ* adding to the overall 'strangeness' of the piece. At the same time, however, the verb *is* in the poem is identical to its modern English counterpart, *brǣcon* in *gebrǣcon* looks like modern *break*, which would fit with its gloss as 'destroyed', and *weorc* (*geweorc*) looks like 'work'. The *burg* in *burgstede* also has echoes of words such as *burgomaster* ('mayor'), which might lead us to make a very reasonable correlation between *burg* and 'city'.[8] Old English is therefore not a completely 'foreign language' for modern English speakers.

3.4.1 Features of OE Spelling and Pronunciation

We begin our description of OE with one of the most immediately noticeable areas of difference from modern English writing: spelling. Since it also appears to bear some relation to pronunciation, OE scholars typically discuss the two together, as we will here. Again, it is worth remembering that what we can say about OE pronunciation is based on reasonable and reasoned approximations – we cannot know with full certainty what OE speakers actually sounded like.

3.4.1.1 OE vowels: graphs and sounds

The graphs or letters used in OE to represent vowel sounds were *a, æ, e, i, o, u, y*. These seven letters were used for both short and long vowel sounds (a total of 14). Texts typically signal the long vowel quality by a line over the letter, as in *ā* (as opposed to *a*). OE speakers also appear to have made use of the unstressed vowel schwa, as well as of four diphthongs, spelt *eo, ēo, ea* and *ēa* (note again the distinctions of length). The vowel graphs and their pronunciations are illustrated in Example 3.2:

Example 3.2 OE vowels

candel	[ɑ]	candle, lantern	*bān*	[ɑ:]	bone
erian	[ɛ]	to plough	*fēdan*	[e:]	to feed
æfter	[æ]	after	*lǣn*	[æ:]	lease
middel	[ɪ]	middle	*blīcan*	[i:]	to shine
hyldan	[y]	to bow, bend down	*fȳr*	[y:]	fire
corn	[ɔ]	corn, seed	*mōdor*	[o:]	mother
unearg	[ʊ]	bold	*dūn*	[u:]	moor, hill
bealocweam	[æə]	baleful death	*cēalf*	[æ:ə]	calf
eorðe	[ɛo]	earth	*lēo*	[e:o]	lion

3.4.1.2 OE consonants: graphs and sounds

OE speakers appear to have made use of largely the same consonantal sounds as modern English speakers, and quite a few of the same letters: the graphs *b, c, d, f, g* (sometimes *ʒ*), *h, l, m, n, p, r* (used to signify a sound similar to the trilled [r] of Scots English (Pyles and Algeo, 1982; Fennell, 2001)), *s, t, w* (sometimes *þ*), *x* all occurred, as did the more rarely used *k* and *z*. There are, however, a few significant points of difference between the orthographic conventions and phonological systems of the two language stages. In terms of spelling, for instance, OE made use of graphs such as *ð* and *þ*, where modern English uses *th*. The graph sequences *sc* and *cg* were used to respectively represent [ʃ] and [ʤ] in OE spellings such as *fisc* 'fish' and *ecg* 'edge'. Finally, there appears to have been a more transparent correlation between graphs and pronunciation in OE than there is in modern English. Thus, OE orthography reflects the pronunciation of consonant clusters (as in *hring* [hr] 'ring', *hwal* [hw] 'whale', *cniʒt* [kn] 'young man' (modern 'knight') and *gnornian* [gn] 'to mourn, grieve'), as well as of lengthened consonants, as in *bedd* (versus *bēd*) and *racca* (versus *raca*). Pyles and Algeo (1982: 109) state that the pronunciation of the same consonant at the beginning and end of two consecutive words is a good indication of what the OE doubled consonants would have sounded like: thus, the <ll> of *fyllan* 'to fill', for example, would have sounded like the pronunciation of *full-length*, and the <cc> of *racca* like that of *book-keeper*. Such lengthening was meaningful in OE: *bēd* meant 'prayer' but *bedd* meant 'bed', and *raca* meant 'rake' but *racca* referred to part of a ship's rigging.

A major point of difference between the OE and modern English consonant systems lies in the fact that certain phonemes in the latter were conditioned allophonic variants in the former. Thus, sounds such as [v], [z], [ð] were word-medial allophones of /f/, /s/ and /θ/ respectively, and [g], [j] and [ɣ] were allophones of /g/ in complementary distribution, as were the [x], [h], [ç] allophones of /h/ and the [k], [ʧ] allophones of /k/. The list in Example 3.3 sets out the distribution of these allophones with examples of OE words:

Example 3.3 Distribution of OE allophones

OE word	pronunciation	environment
(i) in spelling *f*		
heofon 'heaven'	[v]	word-medially
foroft 'very often'	[f]	word-initially
lof 'praise'	[f]	word-finally
(ii) in spelling *s*		
lēosan 'to lose'	[z]	word-medially
snāw 'snow'	[s]	word-initially
mūs 'mouse'	[s]	word-finally
(iii) in spelling *ð* or *þ*		
brōðor 'brother'	[ð]	word-medially
ōþer 'one of two', 'second', 'another'		
ðearle 'violently', 'sorely'	[θ]	word-initially
þearf 'need'		
uncūð 'unknown'	[θ]	word-finally

(iv) in spelling **g/ʒ**

glēaw 'wise', 'prudent'	[g]	before another consonant or
godcund 'religious', 'spiritual'		back vowels
gēac 'cuckoo', *twēgen* 'twain'	[j]	before or between front vowels
lagu 'care'	[ɣ]	between back vowels or
sorgian 'to sorrow'		after [l] or [r]

(v) in spelling **h**

habban 'to have', *hlin* 'maple'	[h]	word-initially
leoht 'light'	[x]	after back vowels
miht 'might', 'could'	[ç]	after front vowels

(vi) in spelling **c**

cnēo 'knee'	[k]	before a consonant or next to a back vowel
cuma 'stranger', 'guest'		
cirice 'church', *rice* 'kingdom'	[tʃ]	next to a front vowel

We should note in relation to the examples in (iv) that there were instances where g was pronounced [g] and not [j] in the environment of front vowels, as in *gēs* 'geese'. The reason for this is historical: the word originally developed from an earlier Germanic form **gōsi*, pronounced with the requisite [g] before back vowels. Through *i-mutation* (see Chapter 1, Section 1.2), long back [o:] was eventually replaced by long front [e:] which, with the loss of final conditioning *–i*, left *gēs*. However, the pronunciation of <g> as [g] remained, a fossilization of a time when it preceded a back vowel.

3.4.2 Features of OE Grammar

In morphological typology, OE is considered a largely synthetic system, or one which makes use of morphs that carry more than one unit of lexical or grammatical information (see Chapter 1, Section 1.5). As we will see in the following discussion, this is not as clear-cut and as tidy a categorization as it might appear: the OE corpus indicates that the language already incorporated analytic-type features and processes and was continuing to change in this direction. Thus texts indicate that inflectional paradigms were involved in a process of reduction, with some inflections disappearing and others falling together in form. These losses were accompanied by a marked preference for fixed word-order – a feature characteristic of analytic systems. In addition, although OE derivational morphology was productive, texts also evidence a high degree of compounding – again, an analytic-type process. It would seem then that OE texts capture a relatively early stage in a long, ongoing transition from the much more synthetic system of the Germanic ancestor of English to one with a more analytic character.

We begin our detailed look at this synthetic but changing system by considering the inflectional systems of OE nouns, pronouns, adjectives and determiners.

3.4.2.1 OE nouns

Modern English nouns tend not to carry a great deal of grammatical information: we mark them for plurality (*plants*) and possession (*Diana's dog*) but not much else. Old English nouns, as we will see, were much more 'weighty' in terms of such information. For instance, OE nouns were gendered masculine, feminine or neuter. This system, inherited from proto-Germanic (and ultimately from PIE), is typically classed as *grammatical*, which means first of all that the gender assignations of nouns did not necessarily coincide with what we might call 'natural'[9] gender, and thus had relevance only within the language system itself; and, second, that all modifiers and referents of the noun showed grammatical agreement with its gender. Thus, an Anglo-Saxon *wif* ('woman', 'wife') was, despite all her female charms, linguistically designated as neuter and in theory, would therefore have had to be referred to as *hit* ('it'), not *hēo* ('she'). Similarly, the *hlāf* ('loaf', 'bread'; masculine) on your table would have been *hē* 'he', and if you were rich enough to own a *bōc* ('book'; feminine), *hēo* 'she' would have been a prized possession in your household.

In trying to explain a system unfamiliar to modern English users, many texts necessarily focus on such examples, which create the impression that OE gender was at the very least, counter-intuitive, or at the very worst, terrifyingly opaque for a student of the language. It may therefore be something of a relief to know that correlations between grammatical and natural gender did in fact occur, and in a significant proportion of cases. Platzer (2001) examined two general categories of noun – those that label human animates (as in *man, woman, boy, girl*) and those that label non-animates (such as *table, chair*). In a statistical analysis of an OE noun sample, based on earlier work by Jones (1988), Platzer (2001: 38) found that 87 out of 90 sample nouns for human animates (96.67%) showed a correlation between grammatical and natural gender. In addition, texts indicate that OE users sometimes shifted to natural gender in their pronoun reference. For example, in Ælfric's *Catholic Homilies* (i.14.27) the anaphoric pronoun for *Ðæt cild* ('the child'; neuter) is *hē*, and that of *ænne wifman* ('a woman'; masculine) is *hēo* (i.14.21) (Mitchell, 1985; cited in Platzer, 2001: 39). Since writing is more conservative than speech, it is highly likely that such pronoun usage in the texts is indicative of a much higher frequency of occurrence in everyday OE talk.

Platzer (ibid.) therefore concludes that the high level of correlation between grammatical and natural genders in human animates, plus the overturning of grammatical agreement in relevant pronouns, means that grammatical gender had become negligible in this type of noun in the late OE period. This is further supported by the treatment of human animate loanwords into OE. As we saw in Chapter 1, loanwords into any language tend to be adapted to the current and productive systems of speakers, and OE was no exception. Loans denoting human animates were invariably assigned natural gender (Welna, 1980; cited in Platzer,

2001: 40–2). Thus, the Latin derived *papa* ('pope') and the Norse loan *hūsbonda* ('householder'; modern 'husband'), for example, were designated masculine, in accordance with the fact that men inevitably filled these roles.

Where mismatches between grammatical and natural gender did occur, however, is in the class of non-animates. In another statistical sample, Platzer (2001: 38) found that of 556 non-animate nouns, only 122 (21.94%) carried neuter gender. The rest were designated as either masculine or feminine, and the system of pronoun reference tended not to shift to the more natural *hit* 'it'. Instead, pronouns mirrored the gender of their nouns, so that a masculine-designated *scyld* ('shield'), for example, was likely to be referred to as *hē*. Loanwords in the non-animate category also conformed to the regular patterns for this class of nouns: of 402 loans, 349 (86.82%) were assigned masculine or feminine gender, and 53 (13.18%) the more 'natural' neuter gender (Welna, 1980; cited in Platzer, 2001: 42). Interestingly, this means that two opposing gender systems co-existed in OE nouns (see Table 3.1), and ultimately had the same effect of marginalizing the neuter.

The neuter, therefore, was very likely the first gender category to disappear in English. Masculine and feminine designations remained for a slightly longer period (although they too had disappeared by the Middle English period) but via opposing tendencies. Platzer (2001: 45) therefore concludes that 'OE gender was neither straightforward nor homogenous and . . . it encompassed trends which were quite conflicting and far from monolithic as the simple epithet "grammatical gender" tends to imply.' In Section 3.5 we will consider how these 'conflicting trends' could be used to dramatic effect.

From proto-Germanic, OE also inherited a large number of inflectional patterns, or *declensions*, for nouns. Reconstruction indicates that proto-Germanic made use of nouns distinguished by vocalic and consonantal stems (that is, their stems ended in either a vowel or consonant). Each noun-type made use of different inflectional declensions and very likely had some correlation with grammatical gender so that, for example, vowel-stem nouns may have also been feminine. This generally Indo-European pattern was possibly already breaking down when English began to emerge, and definitely by the time the extant OE corpus began to appear. Thus, by the ninth–tenth centuries, the original vowels or consonants in the noun-stems had disappeared (so that proto-Germanic *a*-stem **skipa* 'ship', for example, appears in OE as *scip*), but their inflectional patterns had largely survived. Descriptions of OE nouns therefore make use of the historic vocalic and consonantal stem distinctions as a convenient means of distinguishing between the different

Table 3.1 Gender classifications for OE nouns

Noun class	Predominant gender classification	Predominant gender system
human animate	masculine, feminine	'natural'
non-animate	masculine, feminine	'grammatical'

declensions. Some texts also use the labels *weak* and *strong* in this context: the consonantal *n*-stem declension is referred to as the former, and vocalic stem declensions as the latter (see Pyles and Algeo, 1982: 114).

There were four classes of vocalic stem nouns in Old English; namely, those that had respectively ended in –*a*, –*o*, –*u* and –*i* in proto-Germanic. According to Fennell (2001: 65), the –*i* stems coalesced with the *a*-stem nouns, and thus are not typically dealt with as a separate class. Indeed, it seems that the *a*-stem category was something of a default: the majority of OE nouns fell into this grouping, and in time its pattern of inflections was extended to all nouns. In terms of gender, *a*-stem nouns (including old *i*-stems) were either masculine or neuter, *o*-stems were feminine, and *u*-stems were either. Consonantal stem nouns could carry any one of the three genders.

Apart from their stem groupings, noun inflections were also determined by number (singular/plural) and case. OE made use of five cases: the *nominative*, which typically marked subjects, subject complements and direct address; the *accusative*, which was mainly used for direct objects; the *genitive*, which signalled possessives; the *dative*, which marked indirect objects and the object of some prepositions; and the *instrumental*, used in instances where a modern English speaker would use a preposition such as *with*, or *by means of* (as in *I hit him with a stick*). However, as Pyles and Algeo (1982: 111) state, the dative case was typically used to mark the instrumental function in nouns, so we shall not pay much more attention to it here.

Table 3.2 pulls together all these different strands of stem patterns, case and number in the OE noun declensions. The six stem patterns illustrated here are

Table 3.2 OE noun declensions

	vowel stems			consonant stems		
Case and number	Masculine a-stem	Neuter a-stem	o-stem	z-stem	u-stem	Root-consonant stem
	stone	*animal*	*gift*	*child*	*hunter*	*foot*
nominative (singular/ plural)	stān/ stānas	dēor/ dēor	giefu/ giefa	cild/ cildru	hunta/ huntan	fōt/ fet
accusative (singular/ plural)	stān/ stānas	dēor/ dēor	giefe/ giefa	cild/ cildru	huntan/ huntan	fōt/ fēt
dative (singular/ plural)	stāne/ stānum	dēore/ dēorum	giefe/ giefum	cilde/ cildrum	huntan/ huntum	fēt/ fōtum
genitive (singular/ plural)	stānes/ stāna	dēores/ dēora	giefe/ giefa	cildes/ cildra	huntan/ huntena	fōtes/ fōta

those which were most common in OE, or of which parts have survived into modern English.

The possessive –'s and plural –s of modern English are descended from the *a*-stem's genitive singular –*es* and plural –*as* respectively. In fact, as Pyles and Algeo (1982: 113) point out, the use of these two inflections in modern English makes the *a*-stem the only 'living declension', since they are so productive: not only are they used with the majority of already existing nouns, but speakers also invariably apply them to any new nouns that enter the language. Thus, even though we still make use of *n*-stem plurals such as *oxen, children* and the restricted *brethren*, as well as of forms which have no overt plural marking such as *deer* and *sheep* (neuter *a*-stems), they are but fossilizations of now-dead declensions.

You will probably have noticed that many of the noun inflectional endings look identical, sometimes within and across declensions. In addition, some noun forms seem uninflected, as in the singular nominative and accusative forms of the *a*-stem nouns. We could justifiably question at this point how this squares with a system ostensibly built on maintaining inflectional distinctions among its noun types. In other words, what is the point of having different noun declensions with different inflectional patterns if they are more or less the same both within and across paradigms? What is the point of operating a case system when some nouns are not inflected for it?

The most reasonable answer is that this was not always the case. We can only assume that the inflectional patterns for noun-types were once distinct (very likely in Proto-Germanic and earlier ancestral forms, and possibly in early Old English), but that over the course of time they fell together, or underwent *syncretism* for speakers. As we know with hindsight, the majority of these inflectional markings went on to disappear in later stages of English. It is difficult to state with any certainty exactly why such changes occurred, although some scholars (such as Thomason and Kaufman, 1988) have argued that they are a typical result of intergenerational transmission, and others (such as Bailey and Maroldt, 1977) have suggested instead that they result from contact (see Chapter 4, Section 4.5). Whatever the actual reasons, the extraction of paradigms such as those in Table 3.2 from the OE corpus provides a unique snapshot of the progress of a particular change in the language.

3.4.2.2 OE definite articles

The OE definite article, unlike that in modern English, showed agreement with the gender, case and number of the noun it modified. These different forms of *the* are illustrated in Table 3.3.

The corpus indicates that the singular masculine nominative form *se* was changed by OE speakers to *þe*, possibly through analogy with the more common þ- forms, eventually yielding modern *the*. Modern *that* is also derived from the singular neuter nominative and accusative forms *þæt*. Notice the syncretism also evident in these forms – no distinctions of gender are made in the plural forms, the singular dative and genitive forms for the masculine and neuter are identical,

Table 3.3 Forms of the definite article *the*

	Masculine	Feminine	Neuter
sing. nominative	sē, se	sēo	þæt
sing. accusative	þone	þā	þæt
sing. dative	þæm	þære	þæm
sing. genitive	þæs	þære	þæs
plural nominative and accusative	þā	þā	þā
plural dative	þæm	þæm	þæm
plural genitive	þāra	þara	þāra

as are the singular nominative and accusative forms in the neuter, and the singular dative and genitive forms in the feminine.

3.4.2.3 OE adjectives

Adjectives also had to show agreement with the case, gender and number of the nouns they modified. Each adjective also had two forms, strong and weak. Weak forms were used when the noun being modified referred to a definite or specific entity, signalled, for example, by the structure *definite article/demonstrative/personal pronoun + adjective + noun* (as in *the stupid cat, this great book, my lovely house*). Strong forms were used when no such specific reference was meant (as in generic *lovely houses* or *a lovely house is easy to find*).

The strong and weak declensions of the adjective are set out in Tables 3.4–3.6 using *gōd* ('good') in conjunction with the appropriate forms of *the*, as well as of masculine, feminine and neuter nouns. Note again both the lack of, and syncretism of, adjectival endings in some parts of the paradigms.

Even though we no longer have these adjectival declensions in modern English, we have kept the OE comparative and superlative endings <-ra>

Table 3.4 Masculine nouns – strong and weak adjectival declensions

	Masculine noun *guma* 'man'	
	Strong *good man/men*	Weak *the good man/men*
	singular	
nominative	gōd guma	sē gōda guma
accusative	gōdne guman	þone gōdan guman
dative	gōdum guman	þæm gōdan guman
genitive	gōdes guman	þæs gōdan guman
	plural	
nominative and accusative	gōde guman	þā gōdan guman
dative	gōdum gumum	þæm gōdum gumum
genitive	gōdra gumena	þāra gōdra/gōdena gumena

Table 3.5 Feminine nouns – strong and weak adjectival declensions

	Feminine noun *ides* 'woman'	
	Strong *good woman/ women*	Weak *the good woman/ women*
singular		
nominative	gōd ides	sēo gōde ides
accusative	gōde idese	þā gōdan idese
dative	gōdre idese	þǣre gōdan idese
genitive	gōdre idese	þǣre gōdan idese
plural		
nominative and accusative	gōda idesa	þā gōdan idesa
dative	gōdum idesum	þǣm gōdum idesum
genitive	gōdra idesa	þāra gōdra/gōdena idesa

(*heardra* 'harder') and <-ost>/<-est> (*hardost* 'hardest') (see Pyles and Algeo, 1982: 118–9 for more details on the adjective).

3.4.2.4 OE personal pronouns

The personal pronouns in modern (standard) English still largely preserve the distinctions of case, gender and number evident in OE: we have, for example, subject and object pronouns (*I* vs *me*), masculine, feminine and neuter in the third person (*he, she, it*), and singular and plural forms (*I* vs *we*). What we have lost are the OE distinctions of singular and plural in the second person forms (represented in modern English *you*), the dual (pronoun forms used for specific reference to two people), and the OE third person plural *h-* forms,

Table 3.6 Neuter nouns – strong and weak adjectival declensions

	Neuter noun *cild* 'child'	
	Strong *good child/ children*	Weak *the good child/ children*
singular		
nominative	gōd cild	þæt gōde cild
accusative	gōd cild	þæt gōde cild
dative	gōdum cilde	þǣm gōdan cilde
genitive	gōdes cildes	þæs gōdan cildes
plural		
nominative and accusative	gōd cildru	þā gōdan cildru
dative	gōdum cildrum	þǣm gōdum cildrum
genitive	gōdra cildra	þāra gōdra/gōdena cildra

Table 3.7 First, second and dual person pronouns

	First person			Second person		
	Singular	Plural	Dual	Singular	Plural	Dual
nominative	ic 'I'	wē 'we'	wit 'we both'	ðū 'you'	gē 'you all'	git 'you both'
accusative	mē 'me'	ūs 'us'	unc 'us both'	ðē 'you'	ēow 'you all'	inc 'you both'
dative	mē 'me'	ūs 'us'	unc 'us both'	ðē 'you'	ēow 'you all'	inc 'you both'
genitive	mīn 'mine'	ūre 'our(s)'	uncer 'our(s) both'	ðīn 'your(s)'	ēower 'your(s) all'	uncer 'your(s) both'

which were replaced by the Old Norse forms *þai, þeim, þeir(e)* – the ancestors of *they, them, their*.

The OE pronoun forms for the first, second and dual persons are set out in Table 3.7, and those for the third person in Table 3.8.

Again, syncretism is evident: the accusative and dative forms in the first and second persons, for instance, are identical; as are the dative singular forms of the masculine and neuter third person.

3.4.2.5 OE verbs

OE verbs typically fall into two categories *weak* and *strong*, a classification based on the distinct processes by which each type formed preterites and past participles. We will return to this point of difference below, but will first consider areas of similarity between the two verb types.

Both weak and strong infinitive forms carried the suffix *–an* (later superseded by the preposition *to*). In yet another example of syncretism, both verb types also

Table 3.8 Third person pronouns

	Masculine	Feminine	Neuter
	singular		
nominative	hē 'he'	hēo 'she'	hit 'it'
accusative	hine 'him'	hī 'her'	hit 'it'
dative	him 'him'	hire 'her'	him 'it'
genitive	his 'his'	hire 'her(s)'	his 'its'
	plural (no gender distinction)		
nominative	hī 'they'		
accusative	hī 'them'		
dative	him, heom 'them'		
genitive	hira, heora 'their(s)'		

Table 3.9 Present indicative and subjunctive inflections

	Present indicative		Present subjunctive	
	weak verb *ferian* 'to carry'	strong verb *drīfan* 'to drive'	weak verb *ferian* 'to carry'	strong verb *drīfan* 'to drive'
ic	fere	drīfe	fere	drīfe
ðū	ferest	drīfest	fere	drīfe
hē, hēo, hit	fereð	drīfeð	fere	drīfe
wē, gē, hī	ferað	drīfað	feren	drīfen

carried the same inflections for person and number in the present indicative, as well as in the present subjunctive, as can be seen in Table 3.9.

As mentioned earlier, weak and strong differed in their formation of preterites and past participles. OE weak verbs, which were in the majority and of which there were three main classes, did so through the suffixation of –d or –t (as in modern *walk~walked~(have) walked*), whereas strong verbs changed their root vowel, an inherited Indo-European process known as *ablaut* (as in modern *drink~drank~(have) drunk*).

You may see here a parallel between the OE weak/strong and modern English *regular/irregular* distinctions, since the latter terms are often used to distinguish between verbs which form preterites with –ed (regular) and those which do so by changing the stem-vowel (irregular). We should note, however, that the equivalence is by no means a straightforward one. Modern *keep*, for example, is typically described as irregular, but is derived from the OE weak verb *cēpan*. The voiceless final [t] of *kept* resulted from the assimilation of weak –d to the preceding voiceless [p] (OE preterite *cēpte*). Subsequent sound changes have resulted in what seems like a stem-vowel change (*keep* [i:] ~ *kept* [ɛ]), and have obscured the fact that the root vowel remained unchanged throughout the paradigm in OE. Since we associate vowel change with irregular verbs, we have come to assume that *keep* now fits into this latter paradigm.

Tables 3.10 and 3.11 illustrate the basic patterns of preterite and past participle formation in OE weak and strong verbs, and Table 3.12 shows the inflectional conjugation for preterite forms according to the person and number of their subjects. Weak verbs fell into three classes and strong verbs into seven. Some of these also

Table 3.10 Weak verb preterite and past participle forms (one from each main class)

	keep	*end*	*have*
infinitive	cēpan 'to keep'	endian 'to end'	habban 'to have'
preterite	cēpte 'kept'	endode 'ended'	hæfde 'had'
past participle	gecēped 'kept'	geendod 'ended'	gehæfd 'had'

Table 3.11 Strong verbs (one from each main class)

	class 1 *write*	class 2 *creep*	class 3 *sink*	class 4 *steal*	class 5 *speak*	class 6 *go*	class 7 *call, fall*
ablaut pattern	ī, ā, i, i	ēo, ēa, u, o	i, a, u, u	e, æ, ǣ, o	e, æ, ǣ, e	a, ō, ō, a	x, ē, ē, x OR x, ēo, ēo, x
infinitive	wrītan	crēopan	sincan	stelan	sprecan	faran	hātan, feallan
singular preterite	wrāt	crēap	sanc	stæl	spræc	fōr	hēt, fēoll
plural preterite	writon	crup	suncon	stǣlon	sprǣcon	fōron	hēton, fēollon
past participle	gewriten	gecropen	gesuncen	gestolen	gesprecen	gefaren	gehāten, gefeallen

had sub-classes, but we will not explore these here (see, for example, Pyles and Algeo, 1982: 125–8).

Note that certain inflections were used consistently either for both weak and strong verbs, or within one paradigm. Thus, apart from the infinitive inflection –*an* which we have already noted, all plural preterites of weak and strong verbs carried –*on*, and all past participle forms also carried the prefix *ge-* (sometimes known as the *completive prefix*), which disappeared as the past participle came to be consistently preceded by forms of the auxiliary *to have* (as in *I have/had ended the relationship*). All strong verb past participles ended in –*en*, which is still preserved in modern forms such as *written* and *broken*.

Finally, through analogy with the larger number of OE verbs, many strong verbs (of which there were only ever about three hundred) eventually gained weak preterite and past participle forms. Indeed, –*(e)d* has become the *de facto*, productive preterite/past participle suffix for English, as is evidenced by its application to new verbs accepted into the language (see Chapter 1).

Table 3.12 Weak and strong verb preterite conjugations

	weak verb ferian 'to carry' > 'carried'	strong verb drifan 'to drive' > 'drove'
ic	fremede	drāf
ðū	fremedest	drīfe
hē, hēo, hit	fremede	drāf
wē, gē, hī	fremedon	drīfon

Table 3.13 OE *bēon* 'to be'

	Present	Preterite
ic	eom *or* bēo 'am'	wæs 'was'
ðū	eart *or* bist 'are'	wǣre 'were'
hē, hēo, hit	is *or* bið 'is'	wæs 'was'
wē, gē, hī	sindon, sind, sint *or* bēoð 'are'	wǣron 'were'

We cannot leave OE verbs without mentioning the most frequently occurring and most anomalous verb in English, *bēon* 'to be'. The modern forms of this verb – both past and present – seem to follow no discernible pattern whatsoever, largely because they derive from four historically unrelated verbs. This suppletive paradigm (that is, one which combines historically unrelated forms) in OE is illustrated in Table 3.13.

Eom, is and *sindon/sind/sint* forms ultimately derive from a PIE root *es-* (with the forms *esmi, *esti, *senti). *Eart* comes from another PIE root *er-*, meaning 'arise' and *bēo/bist/bið/bēoð* from *bheu-* which possibly meant something like 'become'. The preterite forms are derived from OE *wesan* (Pyles and Algeo, 1982: 129).

3.4.3 Features of OE Syntax: Word Order

Because of features such as case marking and explicit subject–verb agreement, OE word order was much more flexible than that of modern English, allowing for – as we have already mentioned in Chapter 1 (Section 1.6) – both OV and VO structures. By the late years of the Anglo-Saxon period, VO order appears to have increasingly become the norm, very likely in accompaniment to the inflectional reduction we have observed in the last section, which would have eroded morphological signals of case. As we will see, however, there were instances in which V(S)O or OV was preferred, possibly in accordance with developing stylistic conventions in the emerging West Saxon standard. OV order, for example, was common when the object of a verb was a pronoun (see Example 3.4(a)), when an object was topicalized (Example 3.4(b)), or in a subordinate clause introduced by a relative pronoun such as *þæt* 'that' (Example 3.4(c)).

On the other hand, VO was (as stated earlier) the basic, unmarked sentence order in OE (Example 3.4(d)). It was also common in instances where main clauses were introduced by an adverbial such as *þā* 'then' – a frequent occurrence in OE prose narratives and biblical translations. In such cases, the verb would typically precede the subject, giving V(S)O word order (Example 3.4(e)–(f)).

Example 3.4 OE word order
OV word order

(a) hē	hine	geseah
he	*him*	*saw*
S	**O**	**V**

(b) Ðā æfter fēawum dagum	ealle his þing	gegaderode	se gingra sunu
then after a few days	all his things	gathered	the younger son
	O	V	S

(c) God	geseah	ðā	þæt	hit	gōd	wæs
God	saw	then	that	it	good	was
				S	O	V

VO word order

(d) On ðām sixtan dæge	hē	gescēop	eal dēorcynn
On the sixth day	he	made	all kinds of animals
	S	V	O

(e) Ðā	dǣlde	hē	him his ǣhta
then	gave	he	him his property
V	S	O	

(f) Ðā	ārās	hē	from þǣm slǣpe
then	arose	he	from sleep
V	S	O	

In terms of question formation, OE appears to have inverted subjects and verbs (Example 3.4(g)–(h)):

(g) hwæt	sceal	ic	singan?
What	have	I	to sing?

(h) hwæt	segest	þū,	yrðling?
What	say	you,	farmer?

Finally, in negative statements, ne, the negative particle, appeared at the beginning of the clause, and was typically followed by the verb and subject (Example 3.4(i)):

(i) ne	con	ic	nōht	singan
not	know	I	nought	to sing

[I don't know how to sing]

3.4.4 Features of OE Vocabulary

As we noted in Chapter 1 (Section 1.3), English has been no stranger to lexical borrowing throughout its history. In its Anglo-Saxon years, however, English was much more conservative: OE vocabulary was primarily Germanic, with comparatively smaller amounts of loans from Latin, Celtic and Old Norse, and a heavy reliance on compounding and affixation (mainly with native elements) as productive processes of lexical augmentation. We will now briefly consider each in turn, beginning with compounding.

OE compounds comprised mainly nouns and adjectives and as in modern English, their final element typically acted as the head. Thus, a compound such as *hēah-clif* 'high-cliff' (adjective + noun) would have been treated as a noun. Examples from the vast range of OE compounds include formations such as *bōc-cræftig* 'book-crafty' > 'learned', *god-spellere* 'good-newser' > 'evangelist' and *hēah-burg* 'high city' > 'capital'.

These compounds, like those cited in Chapter 1 (Section 1.3), are transparent in that their separate elements are discernible. Modern English has, however, inherited a few amalgamated compounds from OE; that is, words which were once transparent compounds but which, through pronunciation and spelling changes, have fallen together into a seemingly indivisible whole. Examples include *daisy* (*dæges* + *ēage* 'day's eye'), *garlic* (*gār* + *lēac* 'spear leek'), *hussy* (*hūs* + *wīf* 'house wife') and *nostril* (*nosu* + *þyrel* 'nose hole'). Many place names are also the result of such amalgamations: *Boston* (Botulph's stone), *Sussex* (*sūð* + *Seaxe* 'south Saxons') and *Norwich* (*norþ* + *wīc* 'north village') (examples from Pyles and Algeo, 1982: 273).

A final point to note about compounding in OE is that it appears to have been an extremely useful device in poetic composition. The alliterative patterns used in this genre (see Section 3.3) necessitated the availability of a variety of synonyms for the same concept, hence the creation of oft-quoted compounds such as *swanrād* 'swan-road', *hwalrād* 'whale-road' and *ganetes bæð* 'gannet's bath' for the sea. Fennell (2001: 77) also notes that the lexical variety produced by such processes may also have served an aesthetic purpose in keeping the poetry 'fresh and exciting'.

Overall, many OE compounds were replaced by loanwords after the Anglo-Saxon period but as we have seen (Chapter 1, Section 1.3) compounding has remained a productive process of word-formation in English. Indeed, it was even consciously and deliberately espoused as a means of lexical augmentation at a time when native English vocabulary was feared to be under threat from an influx of loanwords. We shall return to this in Chapter 5.

In terms of affixation OE, like modern English, made productive use of prefixes and suffixes. We have already discussed one such affix *–ly* in Chapter 1 (Section 1.6); others include *–dom*, as in *þeowdom* 'slavery'; *–ig* (modern English *–y*), which was used to form adjectives from nouns, as in *mōdig* 'valiant' (*mōd* 'heart', 'mind', 'power'); and *–hād* (modern *–hood*), which formed abstract nouns, as in *cildhād* 'childhood'. Prefixes include *for-*, which generally had a negating quality, as in *forwyrcan* 'to forfeit' (*wyrcan* 'to do'), or an intensifying one, as in *forniman* 'to destroy', 'consume' (*niman* 'to capture'); *mis-*, which also negated the sense of the attached word, as in *misdæd* 'evil deed' (*dæd* 'deed'); *un-* (also still used as a negator), as in *unæþele* 'not noble' (*æþele* 'noble'), and *wið-* 'against', as in *wiðcwepan* 'to refuse' (see Pyles and Algeo, 1982: 264–6 for more examples).

It is important to note that the productivity of the two processes just discussed did not preclude the (albeit relatively minor) incorporation of loanwords, in particular from Latin, Celtic and Old Norse. Borrowings from the latter two sources occurred once the Anglo-Saxons had settled into their new English home – and at early and late stages in the period respectively – but the stages and sources of Latin borrowing were much more diverse. The Germanic ancestors of the Anglo-Saxons had encountered Latin on the Continent as it spread through the expanding Roman Empire, and would certainly have engaged with its speakers in trade and military action. They may have also found themselves living in or near Roman encampments. This contact led to the borrowing of words such as *butter, cheese, -monger* 'trader' (as in *fishmonger*), *pepper, pound, street* and *mile*. These would be preserved in OE and, of course, are still with us. Pyles and Algeo (1982: 293) estimate that approximately 175 words were borrowed from Latin during this period of continental contact.

The contact between the Celts and Romans in England (see Section 3.2) led to Latin borrowings into Celtic. In their early stages of contact with the Celts, the Anglo-Saxons incorporated some of these into their emerging English. Loans include words such as *candle, chester* 'city' (as in *Chester, Manchester*), *mynster* 'monastery', *peru* 'pear' and *port*. After the Anglo-Saxons' conversion to Christianity in the seventh century, religious loans from Latin appeared: *apostle, altar, mass, martyr, demon, temple*. Some of these are ultimately derived from Greek, since Latin had, in its own history, frequently borrowed from this language. Overall, approximately five hundred words from Latin became part of the OE word stock, but many of these have since been lost. Yet, as we have already noted, Latin loans would continue to enter English throughout the centuries, and would play an important role in lexical augmentation in the Early Modern Period (see Chapter 5).

Although five hundred loanwords is a relatively small figure, it is astronomical compared with the number of Celtic borrowings. It has been estimated that perhaps no more than 12 words from Celtic were incorporated into English during the OE period. These included words for geographical features such as *torr* 'peak', *cumb* 'deep valley', *crag*; animals such as *brocc* 'badger'; and miscellaneous words such as *bannuc* 'a bit' and *bratt* 'cloak'. However, many current place names and names of topographical features such as rivers and hills remain as evidence of England's Celtic settlement. *Kent*, where the Jutes initially settled, is derived from Celtic, as is *Devon*, which preserves the name of the tribal *Dumnoni*. *London* is also Celtic, and *Cumberland* means 'land of the Cymry' (which is what the Welsh, or Cymraig, call Wales). *Thames, Avon, Esk, Wye, Usk* are all Celtic river names. The low percentage and domains of borrowing are unsurprising when we consider the socio-historical context of the contact between the early Celtic settlers and the Germanic invaders (see Section 3.2).

The Anglo-Saxons of the eighth and ninth centuries, however, had a very different relationship with the Vikings who invaded and later settled. As stated in Section 3.2, once the bloody hostilities had been put on hold, there seems to have been a period of relatively peaceful settlement in the Danelaw, where these Anglo-Saxon and Viking cousins lived side by side. It is likely that the two languages were also used simultaneously, given their high degree of mutual intelligibility, and as the two groups mixed through marriage, there may also have been extensive lexical mixing. In other words, some Old Norse items may have come to be used synonymously with OE cognates, and eventually either one or the other may have dropped out of use (as in the case of OE *ey* and ON *egg*, which co-existed until well into the fifteenth century); or semantic differentiation may have taken place (as in the case of cognate OE *shirt* and ON *skirt*, both of which originally meant 'garment').

The fact that these two related tongues co-existed closely is borne out by the type of ON words which became part of English. OE borrowed Norse third person plural *th-* forms, prepositions such as *till* and *fro*, and 'everyday' lexical items such as *sister, fellow, hit, law, sky, take, skin, want,* and *scot* 'tax' (as in *scot free*): in each case, examples of borrowing inexplicable without reference to extremely close contact (see Chapter 2).

Some scholars (such as Bailey and Maroldt, 1977) have argued that the contact between ON and OE was intimate enough to not only have caused such lexical transference, but also to have catalyzed creolization which, in their view, produces a new analytic-type system (a claim we will consider more closely in Chapter 4). While contact does sometimes indeed result in the emergence of languages labelled creoles, and while it can sometimes influence the emergence of certain structural features, there is no evidence that the situation between OE and ON speakers was conducive to either. The high degree of mutual intelligibility between OE and ON, plus the fact that ON speakers appear to have assimilated relatively quickly to the English-speaking majority, strongly suggests that the situation necessary for a creole to emerge simply did not exist. In addition, as Thomason and Kaufman's (1988) extensive and detailed analysis shows, the textual evidence indicates not the emergence of a new analytic-type system in the areas that underwent contact but instead the 'continuation' of the relevant English varieties with differing levels of borrowing from Old Norse. They therefore conclude that there is no tangible basis for Bailey and Maroldt's claim (see Fennell, 2001: 86–93; Thomason and Kaufman, 1988: 306–15, for fuller discussion).

3.5 Doing Anglo-Saxon Gender: Heroic Men and Monstrous Women

In this section, we consider the idea that the gendering system of nouns and pronouns in Old English reflected, and reinforced, perceptions of gender roles in Anglo-Saxon society. While this has been a productive line of enquiry in the work of Anglo-Saxon literary scholars (of whom I will say more below), it is typically not addressed in linguistic histories of English. It is, however, of potential interest to socio-historical linguists involved in gender studies for a number of reasons. Sociolinguists' and Anglo-Saxonists' work on gender both tend to make use of the same overarching theoretical frameworks and concepts; and both (albeit with different databases) consider how linguistic usage reflects (and again, reinforces) cultural ideas of what constitutes masculinity and femininity. While modern sociolinguistic studies of gender and the English language do have a historical dimension (for example, introductions to the area typically point out that many nouns associated with feminine roles have historically undergone semantic derogation; that a seventeenth-century parliamentary act made the use of *he* as a generic pronoun the legitimate choice; and more generally, that the authentic female voice is largely absent from the textual record), they tend not to extend as far back as the Anglo-Saxon period, where the gendering system has been viewed mostly as a purely linguistic feature. Anglo-Saxon 'gender scholars', however, have, in their analyses of poems such as *Beowulf*, argued for the same kind of links between language and culture that sociolinguists investigating gender in contemporary society do. There is therefore a great deal of scope for dynamic interaction between the two fields.

The main part of this section will be devoted to the constructions of Anglo-Saxon masculinity and femininity as manifested in *Beowulf* (based primarily on the work of Chance (1991), Overing (2000) and Lees and Overing (2001)). We begin, however, with a closer look at the notion of gender.

In everyday usage, *gender* is quite a common term: we speak of gender differences, gender stereotypes, gender inequality and gender issues. For many, the term signifies the biological division between male and female, a perspective succinctly summarized by Thomas Jefferson (who, interestingly, produced a grammar of Old English): 'the word gender is, in nature, synonymous with sex. To all the subjects of the animal kingdom nature has given sex, and that is twofold only, male or female, masculine or feminine' (quoted in Frantzen, 1993: 459). In this binary perspective, males and females behave, think and even talk in ways that are 'naturally' masculine and feminine respectively: call it sex difference, call it gender difference, call it Men are from Mars, Women are from Venus, it comes to much the same thing, namely that the biological and social differentiation of the sexes is concomitant.

However, as Frantzen (1993: 459) states, this differentiation is a murky business, and we often linguistically contradict this perception of ordered, discrete, biological categories. There are, for example, speakers of English who refer to cars, boats and (in the realm of 'queer-speak') biological males as *she*, computers as *he* and unfamiliar babies as *it*. Cameron (1992: 93) also notes that some Frenchwomen in traditionally male-dominated professions, such as lecturing and medicine, prefer to retain the 'male' titles *le Professeur* and *le Docteur*, instead of forming and adopting ones which reflect their biological sex.

Instances such as these show that biological sex (and lack of it) is not translated in a straightforward, unambiguous manner into cultural life and by extension, into cultural systems such as language. We can, and do, *construct* cultural worlds in which things and people, regardless of biological sex, are imbued with qualities, attributes and behaviours that are designated more or less 'masculine' and 'feminine'. I say 'designated' because what constitutes masculinity and femininity varies culturally and is therefore not a 'natural', universal constant, though we are taught to perceive it as such. Cameron (1992: 83) states that:

> In societies organised around sexual differentiation (which means all known societies) we are led to believe that masculine and feminine are simple categories of the natural world, like plants

and animals . . . the two classes exist and can be defined. Feminist theorists have argued that this is a mistake; or less politely, a con. The only thing that is constant is the assertion of difference.

Thus, in some societies, fishing is considered a masculine activity while weaving is seen as feminine; and in others the complete opposite is true (ibid.: 83). This socio-cultural, not biological, differentiation of the masculine and feminine is what scholars refer to as *gender*: 'although gender presents itself as a given (as something natural, if only because it has been naturalized), "masculinity" and "femininity" are best understood as constructions, as modes of being that depend upon their specific cultural moment to imbue them with meaning' (Cohen, 1995: 3).

This means that conceptions of gender vary not only inter-, but intra-, culturally. Cohen (1995: 3) states for example that 'most people would agree that no inherent value adheres to dying during battle; the act is simply painful. However, certain societies under necessitating conditions represent such a fate as glorious.' Since it is mostly men who engage in and die in battle, this 'behaviour' becomes classified as masculine, and more specifically in the relevant cultural context, heroic masculine:

> The code of behaviour which renders dying in the midst of arms heroic is part of a gender code: it valorizes a masculinity that . . . is altruistic. Heroic masculinity here is wholly dependent upon its generative cultural moment for its codification as a significant means of organizing (and thereby modifying) human behaviour.

(ibid.: 3)

We will return to this relationship between gender construction and cultural context in *Beowulf*.

It is also noteworthy that since gender is more of a cultural construction than a sexual predisposition, whatever a culture has designated masculine and feminine can be performed by both sexes, which can result in a range of 'gender behaviours'. Thus, in Cohen's example, the society that idealizes the 'heroic masculine' can also be home to 'heroic' women and 'unheroic' men. Thus, as Frantzen (1993: 451–2) states,

> [gender] describe[s] both the behaviour expected of men and women and the behaviour not expected of them: it allow[s] for men who '[act] like men' and for those who [do] not (leaving open the possibility that they therefore '[act] like women'), and for women who '[act] like women' and those who [do] not (leaving open the possibility that they therefore '[act] like men'). Gender admits the force of the social into sexual identity that, biologically seen as sex, [is] much less complicated.

In addition, Cohen (1995: 3) argues that in some 'cultural moments', 'performing femininity', for example, can be part of the remit of masculinity: 'according to the taxonomy inherited from the Victorian reception of classical epic, the "traditional" ("masculine") hero is violent and aggressive; the "non-traditional" ("feminized") hero is thoughtful and wily, a deviser of strategies rather than a combatant'. Thus, neither masculinity or femininity is monolithic in itself – each comprises traits, behaviours and attitudes which are not necessarily in binary opposition (so that, for instance, to not perform one type of masculinity does not inevitably equal 'acting like a woman', and vice versa).

Gender construction and performance are therefore 'changeable, adaptive, configurable' and dynamic processes (Cohen, 1995: 3). This has also become the subject of much exploration across various academic disciplines, including sociolinguistics. However, whereas scholars working in the latter field have tended to locate debates and discussions in the context of (at the very least) relatively modern language data, others have been re-examining the historical record, re-analysing texts and data within the framework of gender theories.[10] The particular body of research which is of interest to us here is that undertaken by literary and cultural theory scholars such as Helen Damico, Clare Lees and Gillian Overing, to name but a few, into gender constructions in the Anglo-Saxon period. Lees and Overing (2001: 5) state that the Anglo-Saxon age is one which has traditionally been seen as originary and 'before history' – a distinct and discrete era – whereas the following medieval period has come to be accepted as the beginnings of the modern world, and therefore as one in which questions about 'modern concerns' (such as the construction of gender) can be profitably raised. 'Certain questions' therefore 'have not yet been asked, or are just beginning to be asked, in light of post-modern investigations into the [Anglo-Saxon] period' (ibid.: 4–5). However, because of a continued perception of its 'otherness', work in the Anglo-Saxon field is not well known outside of it. Consequently, there is often very little interplay among scholars in different fields whose theoretical positions overlap:

> an Anglo-Saxonist investigating gender does not necessarily take into account the effect and implications this might have for gender work outside the field, and conversely, those on the outside don't know much if anything about the work on Anglo Saxon gender.

(ibid.: 5)

Historical linguists therefore may not be aware of the fact that one of the areas that scholars like Lees and Overing address concerns how the conflicting trends of OE gender attribution (see Section 3.4) could be manipulated to express a range of 'gender behaviours'. Histories of the language have instead tended to focus on the opacity of grammatical gender attribution in OE, inevitably representing the entire system of gender marking as an unnecessary complication in the language which sometimes contradicted a 'natural' concordance with biological sex. Mitchell (1995: 37), for example, states that 'we are indeed fortunate to have got rid of grammatical gender and [its] oddities' and reassures his readers that it is 'something that you can learn to live with and not worry about . . . so don't give up'. Lees (1990: 15–23) also cites Mitchell's earlier (1985) 'discourse of battle' (echoed by Platzer (2001); see Section 3.3) which represents grammatical gender and 'natural' gender as two systems in conflict, one sometimes 'triumphant' over the other. It is, however, equally plausible to view any such 'conflict' as not problematic but productive: it is possible that the options it made available in the linguistic attribution of gender rendered the latter a useful tool in the textual construction, performance and reinforcement of Anglo-Saxon perceptions of gender behaviour. In so doing, Anglo-Saxon composers and writers managed to capture something of the messiness and ambiguity inherent in gender as a social performance. We will now look at an example of this in *Beowulf*.

Beowulf is definitely one of the best-known pieces of Anglo-Saxon poetry, and probably the one most studied in relation to gender constructions. The story, set in Scandinavia, revolves around Beowulf, a great warrior from the land of the Geats (today southern Sweden) who travels to Heorot in the land of the Danes. The hall at Heorot, ruled by the ageing king Hrothgar, is under attack by a man-eating monster, Grendel, against whom the Danes seem powerless. Beowulf kills both Grendel and later Grendel's mother, who seeks to avenge her son's death on Heorot. He then returns to the Geats in triumph, and eventually rules for 50 years before facing a new threat – a dragon which is terrorizing his homeland. In a final battle, he kills the dragon, but also meets his own end.

Overing (2000: 220) states that *Beowulf* is an 'overwhelmingly masculine poem; it could be seen as a chronicle of male desire, a tale of men dying' and living by a heroic (masculine) code. The major setting is that of the hall which, in Anglo-Saxon heroic poetry, housed a lord and his warriors and represented an 'oasis of comradeship, order, warmth and happiness, in sharp contrast to the threatening chaos of discomfort and danger outside' (Mitchell, 1995: 200). Lord and warriors lived in a mutual obligation of protection and of kin loyalty: the killing of one's comrades and relatives invoked an obligation to seek vengeance. The theme of the blood-feud surfaces constantly in the dynamics of *Beowulf* (and, incidentally, had actually been legalized in late Anglo-Saxon society).

If codes/performance of the masculine are the norm in the patriarchal world created in *Beowulf*, this is offset (and therefore emphasized) by that which is 'other'. In the poem, 'otherness' seems to be embodied in part by the feminine and generally by the monstrous which, in the case of Grendel's mother, is partly constructed through gender ambiguity. This is therefore a world in which the weighting of gender 'worth' is clearly in favour of the masculine.

The linguistic construction of identity in the poem is clearly a mechanism for establishing the masculine norm and feminine 'other'. Overing (2000: 222–3) points out that there is a 'tremendous preoccupation' with genealogy in the poem, specifically, the 'Name-of-the-Father': male offspring are always identified by the father, and then the son is identified by name. The 11 women of the poem, by contrast, are identified largely in terms of their relationships to men – wives, daughters and mothers. Thus, Beowulf's father, Ecgþeow, is named 16 times, but his mother, 'fortunate in her childbearing', remains nameless. Similarly, some of the nameless others are described in a patriarchal determination of feminine roles:

> Hygelac's only daughter is given to Eofor . . . as reward for his battle prowess, along with land and rings . . . Ongenþeow's wife is shuttled back and forth in the battle between the Geats and the Swedes; a nameless Geatish woman mourns at the end of the poem.

(ibid.: 223)

The only women whose names we learn are titled – Waelhþeow, Freawaru, Hygd, Hildeburh, and Thryð. On the whole, these queens, princesses or ladies conform to a particular gender behaviour. They inhabit a world in which they are both the pledges and weavers of peace: they are married as peace-pledges between tribes, and as queens of their lords' halls they 'pass the cup' among retainers, weaving with words, actions and gifts the internal bonds of loyalty that keep the hall secure. The role of *freoðwebbe* ('peace-weaver'; feminine gender), therefore, is not only gendered, but class-specific as well.

The last of the 11 female characters is Grendel's mother. She and her son are neither 'entirely inhuman nor all human' (Hala, 1997: 3); they are 'Cain's kin' (1261ff.) who, cursed by the original, murderous sin of their biblical forebear, inhabit a moral, spiritual and (in the imagery of the poem) physical wasteland of cold, dark and evil. The monsters' space is negative, defined by all that it is not. The mere where Grendel and his mother live can be seen as a hellish inversion of the life-giving warm, unified and morally governed hall of Heorot. Indeed, Grendel is

> introduced as a mock 'hall-retainer' (*healþegn* (142a), *renweard* (770a)) who envies the men of Heorot their joy of community; he subsequently attacks the hall in a raid that is described through the parodic hall ceremonies of feasting, ale-drinking, gift-receiving and singing.
>
> (Chance, 1991: 252)

Just as the monsters' home presents a terrifying ambiguity (it is hall/not hall; physically present but signifying nothingness), Grendel and his dam also embody negative, inverted, ambiguous space: they seem to experience human desires and emotions such as feelings of kinship, the need for revenge and fear, but also participate in inhuman behaviour (such as man-eating) and significantly, lack a potent symbol of humanity – language. The poet tells us that Grendel's patrilineal heritage is unknown but that he has a mother. Although she remains unnamed, which, as we have seen, is not unusual practice, the lack of the Name-of-the-Father immediately marks Grendel as other and outsider to the (patriarchal) rules that govern society. He is therefore one of the poem's 'negative men' (ibid.: 252).

Grendel's mother is, in turn, a 'negative woman', a being caught between the naturalized and idealized feminine behaviour and an 'unnatural' monstrousness, partly derived from her non-human state but also, importantly, from the fact that she (to paraphrase Frantzen, 1993) acts more like a man. This changeable performance of gender is made manifest throughout her appearance in the poem.[11] Early on in our introduction to her, the poet sows doubt as to whether she is an actual female (Hroðgar, the king of Heorot, says to Beowulf that she is 'in the likeness of a woman'). However, at the same time, she is also referred to by terms such as *wīf* and *ides*, feminine-gendered terms which are unreservedly used for human women (Chance, 1991: 251). Indeed *ides*, as used in other literary works, means 'lady' and can therefore be used to refer to a queen or a woman of high social rank. She also conforms in some measure to naturalized performances of femininity – she is 'weaker than a man (1282ff.) and more cowardly, for she flees in fear for her life when discovered in Heorot (1292–3)' (ibid.: 251); she grieves for her lost son and, in the absence of other kin, legitimately takes up the blood-feud in order to avenge his death. On the other hand, she is a fearsome adversary who is much harder than Grendel for Beowulf to kill, and is also labelled by terms typically used for male/masculine figures and linguistically gendered as masculine: *sinningne secg* 'warrior' (1379a); *mihtig manscaða* 'destroyer' (1339a); *gryrelicne grundhyrde* 'male guardian' (2136); *Grendles magan* 'Grendel's kinsman' (1391). Indeed, the connotations of the term *aglæca* (masculine) change according to context: in relation to Grendel's mother (and also to Grendel himself), it means 'monster', but when it is used to refer to Beowulf, for example, it is taken to mean 'fierce adversary' or 'combatant' (ibid.: 251). Interestingly, the poet also moves between masculine and feminine referring pronouns for Grendel's dam, linguistically reflecting and reinforcing the gender ambiguity which is part and parcel of her 'otherness'. Thus, the poem introduces *Grendles modor . . . /se þe wæter-egesan wunian scolde* ('Grendel's mother . . . /he who dwelt in those dreadful waters' (1258–60)); . . . *se ðe floda begong* (lit. 'he [Grendel's mother] who held that expanse of water' (1497b)). In lines 1390–4, Beowulf refers to the female monster in masculine gendered nouns and pronouns:

Aris, rices weard,	uton hraþe feran,
Grendles **magan**	gang sceawigan!
Ic hit þe gehate:	no **hē** on helm losaþ,
ne on foldan tæþm,	ne on fyrgen-holt,
ne on gyfenes grund,	ga þær **hē** wille.

Arise, kingdom's guard, let us quickly go
and inspect the path of Grendel's kin[sman].
I promise you this: he will find no protection –
not in the belly of the earth nor the bottom of the sea,
nor the mountain groves – let him go where he will.

(from Liuzza, 2000: 96)

Yet, when Beowulf finally confronts her in her mere, a battle which will end in her death, the references become unambiguously female, with the use of *sēo*, *hēo* and *hire* (see 1501–69):

It is she who rushes up to meet Beowulf. Her loathsome claws (*atolan clommum*, 1502) cannot penetrate Beowulf's mail. She is described as a 'she-monster of the deep' (*grund wyrgenne*, 1518) as she drags the hero to her lair, a 'mighty water-woman' (*mere-wīf mihtig*, 1519), a 'water-wolf' (*sēo brim wylf*, 1506). Once in the anti-hall, the *ides* literally trips Beowulf up and she ends up astride him slashing at his mail with her knife.

(Hala, 1997: 7)

The language of the poem therefore creates a strong sense of the tensions between not-feminine and feminine behaviours, and implies that their lack of resolution results in a *wīf unhyre* (2120b), a 'monstrous woman' or *ides aglæcwīf* (1259a), a 'lady monster-woman' (Chance, 1991: 251). Chance (ibid.: 252) also points out that the story of Grendel's mother is framed between other narratives which emphasize, and idealize, certain types of feminine behaviour. For example, on the evening that Grendel's mother will attack Heorot to avenge her son's death, the *scōp* recounts the story of the Danish *ides* Hildeburh, who was married to the Frisian lord Finn as a peace-pledge between the two tribes. Her brother is killed by her husband's men, and by the laws of the blood-feud her son is killed in retaliation. Her real role as peace-pledge is as mother to a son of 'united' houses; when her son dies, she loses her primary identity. Hildeburh cannot, by the rules of her society, avenge the death of her son, and she is eventually returned to her original tribe. As soon as this narration ends, Waelhþeow addresses her husband Hroðgar with her concerns about the future of their kingdom. She is anxious that only their actual kinsmen or descendants inherit it, and that whoever does, will see to the welfare of her own sons, Hrethric and Hrothmund (Hroðgar has not fathered an heir). The maternal, passive angst exemplified by Hildeburh and Waelhþeow is in sharp contrast to the (albeit legitimate) but more warrior-like (and therefore 'masculine') response of Grendel's grieving mother who, unlike her human counterparts, takes on the role not of peace-broker but of peace-breaker.

It is arguable that the physicality of the fight between Beowulf and Grendel's mother (cf. Hala, 1997: 7, quoted above) also serves to emphasize the dangers of ambiguous and changeable performances of femininity which in a patriarchal perspective may represent femininity out of control. And, indeed, the discourse of Anglo-Saxon texts generally seeks to define and arguably reinforce a particular idealized representation of the feminine. This is often achieved through a metaphorization of the female body, because it is here, in the realm of imagery and linguistic representation, that it and the feminine can be controlled. Lees and Overing (2001: 153) point out that personification of abstract qualities is a 'major method of signification' in classical and medieval Latin, as well as in the Latin translation of the Bible, the 'other main vehicle of knowledge' in the Anglo-Saxon period. In Latin, a language also with grammatical gender, abstract nouns were mainly grammatically feminine, and it has been assumed that the female personifications that occur in Old English translations and adaptations of Latin rhetoric are a direct transliteration of the Latin source. However, as the authors point out (and as Cohen reminds us to do), when such personifications are considered in the cultural and textual context that produces them, the simple, assumed 'cause and effect' relationship between Latin and English does not seem to hold. Thus, Lees and Overing (2001: 156) draw our attention to Pseudo-Bede's *Collectanea* (a Latin work), whose opening item is 'Tell me, please, who is the woman who offers her breasts to inummerable sons, and who pours forth as much as she is sucked? This woman is wisdom.' In Latin, wisdom, *sapientia*, is grammatically gendered as feminine, but to maintain that this is 'the sole cause and explanation of this spectacularly feminine image of wisdom' and stop there, the authors maintain, 'is simply inadequate', partly because it does not account for the *impact* of the representation. This is not an 'active' female body, nor is the female where wisdom resides – this metaphorical body is one which only yields productively to masculine/male control. In other words, wisdom can only be milked by those who have the right to it, and they are sons, not daughters. Images such as these illustrate how patriarchal discourse 'disciplines and crafts for symbolic use a female body evidently perceived to be otherwise indiscriminate' and potentially out of control (ibid.: 156–7). This interpretation is supported by the *Collectanea* which, like many texts in the clerical tradition, expresses both an idealization of the feminine and a denigration of the female (an ambiguity that is still culturally evident). Thus, it contains juxtapositions such as 'remember always that it was a woman who expelled the first inhabitant of paradise from his inheritance' (item 247)/'there are three daughters of the mind: faith, hope, and charity' (cited in ibid.). In a similar vein, Frantzen (1993: 466) cites the example of 'manly women' in the Anglo-Saxon lives of the saints. St Agatha, for example, loses her physical breast, but retains her metaphorical breast as the seat of her faith. She reaches transcendence in this state of being without breast (masculine), and is later restored. To paraphrase Lees (1990), 'woman' is fine as long as she is not really a woman.

As a final example, we should note, in underlining the fact that the linguistic gendering of personifications of abstract qualities is not simply a 'language process' divorced from its cultural context, that there are instances where Anglo-Saxon scholars made gender choices which differentiated their translations from Latin originals. For example, Alfred reconfigures the feminine personification of Philosophy in Boethius' *Consolation of Philosophy* as a masculine-gendered abstraction. Thus, Philosophy becomes 'divine wisdom' (*se wisdōm*), which is gendered masculine, and Reason (*gesceadwisness*), though it remains feminine, 'is a much more shadowy figure; barely personified' (Lees and Overing, 2001: 160–1). The gender changes are deliberate – the Latin original provides a particular model and as instanced in the *Collectanea*, there was an Anglo-Saxon clerical tradition of personifying wisdom-as-woman. Lees and Overing (ibid.: 160–1) point out that the feminine personifications frequent in the Latin tradition were not regularly kept in Old English translations, which means that both their occurrence and non-occurrence in the latter were deliberately crafted.

Overall, in both feminizing and 'monsterizing' that which can be (and needs to be) controlled, and in masculinizing culturally positive, abstract virtues, such textual representations contribute in no small part to the 'denial, silencing and elision of women's agency in the cultural record' (ibid.: 161) which is still a concern for modern feminists in all disciplines, including linguistics.

3.6 Study Questions

1. The following short excerpt is taken from Aelfric's *Cosmology* (completed around 993). Here, the author details God's creative work on days four–seven.

> On ðām fēorðan dæge gesceōp God twā miccle lēoht þæt is sunne and mōna and betǣhte þæt māre lēoht þæt is sēo sunne tō ðām dæge and þæt lǣsse lēoht þæt is se mōna tō ðǣre nihte. On ðām ylcan dæge hē geworhte ealle steorran and tīda gesette. On ðām fiftan dæge hē gesceōp eal wyrmcynn and ðā micclan hwalas and eal fiscynn . . . On ðām sixtan dæge hē gesceōp eal dēorcynn and ealle nȳtenu þe on feower fōtum gāð and þā twēgen men Adam and Ēuan. On ðām seofoðan dæge hē geendode his weorc and sēo wucu wæs ðā agān.

> (from Burnley, 1992: 44)

On the fourth day made God two great lights that is [the] sun and [the] moon, and assigned the greater light that is the sun to the day and the lesser light that is the moon to the night. On the same day he made all the stars and established the seasons. On the fifth day he created all the race of creeping things and the mighty whales and all the race of fish . . . On the sixth day he made all the race of animals and beasts that on four feet go, and the two humans Adam and Eve. On the seventh day he ended his work and the week was then past.

a. What words and structures in the OE extract are recognizable to a modern English reader? Which are opaque? On balance, would you say that the OE extract has a great deal or very little in common with modern English?

b. What markings of case, gender and number are evident in the following phrases? In phrases that contain adjectives, what inflectional declension (that is, strong or weak) is used?: *ðām fēorðan dæge, sēo sunne, ðām dæge, ðām ylcan dæge, þā twēgen men, se mōna, ðǣre nihte, sēo wucu*.

c. Which principal part of the verb paradigm do the forms *gesceōp, geworhte, geendode* belong to? Is each strong or weak?

d. What inflection is the verb *gāð* carrying?

2. As we have seen in Section 3.4, in OE, the graph sequence *sc* came to be pronounced [ʃ] (as in *fisc* 'fish'). Yet OE also made use of words such as *scathe*, *scorch* and *scrub* in which *sc* was pronounced, as in modern English, [sk]. Similarly, *g* before front vowels was pronounced [j] (as in *year*) and *k* in the same environment as [tʃ] (as in *cild*). Yet OE also has [g] in *gear, geld, gill*, and [k] in *kick, kindle, kilt* (examples from Pyles and Algeo, 1982: 300). In all three cases, why might such exceptions exist?

3. In Section 3.4, we looked at the suppletive paradigm of the verb *to be*. Another English verb with such a paradigm is *to go* (preterite *went*). What are the etymologies of these forms? (A good dictionary will be useful here.)

4. The following place names are found in the county of Yorkshire, England: Shewsby, Kirkby Fell, Foggathorpe, Fridaythorpe, Coneysthorpe, Askrigg, Goodmanham, Oswaldkirk, Halthorpe, Flaxby, Lastingham, Wigginton. Using a good place-name dictionary, such as Ekwall (1960), Fellows Jensen (1972), or Mills (1991) work out what such names can tell us about the settlement history of these areas.

Notes

1. Reported 20 December 2000, BBC news on-line <http://news.bbc.co.uk/1/hi/sci/tech/1080228.stm>. The research was carried out at Macquarie University, Sydney, Australia.

2. It is worth noting, however, that the supposedly elevated nature of Latin, French or even Greek borrowings is not unequivocal: words such as *theatre* (Greek), *angel* (Latin), *restaurant*, *pork, cattle, blue* (French) are now well integrated into everyday use, and it is unlikely that any English speaker would classify the use of such items as 'posh' or intellectual.

3. Scholars now tend to use *Anglo-Saxon* to refer to the culture of the period, and *Old English* to refer to the language spoken at that time.

4. See Mitchell (1995) and Treharne and Pulsiano (2001) for accessible and interesting discussions on the period.

5. The Neolithic settlers are commonly believed to have been non-Indo-European in origin. Baugh and Cable (2002: 45) state that some scholars hold that a modern remnant of this ancient culture is the Basque community in the Pyrenees mountains of Spain. If this is the case, then the Basque language, which does not appear to belong to the PIE family or any other language family now known, may well be a descendant of a Neolithic tongue.

6. The monk Gildas, living in Wales in the sixth century, records it thus in his *The Ruin of Britain*: 'To Aetius, thrice consul, the groans of the Britons . . . The barbarians push us to the sea; the sea pushes us back on to the barbarians. Between these two kinds of death, we are

either drowned or slaughtered' (quoted in Schama, 2000: 44). See also Bede's account in Book I, Chapter XV.

7. The actual date of the mission is unclear. Bede states that it occurred about 150 years after the original Anglo-Saxon invasions (approximately 597–599), but there is no concrete evidence to this end.

8. OE *burg* is glossed as 'dwelling in a fort, enclosure, fort' by Mitchell (1995: 373).

9. I am using 'natural gender' for want of a better term, and also because it is a phrase found in other readings. The quotation marks signify that the concept of gender being a natural or biological endowment is problematic, as we shall see in Section 3.5.

10. As Frantzen (1993: 447) states, early work in this area constituted the 'women in' approach; one in which texts were 're-examined in order to discover "the woman's" point of view', which often 'was the only view in question, and it was re-examined merely to assert that women had been overlooked and undervalued as a group'. The perspective has since been widened to include the examination of the masculine construction as well (since neither the concept of masculinity nor that of femininity exists without the other), within the cultural context that produces them.

11. Interestingly, Heaney's (1999) translation largely avoids this gender ambiguity, referring to Grendel's mother throughout as female. Its only indication lies in Hroðgar's statement to Beowulf that 'One of these things . . . looks like a woman' (ibid.: 45).

4 | Middle English, 1100–1500

4.1 Introduction

The Middle English (ME) period is typically characterized as one of great change, both social and linguistic: the ancient Germanic structures of Old English and of Anglo-Saxon society were tempered with, or displaced by, the Romance influences of the Norman duchy and the Parisian court; and the seeds of modern English society, and of modern English language usage, were sown. The event often cited as a starting point for this transitional period is the Norman Conquest of 1066, which effectively put England into the hands of new and foreign overlords, starting with William, Duke of Normandy. If putting 1066 at the beginning of a timeline of change for the Middle English period gives the impression that English society was calm and peaceful until the Conquest, or that the ascendance of Norman kings to the English throne was an unprecedented surprise to a free Anglo-Saxon nation, then it is worth noting that this was not the case. As we saw in Chapter 3, England had passed into Scandinavian hands at the end of the Old English period, effectively making it a province in a much larger Viking empire. This displacement of the older Anglo-Saxon ruling families, in particular the line of Alfred, plus the resentment in some circles at being ruled by 'foreign' kings (related but nevertheless foreign) meant that England of the late OE and early ME periods was a hotbed of political conspiracy in relation to issues of succession. Anglo-Saxons and Scandinavians were not the only ones embroiled in these intrigues – Emma, the widow of the Anglo-Saxon king Æthelred and wife of the Scandinavian king Cnut, had originally come from Normandy. She and her sons maintained close relations with her connections there, adding yet another dimension to questions of overlordship in England. Thus, the socio-political turbulence that characterizes the ME period had its roots, in large measure, in the quarrels and machinations of the ruling classes in late Anglo-Saxon England.

In terms of language, we would also be wrong in assuming that English remained fairly static until 1066. It is unquestionable that the English of the ME period came to look very different from its Anglo-Saxon antecedent, and that the introduction of Norman French speakers and scribes to England played a role in this. It is, however, important to remember that change also occurred simply through native intergenerational transmission. Features often taken as characteristic of Middle English varieties had begun to emerge long before the Conquest: reduction of inflectional paradigms, for example, had its roots in the ongoing syncretism of the OE period (see Chapter 3). The events of 1066 therefore did not so much begin a period of transformation as add another dimension to the direction of ongoing linguistic (and indeed social) change in the ME period. As we will see in this chapter, the exact nature of those linguistic changes has been a source of contention in analyses of Middle English.

We begin our exploration of this period with the socio-historical background in Section 4.2.

4.2 Social History

As stated in Chapter 3, the Anglo-Saxon period drew to an end with the ascendance of Danish kings to the English throne. Four years into his English reign, Cnut inherited the kingdom of Denmark from his brother, and effectively became ruler of an impressive Balto-Danish empire. Although England was ultimately only a province in this much larger body, Cnut made it his base and devoted a great deal of his energies to ensuring that the political stability and prosperity enjoyed under rulers such as Alfred continued. Cnut shrewdly ran 'England the English way' (Schama, 2000: 70–1), letting the already established councils and governments get on with doing what they had been doing for centuries, and doing well. He also built up a cohort of trusted English advisors including the Earl Godwine, one of Cnut's closest confidants and one of the most richly rewarded in land and title. When Cnut died in 1035, Godwine was very likely one of the most powerful men in England.

With Cnut's demise, the English lost a capable ruler and gained a succession problem that threatened to shatter the 20 years of peace that the old king had established. Cnut had had a son, Harold, with his first wife Ælgifu, and another son Harthacnut with his second spouse, Emma of Normandy. Emma's previous marriage to Æthelred (see Chapter 3, Section 3.2), had borne two sons, Alfred and Edward, both of whom had been sent to Normandy with the resumption of Viking raids at the end of the tenth century. All four of these offspring had legitimate claims to the throne, which did not automatically pass to eldest sons in Danish or Anglo-Saxon law. Decisions of kingship were made by the *witan* (the national council comprising secular and spiritual leaders) who, in this case, named Harold as Cnut's successor.

Alfred and Edward were not initially inclined to forgo their claim: a decision perhaps encouraged by the territorialist sensibilities of the Norman society that had fostered them. The Normans (the label derives from the Old French for 'Northmen') were descendants of Viking invaders who had employed the same intimidatory tactics on France as their kin had on ninth-century Anglo-Saxon England (see Chapter 3, Section 3.2). King Charles the Simple of France had reached terms with the Viking leader Hlófr (or Rollo), granting him and his band the crescent of territory in north-western France that now bears their name. Hlófr became the first duke of Normandy, and his great-great grandson, William, would extend the realm to England.

In the five or so generations that separated Hlófr and William, the Vikings had assimilated in significant measure to their French 'host', 'trading in their longboats for war-horses and . . . stud-farms in Normandy itself . . . the old Norse halls [for] motte-and-bailey castles' (Schama, 2000: 73), and the old Norse gods for the Catholic Church. They also became French speakers, although their variety, known as Norman French, retained Scandinavian influences. But the desire for conquest and land which had driven their forefathers remained, and Emma's sons may well have been encouraged by their Norman guardians to stake their claim to the English throne. In 1036, they arrived in England to consult with their mother on this prospect. Edward, more politically sensitive than his brother, managed to escape the hostility to his claim by returning to Normandy. Alfred, however, stayed – a decision that cost him his life at the hands of Godwine and Harold's men.

Harold died in 1040 and was succeeded by his half-brother Harthacnut, who reigned for only two years. On the *witan's* recommendation, the remaining heir, Edward, was crowned King of England on Easter Day 1043.

Edward's reign was not without personal strife. His mother Emma, for example, explicitly supported the claim of another contender, the Norwegian king Magnus I, to the English throne, and the powerful Godwine, who had engineered the murder of his brother, was a necessary ally. But Edward never lost his animosity to Godwine, nor his sense of affiliation with his Norman kin. It is highly likely that he knew the young William (titled *the Bastard* as the illegitimate son of Duke Robert of Normandy and Herlève, a tanner's daughter) while in Normandy, and may well have maintained contact with him. Edward also built up an entourage of Norman supporters to whom he granted English land and titles. Indeed, with his nephew Earl Ralf (son of his brother Alfred), Edward created 'a little Normandy' in Herefordshire, complete with Norman castles and knights (Schama, 2000: 77). The speculations of modern historians that Edward was deliberately laying the foundations of a Norman succession are therefore unsurprising, but it is equally likely that Edward was attempting, in the face of powerful potential enemies such as Godwine, to buffer himself with loyal subjects.

In the later years of his reign Edward turned increasingly to religion, adopting the ascetic lifestyle that would mythologize him as a miracle-worker and healer, and lead to the title he is known to posterity by, *the Confessor*. He died childless in 1066, and the end of the previous year was recorded in the *Anglo-Saxon Chronicle* as being one of tremendous natural and material destruction: a severe storm had destroyed houses and churches, and wreaked havoc across the countryside. While many may have seen these as portents of the death of the ascetic king, others, with hindsight, may have seen them as warnings of the grim state of affairs to come. In 1064, Harold – one of Godwine's three sons and a renowned military leader – had undertaken a sea journey, the purposes of which still remain unclear. Norman chroniclers maintain that Harold was travelling to Normandy under Edward's instructions to confirm William's succession to the English throne, but this is not indisputable. Harold did indeed land on the French coast and meet with William, but the exact nature of what passed between them is lost to posterity. The possibly retrospective propaganda (ibid.: 80) of the Norman chroniclers has Harold pledging his loyalty to William and swearing to uphold his claim. It is equally possible, however, that Harold had his own royal ambitions. On his return to

England, he took Northumbria from his brother Tostig, installing a more trustworthy ally. It is possible that with such acts Harold had begun to draw together the alliances that would facilitate his election by the *witan*. And sure enough, when Edward died, Harold was offered the throne, and 'the funeral of one king on the Feast of Epiphany 1066 was followed, later that same day, by the coronation of another, Harold II' (Schama, 2000: 89).

The troubles of Harold's short reign began almost immediately. Tostig was now an enemy, and across the Channel William was 'enraged' (William of Jumièges; quoted in Schama, 2000: 91) by Harold's 'usurpation' of the English throne. Both managed to attract significant support – Tostig had joined forces with Harald Hadrada (known as 'the thunderbolt from the north' and once a contender for the English throne), and William had not only put together an army that included contingents from Brittany and other areas in northern France but had also secured papal backing for an invasion. Harold therefore fought two major battles in 1066. While waiting near London for William to land, the king received word that Tostig's army had invaded and sacked towns in northern England. Harold marched his troops in their direction, reaching York in five short days. The English defeated this latest Viking attack, and almost immediately turned south to meet William's offensive. The Battle of Hastings was a resounding defeat for the weary English army, who lost not only king (Harold is said to have been killed by an arrow in the eye), but country.

On Christmas Day 1066, the duke formerly known as *the Bastard* became *the Conqueror*, and was crowned King of England at Westminster. Acceptance, however, was not immediately forthcoming. In the early years of his reign, William faced significant opposition to which he retaliated forcefully, burning and plundering portions of the country, stationing armed troops across the countryside and executing members of the old Anglo-Saxon nobility involved in plots of treason. He also rewarded his supporters and retainers, Norman and otherwise, with the properties, estates and offices of the English nobility (many of whom had been killed at Hastings). Thus, for many of the surviving English who were near enough geographically and socially to the consequences of the Conquest, life changed dramatically:

> the entire governing class of Anglo-Saxon England, some 4000 or 5000 thegns, had been made to vanish and authority, wealth, men and beasts had been given to foreigners. You could survive and still be English. You could even speak the language. But politically, you were now a member of the underclass, the inferior race . . . you lived in England, but it was no longer your country.

> (ibid.: 67–8)

The depletion and displacement of the English in the higher social stations of church and state continued apace, and did not subsequently abate under the respective kingships of William's sons. By 1072, only one of the 12 earldoms in England was actually held by an Englishman, and not for long: he was executed four years later (Baugh and Cable, 2002: 112). The two Archbishoprics of Canterbury and York were granted to Normans, and the English monasterial abbots were similarly replaced. Baugh and Cable (ibid.: 113) note that in 1075,

13 of the 21 abbots were English, but by 1087, only three remained. New monasteries, filled only with Norman monks, were also established under William's patronage.

The presence of Normans and other French migrants was also felt elsewhere. It is likely that the new Norman aristocracy staffed their households with their own retainers and guards, and soldiers from the Continent, as mentioned above, were garrisoned around the country. Merchants and craftsmen also moved their businesses to England. It is impossible to quantify exactly how many of these newcomers, in all walks of life, settled in England under William and his sons, but what is certain is that they never outnumbered the general English population. However, because the Normans largely became members of the governing classes, their 'influence was out of all proportion to their number' (ibid.: 114).

And what of their linguistic influence? At the moment, this is an extremely difficult question to answer: scant reliable evidence exists for the everyday linguistic situation after the Conquest, and we therefore have very little idea of who spoke what language, with whom and for what period of time. In addition, although we know that by the end of the fourteenth century, English had become a native tongue for descendants of the (largely) Norman invaders, we do not know exactly when that process of acquisition began. There are, however, a few clues in the textual and historical records which, along with our increasing contemporary knowledge of contact situations, can lead us through some educated guesswork about the changing linguistic situation after 1066.

Many of the new Norman nobility in England were also landholders in Normandy, and retained strong ties to their native land. It seems safe to assume then that in the early years following the Conquest, the language of communication among this group (who continued to execute their duties in Normandy) was their native variety of French. William's linguistic usage would have also facilitated this continued use. it is said that he tried to learn English but never became fluent in it, apart from – in fulfilment of that stereotype of the essence of Anglo-Saxon – swearing.

The ruling Anglo-Norman[1] classes inevitably transferred their everyday tongue to their official offices, and Anglo-French (that is, the French spoken in England after the Conquest) soon became established alongside the traditional Latin as the language of public state business and of the court. It also became the language of the literature that received royal patronage (see Section 4.3). Thus, English was ousted from public and official roles, and the cultivation of one of its varieties as a literary standard – a process which had begun with West Saxon under Alfred – was halted. English would not make a comeback for about two hundred years.

This is not to say that English was in danger of disappearing while Norman French was so publicly dominant. Nor should we assume that the ruling classes deliberately clamped down on its usage – an occurrence sometimes associated with colonizing activities. The Normans appear to have simply let the English speak the English way, and the language remained the native tongue of the majority of the population. Writing in English also carried on (the *Anglo-Saxon Chronicle*, for example, was continued at monasteries such as Peterborough until 1154) but until about 1250, without the patronage of the court. Thus, in the early post-Conquest years, Norman French became the language of rule not because of a need to implement a linguistic symbol of authority, but simply because it was the native tongue of the people at the top. English simply did not belong to them.

As intimated earlier, the question of exactly when it *did* start becoming used by the upper echelons is ultimately unanswerable. Dahood (1994: 40) points out that before the thirteenth century, evidence for such usage is sparse and mainly documents English use among the ecclesiastical community (we shall return to this below). Consequently, 'early evidence for people outside the church is anecdotal . . . notoriously difficult to interpret' (ibid.: 40), and needs to be treated with caution. For instance, a particular narrative often cited as evidence of English use among the Anglo-Norman upper classes comes from William of Canterbury's Latin *Life of St. Thomas Becket* (*circa* 1173). In Baugh and Cable's (2002: 121) paraphrase of this story, a twelfth-century Anglo-Norman noblewoman Helewise de Morville warns her husband of a supposed impending attack by a young Englishman, Lithulf, with the English words 'Huge de Moreville, ware, ware, ware, Lithulf heth his swerd adrage!' As Dahood (1994: 41) states:

> in the prevailing view the anecdote is accepted as evidence that at least one member of the Anglo-Norman barony born in the first half of the twelfth century understood English or that in one Anglo-Norman baronial household English was familiarly spoken.

No absolute evidence exists, however, for this incident and some scholars have instead suggested that the story is fictional (see Burnley (1992: 425), Dahood (1994: 40–56), for instance). Dahood (ibid.) points for instance to William's vagueness about his source (the story is prefaced only by *ut fertur* 'as is said'), the lack of concrete dates for the event and of evidence for Lithulf's execution (the story states that the latter was boiled to death for supposed insurgence against his superior), as well as parallels with the biblical story of Potiphar's wife and narrations of martyrdom (involving death by boiling) in the hagiographic corpus. We should also note that even if the story is true, the actual linguistic evidence that it presents for English use in the upper classes is extremely minimal. Thus, as either possible fiction or scant fact, the story cannot be taken as definitive proof of language use in the early twelfth century. However, as Dahood (ibid.: 54) points out, it is still of historical and linguistic interest in that 'in 1173 William of Canterbury thought his audience would accept that an Anglo-Norman baroness of the preceding generation and perhaps her husband spoke English'. As such, it may be read as an indication, but not proof, that use of English by the Anglo-Norman nobility was underway by the mid–late twelfth century.

As stated earlier, the only Anglo-Norman sector for which there is some plausible evidence for the early use of English is the ecclesiastic. William's decision to fill the upper church ranks with his own supporters introduced a third language to a body that already made use of Latin and English. Records indicate that certain members of the church in the twelfth century, such as Gilbert Foliot (Bishop of London), Hugh of Nonant (Bishop of Coventry and Norman), Giraldus Cambrensis (Bishop-elect of St David's) and Abbot Sansom (of the abbey at Bury St Edmunds) used all three languages fluently. However, such linguistic dexterity was not widespread – it is unlikely that those at the lower end of the church hierarchy such as local English parish priests, for example, generally had reason to learn French. Documentation also indicates that not all Anglo-Normans affiliated to the church could use English, and that those who did very likely acquired the language for specific 'ecclesiastical duties or scholarly interests'. As such, they were 'in their knowledge of English . . . untypical of the cultured classes' (Dahood, 1994: 40).

As for the linguistic situation in other social strata, we can only move into the realm of conjecture. It seems inevitable that many of those migrants who found themselves, either by choice or design, living in conjunction with the English-speaking majority (such as knights stationed at outposts away from the Norman court, merchants and craftsmen) would have assimilated to this wider community. Stewards and bailiffs on manors may well have started out with (Norman) French ancestry, but their role as go-between for upper-class owners and lower-class workers may well have resulted in their acquisition of English. And finally, the mass of the peasantry, largely native English in origin, would appear to have remained monolingual in their native English varieties, having neither means nor motivation to learn any type of French.

We should also mention here the scribal class which emerged after the Conquest and who were involved in the copying and drafting of (usually official) records. Very little is known about who they actually were: Rothwell (1998: 6) points out, for example, that they may have been native French speakers (from Normandy or elsewhere) who had settled in England, or native English speakers who had learnt French as a foreign language. What does seem to be certain, however, is that they were trilingual in English, French and Latin, moving 'freely from one language to another according to the nature of their work and the company in which they found themselves' (ibid.: 11).[2]

Thus, by the beginning of the thirteenth century, England was a much more multilingual country than we currently imagine, but it is important to note that multilingualism was not widespread; while there was 'a considerable number who were genuinely bilingual', there were also 'some who spoke only French and many more who spoke only English . . . as well as many who had some understanding of both languages while speaking only one' (Baugh and Cable, 2002: 126). As England moved into the thirteenth century, the tide turned increasingly in favour of English, and proficiency in French waned. Indeed, English, as we will see, became intimately associated with notions of distinctive national identity – a process in which French could have no role.

With hindsight, it seems that these notions of 'Englishness' began to coalesce under King John (1199–1216), whose reign saw the creation of the Magna Carta (1215) and the severing of political ties between England and Normandy (1214).[3] The historical record indicates that the Magna Carta, which ultimately sought to limit the potentially despotic power of the monarchy, evolved in reaction to a series of ill-judged political decisions on the part of the king. The essence of the charter was built on the idea of an English 'state', 'of which the king was a part . . . but not the whole' (Schama, 2000: 162). And that state was one of

English people, for some of whom loyalties lay to the land in which they had been born, not the Normandy that their ancestors had come from. When France had taken Normandy in 1214, nobles holding land there as well as in England had had to choose their allegiances. A significant proportion had given up their Norman holdings (and by extension, one of the reasons for maintaining fluency in French). In some cases, their decisions may well have been because their English estates were larger, but we cannot discount the possibility that many now considered themselves English, and were more concerned with internal English affairs. John's misdemeanours, then, ultimately began to give shape to an English polity that saw itself as distinct from its Continental ancestry. Psychologically, this sounded one of the death knells for the use of French in England.

The separation of French and English political interests continued under John's son Henry III, who cultivated the loyalty of his French relations (on his mother's side and through his marriage to Eleanor of Provence) with generous grants of high-ranking appointments, land and titles in England. As a result, London was 'full to overflowing . . . of Poitevins, Romans and Provencals' (Matthew Paris, quoted in Baugh and Cable, 2002: 132). The inevitable backlash to this immigration (issuing primarily from the displaced nobility in England) was enshrined in the Provisions of Oxford (1258), in which a number of Henry's French entourage were stripped of their English holdings and expelled. Schama (2000: 177) asserts that the circumstances out of which these documents emerged struck another nail in the coffin for absolutist monarchy and signalled the beginnings of modern government. Significantly, when they were produced in final form the following year, 'the documents were written, for the first time, not only in Latin and French but in Middle English, the native tongue' (ibid.: 177).

Yet, resentment of French immigrants at the top of English society did not preclude admiration of French courtly culture. By the late thirteenth century, the Parisian court dictated trends and fashions in practically every sphere, including language. Knowledge of what scholars today call Central French (but see Rothwell (1998), Section 4.3.5) therefore became *de rigueur* for members of the higher classes and those who aspired to join them. Anglo-French, which remained one of the languages of official documentation in England until the end of the fourteenth century, was increasingly seen as inferior to the French of the Parisian court, and its decline as a spoken language was no doubt aided by this denigration. Those whose families may once have spoken Norman and later, Anglo-French, natively or as a second tongue, now sought tuition in the fashionable variety, as the multitude of language instruction guides which appear in this period testify. Interestingly, the style and format of these guides indicate strongly that the majority of learners were in fact native speakers of English.

As the thirteenth century progressed into the fourteenth, English gradually became re-established through a concatenation of socio-political circumstances partly catalyzed by natural disasters. The relative prosperity of the twelfth and thirteenth centuries had trebled the country's population to about four million by 1300. Many areas had, as a result, become overpopulated, opening the way to the potentially disastrous effects of famine and disease, especially for the peasantry.

Sure enough, a succession of bad harvests led to a severe famine in 1315–1316, followed by cattle murrain and sheep disease. The decimation caused by the famine was increased when Edward III took England into the Hundred Years War (1337–1453). This not only cost lives on the battlefield but also left fields unploughed, harvests ungathered and animals untended. When bubonic plague hit in 1348 and 1350, it swept easily through the weakened population, leaving thousands dead across Europe by the end of its gruesome run. In England, the impact of this was keenly felt: in the villages around Bury St Edmunds, for example, 60 per cent of the population succumbed to the Black Death in 1348 (Schama, 2000: 235–6). Overall, after the second wave of pestilence, approximately 30 per cent of the overall population of England, particularly the poor, had perished.

An outcome that no-one could have predicted then began to unfold. The decrease in population (particularly among the peasantry) began to shift the economic balance of the country, largely through undermining the old feudal system. Serfs and peasants used to be relied on for manual work and harvesting but after 1350, with labour thin on the ground, the survivors of the old peasantry could set financial and contractual terms that suited them, demanding either pay (or higher rates of pay) and moving to wherever economic and social prospects looked promising.

The plague returned in 1361 and after that, in 20–25-year cycles, all of which were punctuated by increasing taxation demands to finance the war against France. In 1381, frustration at such levies resulted in the Peasants Revolt – a rebellion in south Essex by villagers against the tax commissioners sent to collect payments. Interestingly, it was a revolt 'conspicuous for the absence of peasants' (Schama, 2000: 246). Many of the leaders were members of the village yeomanry (who served as jurors, reeves and constables) who had actually profited from the tragic events of past years since they had been able to take over abandoned lands and estates and increase their personal wealth. They were, however, not prepared to hand over so easily what fortunes they had managed to build up. But they must have seemed exemplary to the villagers on whose behalf they stood, and were a model of what it was now possible to be: 'all [the] sections of the rural community thought of themselves as up and coming' (ibid.: 247).

Throughout the fourteenth century, then, the sense of 'Englishness' continued to evolve and change. When Edward III (the first king to speak English natively since the Conquest) consulted Parliament about the war with France in 1337, the proceedings were conducted not in the language of the potential enemy, but in English. The tolls of the famines, wars, runs of plague and poor leadership were harsh, but they ultimately succeeded in re-structuring English society in ways which favoured those once at the bottom of the socio-economic ladder. This stratum came to have money and for the first time, a public voice. And that voice was English.

In 1362, the Chancellor opened Parliament in English, and in the same year the Statutes of Pleading, which stated that all lawsuits were to be conducted in this language, were passed. When Richard II was deposed in 1399, the articles of accusation were read to Parliament in Latin and English, and his successor

Henry IV made his first regal speech in the latter language. The peasants who had flocked to the towns and cities in search of work turned these places into thriving urban centres, in which their native English flourished. With money also came the potential for education, and many of the offspring of this now up and coming middle class were exposed to tuition. The fact that instruction now had to be given to youngsters whose first language was English, plus the fact that many tutors who had been able to teach French and Latin had been killed by the plague, meant that English became increasingly important in schools.

This is not to say that usage of French (and to a more limited extent, Latin) disappeared quietly overnight. Acquisition of the 'sophisticated' French of Paris was still desirable for those who wanted a courtly or educated veneer, and Anglo-French continued to be used as one of the main languages of legal and ecclesiastical business until 1362. Literature appeared in both French and English, and public records sometimes appeared in Latin, Anglo-French and English. But the language of the English nation ultimately prevailed, and by the fifteenth century, towns and guilds were producing their official records in English only. By 1489, Parliament had stopped using (Anglo-)French completely, and wills and other public texts were produced, with few exceptions, only in English. All in all, by the end of the fifteenth century, English was the conqueror.

4.3 Middle English Literature

The Middle English period was one of significant literary achievement, seeing the production of both translations and original works in both English and French. In the two hundred or so years that French was ascendant, the literature enjoyed and patronized by the court was inevitably composed in this medium. Initially, a significant body of this material was imported from the Continent, but literary works in French soon began to be produced in England itself, including poetry commissioned by various patrons and religious treatises. Despite the early lack of royal patronage, writing in various dialects of English continued much as it had done during the Anglo-Saxon period and indeed, increased in quantity as English became re-established in the public sphere. Thus, the *Anglo-Saxon Chronicle* continued until 1154; compositions such as *Ormulum* (c. 1200), *Ancrene Riwle* (c. 1215), *The Owl and the Nightingale* (early 1200s), as well as Romance poems such as *King Horn* (c. 1225), *Havelock the Dane* (c. 1280–1300) and *Floris and Blanchflur* (c. 1250) were produced in the thirteenth century, as were works such as biblical paraphrases, homilies and saints' lives. The late twelfth century also saw translations of French texts. Laȝamon's well-known *Brut* (c. early thirteenth century), based on the Norman poet Wace's translation of Geoffrey of Monmouth's Latin *History of the Kings of Britain*, belongs to this tradition.

The fourteenth and fifteenth centuries saw a wealth of literary production, of which we will cite only a sample, including *Athelstan* (c. 1355–80), *Sir Orfeo* (early 1300s), *The Earl of Toulouse* (c. 1400) and *King Edward and the Shepherd* (late 1300s). Chaucer's *Boethius, Treatise on the Astrolabe, Troilus and Criseyde*, as well as *The Canterbury Tales* all emerged in the fourteenth century, as did Langland's

Piers Plowman, anonymous poems such as *Sir Gawain and the Green Knight, Pearl, Cleanness (or Purity)* and *Patience*, and the medieval mystery plays of the Wakefield and York cycles which also began to be performed during this period. John Gower's *Confessio Amantis* (1390–1393) dates from the fourteenth century, as does Julian of Norwich's (1342–c. 1416) *A Revelation of Love* and Margery Kempe's (c. 1373–1438) *The Book of Margery Kempe*. The inflammatory religious prose and biblical translations of Wycliffe and his followers also emerged in this period.

The fifteenth century saw the work of Scottish poets such as William Dunbar (1460–1522), who wrote *The Tretis of the Twa Marrit Women and the Wedo*, Arthurian romances such as *The Avowinge of King Arthur* (c. 1425) and Malory's *Morte d'Arthur* (late 1400s). Finally, the ME period has also left a significant textual record in terms of legal and medical documents, sermons, macaronic poems (or poems where more than one language is used for composition, such as *On the Times* and *On the King's Breaking of the Magna Charta*), lyrics (such as *Alisoun, Fowles in the Frith* and *My Lief is Foren in Londe*) and personal and public correspondence (such as the Paston letters).

Let us now turn to a consideration of the linguistic features of ME usage that such texts have shed light on.

4.4 The Language of Middle English

Even with the proviso that it does not accurately record contemporary speech, the ME corpus has proved an invaluable and impressive database for historians of the language. The fact that it spans most of the period – a period in which, crucially, no literary standard existed – and is dialectally diverse means that it lends itself easily to both diachronic and synchronic study, allowing observations about both language change through time and variation at particular points in time. We will note instances of variation and change where relevant in the following sections (see also Fennell, 2001: 110–13; Burnley, 1992: 63–196).

Before beginning our description of ME, we should take note of its main dialects. Five are generally recognized: Northern, Midland (East and West), South-Eastern and South-Western. Northern (derived from the OE Northumbrian dialect) stretched from the middle of Yorkshire to Scotland and so subsumed Scots, the English variety of the lowlands. Scots came to be used as a literary standard in Scotland from the late fourteenth century onwards, and has been especially noted as the medium for the work of the fifteenth-century 'Chaucerian poets' of the Scottish court. We will not pursue the history of Scots here, but the interested reader is referred to Barber (1993), Görlach (1991) and Wales (2002).

As to the other dialects, South-Eastern derived from OE Kentish and South-Western from OE West Saxon. Mercian was the OE antecedent of Midland (stretching from London to Gloucestershire), which is traditionally separated into East Midland and West Midland. Fennell (2001: 109) also distinguishes a sixth dialect, East Anglian, stating that texts from that particular area show marked differences from its neighbouring East Midlands variety.

4.4.1 Features of ME Spelling

In the ME period, quite a few changes were made to spelling conventions, one of the results of which, for the modern reader, is to make English seem much more familiar. Some of these resulted from the influence of Norman scribes, and others were re-introductions of orthographic practice which had become obsolete during the OE period. The most significant re-introductions were the substitution of *th* (used before 900) for OE *þ* and *ð*, and of *w* in place of the runic wynn *ƿ* for [w]. Early OE scribes had used *uu* for this sound, but the Norman scribes introduced the joined-up, double-u we use today.

In early ME spelling, the three allophonic values of /g/ – [g], [ɣ] and [j] – were represented by both *g* and *yogh*, *ȝ* (a retention of Anglo-Saxon *ȝ*). In general, the graph *g* represented [g] (as in ME *gome* 'man'), and *ȝ* [ɣ] and [j] (as in ME *cniȝt* and *ȝelde(n)*). By late ME, [ɣ] was represented by *gh* and [j] by *y*, hence later ME spelling of the latter two examples as *knight* 'knight' and *yelde(n)* 'yield', 'give'.

Anglo-Norman scribes also introduced the use of the graph *v* for [v], which in OE had been represented by *f*, as in OE *drifan* ('to drive') and *seofan* ('seven'). They also followed the continental practice of using *v* and *u* for both consonant and vowel sounds. As a general rule, *v* was used word-initially and *u* elsewhere, yielding ME spellings such as *euer* ('ever'), *euil* ('evil') and *vndeþ* ('undeep' > 'shallow').

The allophones of OE *c*, namely [tʃ] and [k] (see Chapter 3, Section 3.4.1) were orthographically disambiguated in ME. The spelling *ch* was introduced to represent the palatal sound, which occurred next to front vowels (thus, OE *cild* [tʃ] > ME *child*), and *c* was retained for [k], which primarily occurred with back vowels and consonants, hence ME spellings such as *care* ('unhappiness'), *cofre* ('coffin'), *cunde* ('nature') and *clerc* ('priest', 'cleric'). In the few instances where *c* did represent [k] before front vowels, the symbol was changed to *k*, hence modern *kin* (OE *cyn/cynne*) and *king* (OE *cyning*).

Other significant changes include that of OE *hw* to *wh* (as in OE *hwæt* > *what*), as well as the replacement of OE *sc*, which represented [ʃ] (as in *fisc* 'fish'), by the more transparent *sh* (sometimes *ss* or *sch*), OE *cw* [kw] (as in *cwēn* 'queen') by French *qu* (inherited from Latin), and OE *cg* [dʒ] (as in *ecg* 'edge') by *gg* and later *dg(e)*.

In terms of vowels, the main spelling changes to note were that scribes frequently used double vowels to indicate vowel length, as in *rood* ('cross'); and that final unstressed *e* after a consonant also indicated that the main vowel in the word was long, as in *fode* ('food'). The French spelling *ou* came to be used for long *ū* [uː], as in OE *hūs* > ME *hous*. It is worth remembering at this point that even though such vowel spellings look a great deal more familiar, the sounds they represented did not yet have their modern values. Thus, *hous* was still pronounced [huːs] at this point, and *fode* as [fɔːd]. The shifts that would take these vowels to their modern values would not occur until much later (see Chapter 5).

4.4.2 Features of ME Pronunciation

The ME corpus indicates that the consonantal system remained relatively stable during the period, experiencing a few significant changes from OE. The vowel system, however, underwent many more changes, some of which (as we will see later) would have far-reaching consequences for the inflectional structures of English.

We begin with the consonants.

4.4.2.1 ME consonants

As discussed in Chapter 3 (Section 3.4.1), OE speakers appear to have made use of word-initial consonant clusters including h, as in hl, hn and hr. ME spelling indicates that the pronunciation of this initial h disappeared, as can be seen in Example 4.1:

Example 4.1 Disappearance of initial h

OE		ME	
hlēor [hl]	>	lere [l]	'complexion'
hnappian [hn]	>	nappe [n]	'to sleep'
hraþor [hr]	>	rather [r]	'sooner'

The loss of [h] in wh clusters (from OE hw), apart from when it preceded a back vowel, initially began in the southern dialect areas and later spread to other ME regions. Thus h-less pronunciations in words such as what and where (OE hwǣr) are commonplace today, but who (OE hwā/ME ho) retains [h] and not [w].

Other OE word-initial consonant clusters which underwent pronunciation change in ME include sw and tw. Where these clusters came to precede a back vowel (as a result of sound changes), the pronunciation of w was lost. Thus OE swā ([sw]) and twā ([tw]) became ME so ([s]) and two ([t]) respectively.

As noted in Chapter 3 (Section 3.4.1), [f]/[v], [s]/[z] and [θ]/[ð] were voiceless/voiced allophones, the first in each pair occurring word-initially and word-finally, and the second, word-medially. In ME, this distribution became blurred for two main reasons. First, English borrowed French and Latin loans with initial voiced [v] and [z], such as (in their modern forms) veal, virtue; zeal, zodiac. In analogy with this pattern, initial f, s, ð and þ in native English words become voiced – a change that first began in the southern ME dialects. Our modern pronunciations of this and they, for example, are the result of this voicing, as are words such as vixen, which derives from OE fyxe ('female fox').

Second, many of the OE inflectional endings were reduced and lost during the ME period (discussed in more detail below). Thus, in words such as giefan ('to give'), the final –an inflection was reduced to the unstressed vowel schwa and then ultimately lost in pronunciation, although it survives orthographically in final –e. This meant that the OE voiced medial f in words like giefan become word-final in ME (as in gif [v]). The same principle applied to the pronunciation of words such as lose [z] (OE losian) and bathe [ð] (OE baþian). The loss of complementary distribution in these allophonic pairs (that is, their occurrence in mutually exclusive environments in the word) paved the way for their eventual adoption as phonemes.

Finally, the –n [n] of OE inflections such as verb infinitive –an (as in giefan), n-stem plurals (as in huntan), and adjectives in a weak declension (see Chapter 3, Section 3.4.2) began to be gradually lost in pronunciation (and spelling) in the

ME period – a development which affected the language's grammatical and syntactic systems. In possessive pronouns such as *min(e)* and *thin(e)*, final *–n* was also lost before a consonant, as in OE *min fæder* > ME *my fæder* (but *myn eye*).

4.4.2.2 ME vowels

In syllables that carried stress, the OE short vowels spelt *a, e, i, o, u* ([ɑ], [ɛ], [ɪ], [ɔ] and [ʊ]; see Chapter 3, Section 3.4.1) remained unchanged in ME, although some underwent lengthening in certain environments (see below). Short [æ] (*æ*), on the other hand, was lowered to [ɑ], as reflected in the ME spelling *glad* (from OE *glæd*). This change initially occurred only in some ME dialects – texts from the South-west Midland and Kentish dialect areas spell the same word *gled*. Pyles and Algeo (1982: 149) postulate that this indicates little variation from the OE [æ] sound in these areas.

Short [y] (*y*) was also unrounded in ME to [ɪ], as indicated by spellings such as *brittened* from OE *brytnian* 'destroyed'. This change occurred first in the Northern and East Midland dialect areas.

In terms of the OE long vowels in stressed syllables, three important changes took place. First, south of the Humber, words with OE long [ɑ:] (*ā*) rounded to [ɔ:] in pronunciation, as indicated in the ME spellings *bon* and *stoon* (OE *bān* 'bone' and *stān* 'stone', respectively). In the North, the OE value was retained for a longer period, and evolved into [e:] in modern Scots, as indicated by spellings such as *hame* ('home') and *stane* ('stone').

Second, in the Northern and East Midland dialect areas, long [y:] (*ȳ*) was unrounded (like its short counterpart) to [i:]. In the later years of the fourteenth century, this change eventually spread to the West Midland and South-west areas. In Kent and the South-east regions [y:] became [e:]. Thus, where texts from the Northern and East Midland areas use spellings such as *hiden*, those from Kent and the South-east render the same word as *heden* ('to hide', from OE *hȳdan*).

Third, the pronunciation of OE long *æ* and *ēa* fell together as [ɛ:], and that of OE *ē* and *ēo* as [e:], in the ME period. ME orthographic conventions, however, did not typically disambiguate the two, as can be seen in ME spellings such as *seen* [e:] 'to see' (< OE *sēon*) and *leef* [ɛ:] 'leaf' (< OE *lēaf*). However, *ea/ei* for [ɛ:] and *ee/ie* [e:] did later come to be used in the Early Modern Period. Eventually [ɛ:] and [e:] also fell together, as can be heard in modern pronunciations of *sea* (from OE *sǣ*) and *see* (OE *sēon*) (from Barber, 1993: 154).

ME vowels also appear to have also undergone quantitative changes in pronunciation, meaning that they were either lengthened or shortened depending on environment. For instance, OE short vowels which occurred before certain consonant clusters (namely, *mb, ld, rd, nd* and *rð*) were lengthened. Thus, short [ɪ] in words such as *milde, climben,* and *binden* became [i:]. If the cluster was followed by a third consonant, however, lengthening did not occur. OE *cilde* ([ɪ]) for example, therefore came to be pronounced with long [i:] in ME, but remained short in *children*.

Another important case of lengthening occurred with short [ɑ], [ɛ] and [ɔ] (*a, e, o*) in open syllables (that is, syllables which end in a vowel). Hence OE words such as *bacan* [ɑ] ('to bake') became pronounced with long [ɑ:] in ME, OE *stelan* [ɛ] ('to steal') with long [ɛ:] and OE *þrote* [ɔ] with long [ɔ:] (examples from Pyles and Algeo, 1982: 151).

Conversely, long vowels which in OE preceded double consonants, as in *hỹdde*, shortened in ME pronunciation, as did long vowels before consonant clusters such as *pt* (*kepte*, from OE *cēpte*) and *nt* (*twentig*, from OE *twēntig*). If a long vowel occurred in the first (typically stressed) syllable of a trisyllabic word in OE, then it was also shortened in ME, as occurred with OE *hǣligdæg* ([æ:]) 'holiday'.

The diphthongs of OE (*eo, ēo, ea, ēa*) essentially became monophthongized in the ME period. Short *eo* and *ea* were replaced in spelling by *a* and *e* respectively, yielding forms such as *yaf* (OE *geaf* 'gave') and *herte* (OE *heorte* 'heart'). The long diphthongs *ēo* and *ēa* became, as seen earlier, monophthongal [e:] and [ɛ:], respectively. New diphthongs did however emerge, partly through the incorporation of French loanwords, but also primarily through combinations of vowels and glides such as [j] and [w]. Thus, borrowings such as *joie* and *cloister* yielded [ɔɪ] and others such as *boilen* and *poisen* [ʊɪ]. This has of course changed – modern English users typically pronounce *boil* and *poison* with [ɔɪ].

Other new ME diphthongs – [aʊ], [ɔʊ], [ɛʊ], [ɪʊ] – developed from different sources. The vocalization of *w* after vowels, for instance, produced all four, as occurred in the ME pronunciations of words such as *clawe* [aʊ] 'claw', *flowe* [ɔʊ] 'flow', *lewed* [ɛʊ] 'unlearned' and *nīwe* 'new' [ɪʊ]. However, [aʊ] and [ɔʊ] also emerged from combinations of back vowels and the voiced velar fricative [ɣ] which vocalized and became represented in spelling by *w*. Thus, OE *lagu* and *boga* became ME *lawe* [aʊ] 'law' and *bowe* [ɔʊ] 'bow', respectively. Finally, the combination of front vowels and [j] produced [aɪ] and [eɪ] – a development which, according to Pyles and Algeo (1982: 149), had begun in the OE period. Thus, OE *maegn* 'might', 'power' became ME *mayn* [aɪ] 'great', 'strong' and OE *plegian*, ME *pleie, play* [eɪ] 'to play'. The two qualities fell together in the late ME period.

Last but by no means least, vowels in unstressed syllables underwent levelling in ME (a process which may well have begun in the Anglo-Saxon period). A significant consequence of this was that the myriad (typically unstressed) inflectional endings we looked at in Chapter 3 (Section 3.4.2) eventually fell together in pronunciation as schwa – and as *–e* in spelling – losing their function as morphological signals for number, case (apart from the genitive) and gender distinctions. Thus, nominative singular *oxa* 'ox' became *oxe*, plural accusative *hundas, hundes* 'dogs', and singular masculine *gōda* (adjective in weak declension), *gode* 'good'. Plural marking, however, remained salient but the different endings available in OE were quantitatively reduced. We consider these points in more detail in Section 4.4.3.

4.4.3 Features of ME Grammar

We should note that although inflectional reduction is usually cited as one of the most salient and distinctive characteristics of ME, it is very likely to have begun in earlier stages of the language – witness, for example, the syncretism of certain inflectional paradigms in Old English (see Chapter 3, Section 3.4.2). The extensive ME database does, however, offer a much clearer view than the OE corpus of such change in progress. Consider for instance the extracts in Example 4.2 (a)–(c), which are taken from different periods of Middle English writing (Burnley, 1992).

Example 4.2 ME texts

a. And se kyng of France brohte þone eorles sunu Willelm of Normandi, and iæf hine þone eorldom, and þet landfolc him wið toc.

And the King of France brought the earl's son, William of Normandy, and gave the earldom to him, and the people of that land accepted.

(from the Peterborough Chronicle, First Continuation 1127)

b. þa þe king Stephne to Englalande com, þa macod he his gadering æt Oxeneford; and þar he nam þe biscop Roger of Serebyri, and Alexander biscop of Lincol, and te canceler Roger, his neues, and dide ælle in prisun til hi iafen up here castles.

When King Stephen came to England, he held a parliament at Oxford, and there he took Roger, Bishop of Salisbury, and Alexander, Bishop of Lincoln, the Chancellor Roger, his nephews, and imprisoned them until they surrendered their castles.

(from the Peterborough Chronicle, Final Continuation 1154)

c. For the difficulte of the processe, it briefly can not be expowned what the pagans, otherwise called the paynyms, supposed of their goddis, and what they were that first gaaue enformacion to haue theyr goddes in reuerence and worshipp, and what oppynyon they hadde of their immortalite.

(from John Skelton's translation of the Bibliotheca
Historica of Diodorus Seculus; fifteenth century)

Text 4.2(a) makes use of inflected forms of the definite article in phrases such as *se kyng* (masculine nominative singular), *þone eorles sunu* and *þone eorldom* (both masculine accusative singular). *Eorles* in *eorles sunu* carries the common OE genitive singular inflection. The writer also maintains a distinction between third person singular accusative masculine *hine* and dative masculine *him* (see Chapter 3, Section 3.4.2). By the time of text 4.2(b), the inflected forms of the definite article have been replaced by *þe* (sometimes spelt *te*, as in *te canceler*). The plural nouns in this text (*neues* and *castles*) carry –*(e)s* inflection. The third person plural pronouns, however, still retain their OE forms, namely *hi* 'they' and *here* 'their'. By the time of Skelton's translation, all plurals end in –*(e/i)s* (*pagans, paynyms, goddes/goddis*) and the third person plural pronouns are those inherited from Old Norse, namely *they, theyr/their*.

We will consider such changes (and others) in the following discussion (see also Burrow and Turville-Petre (1996: Chapters 4 and 5) for a detailed description).

4.4.3.1 ME nouns

By the end of the twelfth century, levelling and inflectional reduction to schwa (and –*e*) had largely erased the case, number and gender inflectional paradigms of OE nouns. In the case of inflectional endings with a final nasal, such as the plural dative –*um*, the nasal appears to have been lost before the vowel change to schwa.

Nouns did, however, continue to mark plurals and genitives, using inflections inherited from OE declensional patterns and extending them to paradigms to which they did not historically belong. Thus, ME plural forms (apart from historically 'irregular' forms such as *i*-mutated and zero-marked plurals, as in *feet* and *deer*) were generally formed with either –*es* (from OE –*as*, *a*-stem declension) or –*en* (from OE –*an*, *n*-stem declension) (see Chapter 3, Section 3.4.2). The use of these inflections tended to conform to dialectal divisions in ME: southern dialects appear to have favoured the –*en* plural, while the –*es* plural was used elsewhere, particularly in the northern dialects. Thus, ME texts record alternate plurals such as *deoflen* and *deuils*, *kine* and *cows*, *eyen* and *eyes*. As we know, –*en* eventually ceased to be employed as a productive plural marker.

The genitive singular –*es* inflection (from OE –*es*, *a*-stem declension) was also extended to general use with ME nouns, but was indistinguishable in writing and speech from the plural –*es* inflection where the latter was used: *eorles*, for example, could mean 'earls' or 'earl's'. However, context would have helped disambiguate such instances, so we know that *eorles*, for example, is a genitive in the extract from the *Peterborough Chronicle* quoted in Example 4.2 (a) because it occurs in conjunction with *sunu* (*eorles sunu*). This formula of *possessor noun-genitive inflection + possessed noun* has of course continued into modern English (with the introduction of the apostrophe in spelling).

Some nouns in ME, however, did not carry genitive marking, such as those which denoted family relationships and ended in <-*er*>, as in *fader bone* 'father's murderer', nouns which had been feminine in OE (*his lady grace*), and proper names, as in *Adam kynde*, *God hert* (Burrow and Turville-Petre, 1996: 24).

The ME corpus also indicates increasing use of other types of possessive marking. *Of*-phrases, as in *þe termes of Judé*, began to appear, as well as a *his* genitive, which would become more popular in the Early Modern Period. In the latter construction, *his* functioned as the possessive marker, as in *Seint Gregore hys bokes Dialoges* 'St. Gregory's books *The Dialogues*' (Burrow and Turville-Petre, 1996: 40). We will return to examples of this process in Chapter 5.

4.4.3.2 ME pronouns

ME pronouns, like their OE antecedents, continued to retain distinctions of person, case, number and gender. The major points of difference lay in the loss of the OE dual forms, and the falling together of OE accusative and dative third person singular forms (such as *hine* and *him*) – a process that had already occurred for OE first and second person singular and plural forms (see Chapter 3, Table 3.7).

The ME corpus displays a wide range of dialectal variation in the actual pronoun forms. Tables 4.1 and 4.2 illustrate some of these (examples from Pyles and Algeo, 1982: 157).

The southern dialects maintained the OE third person accusative–dative distinction longest, but eventually followed the rest of the dialect areas in opting for one object pronoun form. In addition, as Table 4.2 shows, the Scandinavian

Table 4.1 ME pronouns – first and second persons

	First person		Second person	
	Singular	Plural	Singular	Plural
nominative	ic, I, ik	we	thou	ye
object	me	us	thee	you
genitive	mi, min(e)	our(e), oures	thi, thin(e)	your(e), yours

th-third person plural forms which are commonplace today were merely variants in the ME period, surfacing first in texts from the Northern and Midland dialect areas – regions which had once encompassed the ninth-century Danelaw settlements. Eventually, as we know, these forms would dominate and replace the Anglo-Saxon *h*- pronouns.

4.4.3.3 ME definite article

With the inflectional losses in the noun system, the OE forms of the definite article, which varied according to case, gender and number, were all eventually replaced by *the* in early ME (see Example 4.2 (b)). By the end of the period, the modern system whereby the definite article remains invariant, regardless of the inflectional marking on the noun (here plural or possessive) as well as of its function in the sentence, had been well and truly established.

4.4.3.4 ME adjectives

The OE inflectional paradigms marking case, number and gender in adjectives – which comprised either a vowel, or vowel plus –*n* (see Chapter 3, Section 3.4.2) – also underwent reduction in the ME period, again through the loss of inflectional –*n* and vowel levelling. The southern dialects, however, did retain for a time a distinction between weak and strong forms, as well as of number in certain types of adjective. When a monosyllabic adjective, or one which ended in a consonant (such as *old*, which fulfils both criteria) pre-modified a noun with a demonstrative (an OE weak declension) –*e* was added word-finally. This also applied when the adjective modified a plural noun. Hence, in texts from southern

Table 4.2 ME pronouns – third person

	Singular			Plural
	masculine	feminine	neuter	
nominative	he	she, scæ, ho, hye, scho, he	hit, it	hi, they, thai
object	hine, him	hir(e), her(e), hi	hit, it	hem, heom, the(i)m, thaim
genitive	his	hir(e), her(e), hires	his	her(e), heres, their(e), theires

dialect areas, it is not unusual to find structures such as *god man* ('good man'), but *the gode man* (weak declension) and *gode men* (plural).

ME adjectives also retained OE comparative and superlative inflections, but in slightly different forms. The OE comparative *–ra*, being an unstressed syllable, also underwent reduction of the vowel to schwa. In spelling, the ending therefore became *–re*, and later, the *–er* still used in modern English. The superlative inflections *–ost* and *–est* also underwent vowel reduction, ending up in spelling as *–est*. Some texts indicate that if the root vowel of the adjective was long, it often became shortened when these inflections were added, and the root consonant doubled in spelling. Hence the superlative form of *greet* (great) is represented orthographically as *grettest* (Burrow and Turville-Petre, 1996: 30).

4.4.3.5 ME verbs

The OE distinction between weak and strong verb classes survived into Middle English dialects, as did a great many of the inflectional characteristics we considered in Chapter 3. The ME corpus does, however, also show that inflectional changes were under way. For instance, the infinitive *–an* suffix (see Chapter 3, Section 3.4.2) underwent the ubiquitous loss of final *–n* and vowel levelling to schwa. In southern ME dialects, the inflection was retained in writing for a time as *–en*, but as *–e* in the North, hence southern *heren* ('to hear') and northern *here*. ME texts indicate that as the inflection lost its morphological usefulness, prepositions such as *to* and *for* increasingly took over its function.

The OE shared present indicative and present subjunctive inflections for weak and strong verbs (see Chapter 3, Section 3.4.2) survived into ME, but were also subject to levelling. Table 4.3 compares the inflectional endings typically found in southern and northern dialects, using the weak verb *to heren/here* ('to hear'). The ME southern dialectal data is taken from the *Ancrene Wisse* (early thirteenth

Table 4.3 ME present indicative and subjunctive inflections

		Present indicative	
	OE endings	ME endings	
		Ancrene Wisse **Infinitive** *heren*	*Gawain* **Infinitive** *here*
I	-e	here	here
thou	-est	her**est**	heres
he, she, it	-eð	here**ð**	heres
we, ye, they	-að	here**ð**	here(**n**), heres

	Subjunctive	
	OE endings	ME endings (northern and southern)
I, thou, he, she, it	-e	here
we, ye, they	-en	heren

century, South-West Midlands), and the northern is taken from the *Gawain* manuscript (late fourteenth century, North-West Midlands) (cited in Burrow and Turville-Petre, 1996: 32–3).

The *–en* ending of indicative and subjunctive plural forms gradually disappeared during the ME period and was replaced in pronunciation and spelling by schwa and *–e* respectively. Overall (and as we know) modern English retains none of these inflections apart from the third person singular present *–s* (*he, she, it hears*): a descendant of the northern *–es*.

Weak and strong verb preterite conjugations continued into ME, and strong verbs generally retained their OE ablaut patterns, as can be seen in Table 4.4 (data from Burrow and Turville-Petre, 1996: 34–5).

The *–e* and *–en* suffixes continued to undergo levelling in the ME period and eventually disappeared, as did the weak *–dest* suffix of the second person singular (*–des, –dez* or *–de* in Northern and Northern Midland dialects). The movement towards the use of one preterite form for all persons and numbers of the subject (as in modern English *I/we, you* (singular and plural), *he, she, it/they* **heard/drove**) appears to have begun in the ME period first in the northern dialect areas. The *Gawain* manuscript seemingly records this change in progress, sometimes not only using one preterite form regardless of subject (in this case, *drof*), but also the older OE singular and plural preterite forms indiscriminately, indicating that the distinction was increasingly becoming less salient. Thus *ran* (preterite singular) and *runnen* (preterite plural) are both used with plural subjects. The southern dialects, however, appear to have been quite conservative in terms of this feature (as indeed they were in so many others, as we have seen), and maintained the distinction between singular and plural preterite forms for much longer (see Burrow and Turville-Petre, 1996: 36).

In terms of the past participle, the completive prefix *ge-* of both weak and strong verbs was reduced in pronunciation, as can be seen in its spellings as *y-* or *i-* in ME *ibolwe* (OE *gebolgen* 'puffed up') and *ibeot* (OE *gebēot* 'boast'). ME texts also show dialectal variation in strong verb past participle forms. The *–en* ending was maintained in the northern dialects, but not in the South and Midlands (as

Table 4.4 ME preterite conjugations in weak and strong verbs

	Weak verb *heren/here* 'to hear'		Strong verb *drifan* 'to drive'	
	OE endings	ME endings (*Ancrene Wisse*)	OE forms	ME forms (*Ancrene Wisse*)
I	-de	her**de** 'heard'	drāf	draf 'drove'
thou	-dest	her**dest**	drīfe	drive
he, she, it	-de	her**de**	drāf	draf
we, ye, they	-don	her**den**	drīfon	driven

in *ynome* 'taken', *ydrawe* 'drawn' and *ycore* 'chosen'). Some of these variants survived while others did not; hence modern English has inherited *–en* forms such as *broken* and *eaten*, but also *–en*-less forms such as *drunk* and *sung*. In some cases, both variants still exist: *got* and *gotten* are used by modern speakers, although the former is now considered typical of British usage, and the latter of American.

As mentioned in Chapter 3, many strong verbs in ME developed weak past and past participle forms through analogy with the more widespread paradigm. In quite a few cases, the weak forms dominated, and have been inherited by modern English. Thus *crēap/crupon/gecrupen* gave way to *crept* and *healp/hulpon/geholpen* to *helped*. Finally, one more feature of note for the ME verb concerns dialectal variation in the present participle inflection. Our modern English ending *–ing* (as in *dancing* and *talking*) is inherited from the form used in the southern ME dialects. Others, such as *–and(e)* (Northern), *-inde* (South-West Midlands) and *–ende* (East), were all used throughout the ME period, but eventually disappeared from the language.

4.4.4 Features of ME syntax

The preference for VO word-order evident in the OE corpus (see Chapter 3, Section 3.4.3) continued into the ME period, as did the comparatively less frequent use of OV structures. If the object of a sentence was a pronoun, word order was typically OV, as in Example 4.3(a). Subject–verb inversion (in structures with basic VO order) occurred in imperatives and after adverbs of place, time and manner, as illustrated in Example 4.3(b)–(c):

Example 4.3 ME word order
Object pronoun
(a) Yef   thou   me   zayst
             S   O   V

if you say to me . . .

Imperatives
(b) Clothe   ye   him,   brynge   ye   a fat calf . . .
    V   S   O /   V   S   O

(you) clothe him and (you) bring a fatted calf

After adverbs of place, time, manner
(c) here   lieþ   counforte
         V   S

here lies comfort

Another ME structural feature we should note concerns the placement of modifying adjectives in noun phrases. Adjectives tended to pre-modify nouns (as they do in modern English), but in ME verse they sometimes followed them, as in *sceld deore* 'beloved shield'. In cases where more than one adjective was used in a noun phrase, one would typically function as a pre-modifier, and the other (or others) as post-modifiers, as in *he milde man was and softe and god* ('he was a gentle man and soft and good').

The ME corpus also shows an increasing use of *to be* as the auxiliary verb in passive constructions, as well as the use of *by* to introduce the agent of the action (as in modern *my car **was** destroyed **by** my little brother*). Alternative structures did, however, exist: *worthe* ('to be', 'to come to be'), as in *blessid þou worth* ('may you be blessed'), was used, for example, until the fourteenth century (Burrow and Turville-Petre, 1996: 52). In early ME, an indefinite pronoun *men* (in unstressed form *me*) was often used to express the passive, as in *me henged up bi the fet and smoked heom mid ful smoke* ('they were hung up by the feet and smoked with foul smoke'; *The Peterborough Chronicle*, Final Continuation 1154).

The verb *do* also began to develop a variety of functions in ME. It retained its OE function as a 'substitute verb' in sentences such as modern *Mark loves watching TV and I **do** too*. In some ME dialects, *do* also meant 'make' or 'have' – a usage still retained in phrases such as *let's do lunch*. The past tense form *did* was sometimes used to signal past tense (as in *did carye* 'carried'), a construction which was used productively in Early Modern English (see Chapter 5). Its other uses, such as as an auxiliary in negative statements and questions, which have become part of modern English usage (as in *they don't eat liver* and *do you hate cats too?*), had begun to appear, but would not become a consistent part of usage until approximately the seventeenth century.

Finally, as the importance of prepositions grew in ME (as the synthetic nature of English diminished), new creations joined this word class. Many emerged through semantic change, as in the case of *among*, whose OE antecedent *gemong* meant 'in a crowd', or through compounding (as in *in + to*) and borrowing, as in the case of *till* (borrowed from Old Norse) and *except*, from Latin (Fennell, 2001: 102).

4.4.5 Features of ME vocabulary

Whereas the lexical stock of Old English had been largely Germanic, that of Middle English was somewhat more Romantic in nature. English borrowed significantly from French in this period (a typical estimate is about 10,000 loans), and it is traditionally held that these loanwords entered the language in two main phases divided approximately by 1250. In the first early stage of borrowing, a relatively small number of loanwords entered English primarily from Norman French, their nature reflecting the social positions held by the newcomers from the Continent. For example, some of the earliest loans include words such as (in their modern form), *government, administer, castle, prison, service, attorney, court, jury* and *felon*. In the church, the new *clergy* also gained new *abbots*, and administered the *sacrament*. The court gained *princes, dukes, counts* and *countesses, barons, marquesses* and *dukes*, although the Anglo-Saxon titles *king, queen, earl, lord* and *lady* remained. A *soldier* in the newly re-formed *army* took his orders from *captains, corporals, lieutenants* and *sergeants*. *Beef, pork, mutton* and *veal* were now served to table, sometimes as meals which have now become synonymous with British cooking: a *roast* or a *fry* up.

After 1250, it is thought that the majority of loanwords derived from the fashionable French of the Parisian court (or Central French), in vogue at most thirteenth-century European courts as a symbol of 'chivalrous society in its most polished form' (Baugh and Cable, 2002: 134), including that presided over in England by Henry II and Eleanor of Provence (see Section 4.2). Thus, borrowings continued in the domains mentioned above but also entered fashion (*fashion, dress, cape, coat, petticoat, lace, boot, mitten, blue, scarlet, jewel, brooch, diamond*), domestic settings (*arras, curtain, towel, chandelier, blanket, basin*), social life (*recreation, leisure, dance, minstrel, juggler, melody, music, conversation*), hunting and riding (*rein, stallion, trot, stable, falcon, merlin, forest, tournament*), art (*sculpture, beauty, colour, image, tone*), architecture (*cathedral, palace, chamber, ceiling, turret, porch, pillar*), literature (*poet, prose, romance, story, chronicle, title, chapter*) and medicine (*physician, surgeon, malady, plague, pestilence, anatomy, balm, sulphur, ointment*).

Various sources (such as Baugh and Cable, 2002; Fennell, 2001; Pyles and Algeo, 1982) state that ME speakers sometimes borrowed the same word twice, once in each phase. This is based on the assumption that regular sound correspondences obtained between the two varieties of Norman and Central French, which resulted in the same word having somewhat different phonetic forms. Thus, where Norman French had [w], Central French had [g]; and Norman French [k] and [tʃ] corresponded to Central French [tʃ] and [s] respectively. English therefore borrowed *warranty* and *warden* from Norman French and later, their Central French counterparts *guarantee* and *guardian*; *catch* and *launch* from the Normans and *chase* and *lance* from the Parisian court. Whereas the difference between these forms in the two varieties of French was purely phonetic, the primary distinction in English is semantic: to *catch*, for example, is not the same as to *chase*, even if both activities are related.

One scholar who challenges the idea of two phases of borrowing from two distinct sources is William Rothwell (1998). He argues that this position, replicated unquestioningly in many discussions of French loanwords in the ME period, is based on material compiled in the early twentieth century, when relevant data and analysis were sparse. Recent progress, however, in the form of publications of the *Middle English Dictionary*, the *Anglo-Norman Dictionary* and other such sources, has rendered much of the earlier suppositions and theories about borrowing obsolete, particularly the notion of a second wave of borrowing from Central French.

The main thrust of Rothwell's argument is that Anglo-French was much more influential a source of borrowing than Central French. He points out that there is no evidence that the diverse French retinue favoured by Henry and Eleanor actually spoke a variety which 'corresponded to what modern philologists are pleased to call *Central French*' (Rothwell, 1998: 6). Anglo-French, on the other hand, was very much a reality, and was well established in usage. Rothwell therefore believes that English was much more likely to borrow from this more familiar source on its doorstep.

Rothwell's article provides a range of supporting examples, of which we will consider two. He postulates that if certain loans in English were in fact from Central French, then we should see a significantly close correspondence in form and meaning between the two. Thus, our modern English *customs* (as in *customs and excise*), allegedly borrowed in the ME period from Central French, should have an identical or similar counterpart in the latter's modern descendant, standard French. This is, however, not the case – today, travellers to France must pass through the *douane*. Thirteenth-century Anglo-French texts record a verb *custumer* 'to pay customs duty', very likely derived from the noun *custume* 'customs duty'. On the Continent, however, the French paid *droits de douane* from about 1372, *douane* itself being a borrowing from Arabic, and a reflection of the productive trade that France carried on in the Mediterranean at that time.

Another example is that of English *dungeon*, ostensibly a borrowing in ME from Parisian *donjon*. However, English *dungeon* is semantically closer to the Anglo-French *donjun*. A person in a Parisian *donjon* would be enclosed in the centre of a castle but in an English *dungeon*, in an underground cell. Rothwell (ibid.: 13) argues that the Continental meaning of *donjon* has remained stable for about eight hundred years, but that that of Anglo-French shifted during the thirteenth century. Thus, Anglo-French texts from the twelfth and mid-thirteenth centuries show that the word was being used in the sense still preserved on the Continent, as can be seen in Example 4.4 (a)–(b). However, thirteenth-century texts also indicate a growing use of the word without the sense of elevation (but still with the earlier senses of strength and security (Example 4.4 (c)). By the first half of the fourteenth century, the sense of being underground was explicit in the use of *donjun*, strongly suggesting it as the source of the English word (Example 4.4 (d)).

Example 4.4 Use of *donjun*

(a) La reine . . . a tant devale le dungun
   'the queen . . . thereupon comes down from the keep' (*The Life of St Catherine*, twelfth century)
(b) les treis bailles du chastel Ki . . . defendent le dongon
   'the three baileys of the castle which . . . protect the keep [the strongest part of the castle]' (*Le Chasteau d'Amour*, thirteenth century)
(c) Il est bricum, E clostre dust estre, ou en dungun
   'he is a fool; he ought to be in a cloister or a dungeon' (*Le Manuel de Pechez*, thirteenth century)
(d) Ly roi descendist en un bas dongoun
   'the king went down into a deep dungeon' (*Chronicle of Peter of Langtoft*, fourteenth century)

Finally, Rothwell (1998) makes an interesting and challenging point about words such as *catch* and *chase* which, as we have seen, have been accepted as having entered English from two different sources in two different periods. He states that:

> the distinction between 'Norman' spellings of words taken into Middle English during the early period, and the 'Central French' spellings attached to words adopted later, is far from being as clear-cut as it is made out to be in reference books.

The repercussions of this are significant, since the differences in spelling, which are taken to indicate differences in pronunciation, have been key in maintaining the argument for two different waves of borrowing. Take, for example, the alleged equivalence of Norman French [k] (spelt *c*) and Central French [tʃ] (*ch*) before *a* and *o* (see above). At its most straightforward, this means that *ch* before these two vowel graphs should not appear in 'Norman texts'. This is, however, not the case. Anglo-French texts written in the early years after the Conquest (the first appear about 50 years after 1066), and which should therefore show a heavy Norman influence, contain spellings which have been classified as indicative of Central French provenance. Thus the early twelfth-century *Leis Wilheme* ('The Laws of William'), the earliest body of law written in French in England, and 'as "Norman" and as "official" a text as it is possible to find' (Rothwell, 1998: 8), uses 'Central French spellings', such as *chalenjeurs*, *chambre* and *cheval*. Similarly, the *Estoire des Engleis* (1135–40) uses *chalengier* and *champaigne* alongside *cacier* and *campiun*; and *Li Quatre Livre des Reis* (1170) has *chaldes* and *champiuns*, but also *cancelant* and *kachevels* (ibid.: 8). As Rothwell (ibid.) points out, texts written in Anglo-French were no more standardized in spelling than those written in Middle English, and we may have been naïve in never considering this as a factor. Overall, if Rothwell's analyses are correct (and we have as yet no reason to believe they are not), then the assumptions of two discrete phases of borrowing during the ME period may have to be re-thought. Closer interfaces with the work of Anglo-French scholars may very well hold the key to linguists formulating a more accurate understanding of borrowing during this period.

4.5 Contact and Change: Middle English Creolization?

As we have seen, the Norman Conquest created a context for contact between speakers of English and French. While language contact was certainly not new in the history of English, or even in the history of England, the relationship between French and English has retained a particular fascination for sociohistorical linguists, particularly since the period is also one in which English as a whole appears to change considerably from its Old English predecessor. An assumed correlation between language contact and language change in the ME period is not unreasonable: modern sociolinguistic studies, for example, can often demonstrate a link between the two (see Thomason and Kaufman, 1988, for numerous case studies). Given this context, the linguist piecing together a diachronic narrative of English can very easily see the phase in which French and English co-existed functioning like a transformation device between the Anglo-Saxon and ME periods: late OE goes in one end around 1066, and an English much more recognizable to the modern eye emerges from the other around the thirteenth century.

The question that this brings modern researchers to concerns the nature of the contact situation between French and English. Was it, for example, the kind of context which allows for each language, or one language, to impact structurally on the other, or was it one in which the languages co-existed discretely but with the opportunity for limited lexical borrowing in certain domains? Many scholars have opted for the latter scenario as the more plausible (a perspective presented by well-known histories of English such as those of Baugh and Cable (2002) Barber (1993) and Fennell (2001)), but others such as Bailey and Maroldt (1977) have famously (or notoriously) argued instead for the former kind of contact situation, postulating that French and English had in fact participated in processes of creolization. Their position has been widely discredited, but it and proposed counter-arguments are frequently mentioned in discussions of the ME period as an important example of language contact analysis (albeit a failed one). The debate therefore deserves some attention here, and the following discussion – which begins by outlining Bailey and Maroldt's position – will incorporate current perspectives from creole studies that have inevitably not been included in seminal treatments such as that of Thomason and Kaufman (1988) and subsequent summaries such as Fennell (2001).

Bailey and Maroldt (1977: 21) define *creolization* as 'the gradient mixture of two or more languages' which occurs in situations of contact. A *creole* emerges when 'the result of mixing . . . is substantial enough to result in a new system, a system that is separate from its antecedent parent systems' (ibid.). The authors argue that the linguistic make-up of ME is testimony to this mixing: (1) it combines features of English and French; (2) it uses English elements in French functions; and (3) it shows the influence of French in certain grammatical developments.

In relation to (1), Bailey and Maroldt (1977: 52) argue, for example, that the majority of derivational affixes used in ME came from French loanwords, although a 'not inconsiderable volume' was also inherited from Anglo-Saxon. In addition, ME vocabulary contained a 'very considerable' number of loans from French, which are significant both quantitatively and qualitatively. In terms of quantity they state, for example, that in 1460, 40 per cent of ME vocabulary was derived from French; and in terms of quality, that while French loans in ME largely fell into certain cultural domains (see Section 4.4.5), they also included 'basic' borrowings, such as *uncle, aunt, nephew, niece, danger, doubt, trouble* and *cause* (ibid.: 34–5). However, ME also made use of Anglo-Saxon vocabulary, including a high degree of 'basic' lexis, including 'most functional elements' (such as prepositions, demonstratives, conjunctions) (ibid.: 52).

In terms of (2), Bailey and Maroldt state, for instance, that many verb constructions in Middle English use English words but are modelled on French constructions. Hence English perfect aspect, as in *she has broken the window*, is based on the French pattern *avoir* ('to have') + *main verb past participle*. Go + *infinitive main verb* (as in *I'm going to eat crisps all night*) is allegedly also modelled on French *aller* + *infinitive*. Similarly, the authors argue that the use of *of*-genitives in ME was based on French *de*-possessives (as in *la voiture de Guillaume* 'William's car'), just as the use of *to* before an indirect object in a sentence derived from the use of French *à* (as in *donnes le livre à Robert* 'give the book to Robert').

Finally, in terms of (3), Bailey and Maroldt argue that the Middle English loss of OE case and gender inflections in nouns, determiners and adjectives (the authors do not mention number) was largely determined by the 'clash' with the entirely different inflectional systems in French, which rendered the use of the OE morphological signals 'so utterly complex . . . [they] had to be given up'. As further support for statement (3), the authors also propose that French SVO word order came to predominate in ME, and that constructions such as *it is me* and *it is him*, where object pronouns are used instead of the subject pronouns *I* and *he*, are 'clearly French' (ibid.: 46).

Overall, Bailey and Maroldt (ibid.: 21, 22) claim that 'at least forty percent of each component [of ME] – lexicon, semantax, phonetology [*sic*], and morphology – is mixed', making it 'a mixed language, or creole'. The salient question for the authors is therefore whether 'Old French was creolized with Anglo-Saxon . . . whether Anglo-Saxon was creolized with Old French, or whether the mixture was of so thorough-going a nature that it makes little sense even to pose the question at all' (ibid.: 22–3). This is not addressed in specific detail but in all fairness, the authors state that the analyses they present are provisional.

What they do argue about the assumed process of creolization is that it took place in stages, the first of which involved Old Norse and Old English contact in the late Anglo-Saxon period. This 'Norse creolization' resulted in 'linguistic instability' that in turn paved the way for later creolization involving French (ibid.: 26). Given that contact between Norse and English speakers took place in Danelaw areas, removed from London and the southern regions which would later be the focus of contact between French and English, this purported influence of Norse creolization seems odd. However, the authors postulate that substantial immigration to London from the Danelaw in the fourteenth century had a significant linguistic impact on the English varieties of the capital.

Norse creolization was followed by two stages of French and English creolization: a pre-1200 'major creolization', and a minor one involving substantial borrowing from Central French in the thirteenth and fourteenth centuries. Bailey and Maroldt (ibid.: 30) therefore argue that the 'English' being spoken by the end of the Middle English period was 'certainly not a variety of Anglo-Saxon'.

Bailey and Maroldt's position, however, is undermined both by inconsistencies and ambiguities, as well as by the fact that their definitions of creoles and creolization have little or no currency in creole studies itself. In addition, their analysis of ME as a 'mixed, analytic language' is problematic. The following discussion outlines some of the main problems which fall into each or all of these categories.

One immediate problem concerns the question of Norse creolization in the Danelaw which 'prepared' (southern) English for further creolization with French. The 'major creolization phase' of French and English, however, allegedly occurred between 1066 and 1200, thus pre-dating the supposedly influential fourteenth-century immigration of Danelaw populations into London. Even if we assume that the migrations were supposed to have influenced the 'minor creolization' phase, the causative link between tenth-century and thirteenth–fourteenth-century creolizations is tenuous. For the authors, this link is 'linguistic instability', which 'prepares the ground' for further creolization (ibid.: 26). There are two problematic issues here: a seemingly indiscriminate assumption that creolization is the generic outcome of contact situations where languages impact on each other (see their open-ended definition of creolization cited earlier), and an assumed link between linguistic instability and creolization. Sociolinguistic studies have repeatedly demonstrated that all situations of language contact, and the motivations of relevant speakers, are not identical; and it would seem naïve to therefore assume that they all have the same linguistic result. Depending on the circumstances, contact can create a wide range of linguistic outcomes: among others, it can cause the emergence of systems such as a pidgin or creole, or contribute to the obsolescence of one language, or to heavy lexical and structural borrowing in another. To say that contact generally boils down to the same effect – creolization – is, as Thomason and Kaufman (1988: 307) point out, to virtually render the term meaningless and also to reduce all situations of contact to a common denominator: an act not only demeaning to the communities involved but also descriptively unhelpful.

Furthermore, the term 'linguistic instability' is ambiguous and unquantifiable: does it imply that the usage of one speaker varied considerably and erratically from another's, or that norms of linguistic and social usage are violated? Even if 'linguistic instability' could be delimited, its existence in the sociolinguistic context Bailey and Maroldt describe is still problematic: by the time 'linguistically unstable' Norse creoles arrived in London, they would have been established as 'stable' first languages in speech communities for generations. If Bailey and Maroldt are in fact suggesting that creoles are inherently 'unstable' systems that are erratic and highly variable, then they are wrong. As I will explain below, creoles are native languages which are distinguished not by any 'linguistic peculiarities' but primarily by the socio-historical context of their origins. They are therefore no more 'linguistically unstable' than any other living language.

Bailey and Maroldt's assumption of English–Norse creolization is also, in itself, tenuous. The extensive analysis carried out by Thomason and Kaufman (1988: 274–304) on English varieties spoken in areas of the Danelaw shows that Norse impacted primarily on English lexis, simply adding 'a few subtleties of meaning and a large number of new ways of saying old things, often by replacing an English item of similar but not identical sound' (ibid.: 302; 303; see also Chapter 3, Section 3.4.4). These authors also maintain that there was no social and linguistic motivation for Norse creolization to occur, an issue to which we will return.

Another problematic dimension of Bailey and Maroldt's thesis lies in the fact that their analysis of ME features influenced by or derived from French typically contains very little or no supporting evidence. For example, the authors state that 'it is clear that the Middle English tense-and-aspect system was a *tertium quid* which resembled French rather more than Anglo-Saxon' (Bailey and Maroldt, 1977: 42), or that constructions such as *it is me* are 'clearly French and always have been' (ibid.: 46). It is not clear, however, why these correlations are presented as indisputable. The authors do not make available any evidence that constructions such as *aller + infinitive*, or *avoir + main verb present participle*, for example, actually existed in the French varieties of post-Conquest England. Equally importantly, there is also no evidence that the equivalents of such constructions did not already exist in English. Indeed, Bailey and Maroldt (ibid.: 41) state that such constructions had existed 'superficially' as 'optional variants' in Old English. In the authors' argument, these options 'won out' in ME because they received reinforcement from allegedly similar patterns in the French of the period. This, however, contradicts characteristic (2) of Middle English (see above): if such constructions already existed in English, then they cannot have been, as the authors argue, 'Anglo-Saxon elements in French functions' (ibid.: 51).

A related issue here is the authors' presentation of certain (allegedly French-influenced) features as unmarked in the 'new' and different system of Middle English. Thus, growing use of *thou* and *you* as informal/formal pronouns of address, for example, and the use of the *of*-genitive are discussed as basic, unmarked features of Middle English, without explicit acknowledgement of their development and function within the English system. Thus, although *thou* and *you* began to be used to indicate social distance between speakers (a usage that continued and developed during the Early Modern period; see Chapter 5), they also still retained their previous Anglo-Saxon functions of denoting number in the second person pronoun (a usage that also continued beyond the ME period). While the *of*-genitive was used during ME, it was (as we saw in Section 4.4.3) one of many options, not an absolute, for possessive marking.

Bailey and Maroldt (ibid.: 21) also claim that ME exhibits 'analyticity', a 'special identifying trait' of creole morphology. 'Analyticity', the authors state, is a 'universal loss of inflections' (ibid.: 51); a definition that does not quite match the accepted understanding of analytic systems (see Chapter 1, Section 1.5). Even if the authors' definition of analytic structure were assumed, this description of ME would still be problematic. As we saw in Section 4.4.3, ME underwent not wholesale inflectional *loss* but inflectional *reduction*. Thus, nouns continued to carry case (genitive) and number (plural) marking; pronouns retained the synthetic nature of their OE antecedents, signalling case, gender, number and person; verbs continued to carry present indicative, subjunctive, preterite and participle inflections; and adjectives retained for a time weak and strong declensional forms as well as comparative and superlative suffixes. ME is, therefore, in the authors' definition of 'analyticity', definitely not an analytic system. Furthermore, the southern and London varieties of ME, speakers of which would have had the most contact with French, appear to have been more inflectionally conservative than other varieties, another problematic issue for the blanket assumption that contact equals inflectional loss. Incidentally, we might also reasonably ask how ME can exhibit 'loss' of anything, considering the authors' argument that it is a new and independent system.

A final point we can make here about the 'analyticity' of ME is that here too, the authors do not consider the developments in the inflectional systems of ME in the general context of English language history. The authors assume, as stated earlier, that the meeting of different English and French inflectional paradigms caused such confusion that speakers abandoned them. However, as we saw in Chapter 3, inflectional reduction was well under way in OE by the ninth century and indeed, is very likely to have begun much earlier. There is therefore no reason to assume that the processes of levelling and reduction in ME were anything but a continuation of tendencies already clearly observable in preceding stages. Overall, as Thomason and Kaufman (1988: 308; 312) state, 'the reasonable assumption is that gradual change [from OE to ME] was going on' from generation to generation. Contact and conflict, therefore, are not the unequivocal catalysts of change in this context that Bailey and Maroldt present them as being.

A further area of ambiguity and inconsistency in Bailey and Maroldt's thesis lies in their conceptualization of certain qualities. For example, they state, quite rightly, that some assessments of characteristics in linguistic systems are necessarily variable and have to be judged not comparatively, but independently. Thus, a claim of 'substantial language mixing', for instance, has to be 'judged on the basis of the result' before it can come close to being quantifiable (1977: 21). However, the authors themselves do not consistently adhere to this principle. They cite, for example, as evidence of 'substantial language mixing' the fact that ME contains a 'very considerable' vocabulary borrowed from French (ibid.: 52). While there is indeed a high proportion of French loans in ME, these words were ultimately a component of a much bigger, predominantly Germanic lexicon. In addition, while statistical counts may give the impression that the proportion of French words was extremely high in actual usage (Bailey and Maroldt (1977: 32), for example, cite an occurrence of 50 per cent in Chaucer), we should bear in mind the contexts in which texts (our only source of data) were written:

> It was probably not only an author's audience, but also his own background endowments and tastes that determined the number of adoptions from [French] that he used. This is one of the reasons why the first record of a French word in ME should not necessarily be assumed (as is commonly done) to imply that it was, or even soon became, generally current in the 'language'. In fact, so long as we are dealing with any one ME work, the influence of French vocabulary on the 'language' is an abstraction: such a notion applies only to words which are found, on analysis of many works, to recur in several of them.
>
> (G.V. Smithers, 1968: lii; quoted in Thomason and Kaufman, 1988: 314)

'Substantial' therefore may not be so big after all.

From a creolist perspective, Bailey and Maroldt's definitions of *creoles* and *creolization* – in particular the claims of language mixing and the generation of a specific structural language type – are perhaps the most problematic aspect of their thesis. While critical discussions such as that of Thomason and Kaufman (1988) and Fennell (2001) explicitly take issue with the authors' assumptions about language contact situations, they do not really question the idea of creolization as a process which creates particular structural characteristics. These concepts, once current in linguistic thought (and in all fairness, at the time Bailey and Maroldt were writing), have long since been revised.[4] However, these more recent perspectives do not always find their way into critical summaries of the ME creolization hypothesis which tend to still use the same discourses as Bailey and Maroldt, mainly by focusing on the lack of 'creole features' in ME or in arguing that ME does not have the 'morphological simplicity' of creoles. It is therefore perhaps time to update the critical stance by looking at current perspectives in creole studies.

Numerous theories of creole genesis and creolization have been formulated since these languages first began to be recorded and studied in the seventeenth century.[5] However, as Chaudenson (2001: 43) points out, these have tended to fall somewhere between two polar extremes, both of which posit creolization as a purely linguistic process:

(a) Creoles allegedly developed from the interference of two or several linguistic systems.
(b) Creoles are putatively the results of the restructuring of European languages.

In both types of explanation, creolization has been typically associated with contexts of language contact created by colonizing practices (particularly slavery and indentureship), which often brought ethnically diverse groups, speaking mutually unintelligible languages, together in exogenous settings. In such situations, a *superstratal* group, typically comprising members of the colonizing nation, were socio-politically dominant over a numerically larger but culturally and linguistically diverse *substratal* group who were socio-politically powerless (such as slaves and indentured labourers). The hostility and distance between the two main groups, plus the imposition and maintenance of an unequal dynamic of power, were therefore not conducive to, for example, assimilation of one set of speakers to another, or to multi-lingualism but instead to creolization.

Bailey and Maroldt's assumption of language mixing – an accepted theory of creolization in the late nineteenth–mid-twentieth centuries – falls into Chaudenson's category (a). Proponents of this theory typically maintained that creoles combined a grammatical system derived from the substrata, and a lexicon from the superstratal language: Sylvain (1936: 178; quoted in Chaudenson, 2001: 44), for example, stated that Haitian French Creole combined 'African syntax' and French vocabulary. Popular theories of creolization from the 1950s to the 1970s, such as that of *monogenesis* and *relexification*,[6] were based on this idea of language mixing, and were therefore very likely to have influenced Bailey and Maroldt's own view of the process (although we must point out that it has always had its detractors). Such positions have now largely been discredited, mainly because there is scant evidence for them, and also because assumptions of generic entities such as 'African syntax' are untenable and in Chaudenson's words, 'outlandish'. Yet, putting aside its current marginalization in creole studies, Bailey and Maroldt's view of language mixing does not conform to that once accepted in the field. We might have expected them to posit (in accordance with stances such as Sylvain's) that 'mixed language' or creole ME comprised a substratal English grammatical system, and a superstratal French lexicon. Yet this is not their position. Although they repeatedly claim language mixture and the production of a new, creole system, the stance that their analysis instead seems to feed is change in English under the influence of French – a position which we have already seen as problematic in other ways.

A related issue here is the assumption that creoles are a specific structural type, namely languages with 'analyticity'. We have also seen that this analysis of ME is erroneous, but even if it were not, it would involve inaccurate assumptions about the structural nature of creoles. Chaudenson (2001: 48–9), quoting Whinnom (1965: 522), lists structural features thought to be common and peculiar to creoles formed in European-driven colonial contexts. Some of these are listed below.

Creoles show:

1. Elimination of inflections for number in nouns and for gender and case in pronouns.
2. A system of preverbal particles to express tense, mood and aspect (as in *mi bin go tell am* ('I would have told him'); Guyanese English creole data from Bickerton (1986: 24).

Bin expresses tense (here, past); *go* expresses mood (here, future and conditionals); *tel* – main active verb. For a fuller explanation, see Singh (2000: 57).

3. Identity of adverb and adjective (as in *come quick* (adverb); *a quick job* (adjective)).
4. Iteration for intensification of adverb-adjectives (as in *she pretty pretty* 'she is very pretty' (adjective)).
5. The use of an all-purpose preposition *na* (as in *you no see one man kill one tarra one na Cowra tarra day?* 'didn't you see that one man killed another in/at/near Cowra the other day?').
6. Development of compound prepositions of the type *na* + noun + *de*, or some other genitive marker (as *foe* in Sranan).
7. The word for 'thing' as interrogative (*sani* in Sranan).
8. The word for 'much' derives from a model language word that means 'too much': *tro, tumsi, maisa*.
9. The overall simplicity of these languages as such.

(adapted from Chaudenson, 2001; creole data from Trinidad English creole)

While some of these structures do occur in creole languages, they are not peculiar to them, and they are certainly not common to all. For example, (1)–(4) and (8) occur in 'lingua franca varieties of many languages' and can also be found in regional varieties of French (Chaudenson, 2001: 49); and (1) and (3) occur in regional non-standard varieties of English in the United Kingdom. Structures (5) and (6) are not found in French creoles (ibid.), and while (5) appears to have been used in the nineteenth-century English creole in Trinidad, it has since dropped out of use (Singh, 1997). Feature (7) does not occur in current usage in French creoles, nor in English creoles in the Caribbean. Chaudenson (2001: 49) also points out that a feature such as (9) is so general in reference as to be inconclusive. In addition, 'simplicity' as a defining characteristic is particularly unhelpful and ambiguous. It remains largely undefined in linguistics, mainly because it is has no fixed criteria which can delimit it objectively and, as such, has been used variously to describe (sometimes subjectively) very different processes and features. In terms of creole description, 'simplicity' is problematic because it has been used in the past, in its sense of 'simple-mindedness' and 'lack of sophistication', to denigrate these languages and their speakers.

It has also been used in reference to creoles as 'young' languages – a perspective which seems to underlie Bailey and Maroldt's assumption of morphological simplicity. It has long been assumed that since known creoles have emerged relatively late in linguistic history, they have not had time to 'evolve' like older, established languages. They are therefore construed as 'simpler' (younger) languages which have not developed 'complexities' such as highly inflected systems. This, however, assumes that creoles are static – even if they began life as predominantly 'inflection-less' systems as in Bailey and Maroldt's definition of 'analyticity' (and it is not a given that they do), they will, like other living languages, have undergone (and be undergoing) processes of change which potentially result in what might be termed more 'complex' features. Grammaticalization, for example, could produce derivational or inflectional morphemes, as could the borrowing of loanwords (see Chapter 1).[7] Indeed, creole speakers do make use of 'complex' inflectional structures: urban as well as formal varieties of Trinidad English creole, for example, make varying degrees of use of English preterite, plural and possessive inflections, as in *he went by Ravi* ('he went to Ravi's'), or *where meh books?* ('where are my books?'), or *she used to be mom's boss* (personal data collection, 2002). To ascribe a blanket description of 'simplicity' to creoles is therefore to ignore a dynamic, changing system.

Bailey and Maroldt's (1977) assumption that creolization produces identifying structural traits, including 'analyticity' (or 'simplicity') – an assumption, it should be noted, which is shared by their critics – is presently considered untenable by influential creolists such as Mufwene, Chaudenson and DeGraff to name but a few. Indeed, with regard to this particular issue, Chaudenson (2001) and Mufwene (2001) both maintain that creolization is not so much a linguistic restructuring process as 'a social phenomenon' (Mufwene, 2001: 113); 'a human and social tragedy characterized by unity of time, place and action' (Chaudenson, 2001: 34). As Mufwene (2001: 138) summarizes:

> The most adequate interpretation of *creolisation* – if such a process must be posited – appears to be the social marking of a particular colonial vernacular of the seventeenth to the nineteenth centuries from other colonial varieties because of the ethnic/racial affiliation of its primary speakers . . . Having been restricted historically to (sub) tropical European colonies of the past few centuries, creoles are far from being a general structural type of language although they form a special sociohistorically defined group of vernaculars.

We will return to creolization in Chapter 5. One final but important point about Bailey and Maroldt's thesis concerns the social context for creolization. The authors, in accordance with established theories of creolization such as those cited earlier, assume the presence of superstratal (French) and substratal (English) groups in the Middle English period but with none of the social distance that would typify a context of creolization. Indeed, the authors themselves state that: 'There is no cogent reason to assume that any socially relevant groups had a pro-Anglo-Saxon or anti-French attitude before the time when the dominant classes themselves turned to English as their mother language' (Bailey and Maroldt, 1977: 30). If this were the case, then surely there is 'no cogent reason' to assume that a creole, a language seeded in social distance, ever emerged. Instead, as we have seen, it is perhaps more likely that bilingualism for sectors of the population was the likely outcome, with assimilation to the larger settled English-speaking population occurring within a few generations of English-born Norman descendants.

Overall, Bailey and Maroldt's creolization hypothesis, in the amount of critical attention it has received, has contributed to productive debates on the varying nature of language contact and its outcomes. It also extended the concepts of *creoles* and *creolization* (flaws apart) outside of the situations with which they have been typically (and sometimes derogatorily) associated. By suggesting that creolization was a product of language contact and could therefore arise anywhere if the situation was right, they implied that creoles were not marginal or unusual systems – a derogatory perspective that retained currency for a long time in discourses on the subject. Thus, in principle, there were perhaps some beneficial aspects to their thesis. However, as we have seen, the high degree of inconsistencies and inaccuracies put forward in their paper greatly undermined their position. To paraphrase the authors, ultimately, it perhaps made 'little sense even to pose the question at all' (Bailey and Maroldt, 1977: 23).

4.6 Study Questions

1. In Section 4.4.1 we saw that *c* typically represented [ʧ] before front vowels in ME. There are, however, cases in which its value is [s], as in ME *citee* 'city', *ceptre* 'sceptre', *cessyd* 'ceased', 'ended'. What is the reason for such exceptions?

2. What are the origins of the modern demonstrative pronouns *this*, *that*, *these* and *those*? A good dictionary with etymological sources will be useful here.

3. The following passages (i) and (ii) are taken from two varieties of fourteenth-century ME.

(i) Chaucer *The Nun's Priest's Tale* (fourteenth century; London (East Midlands dialect))

A povre widwe, somedeel stape in age
Was whilom dwellynge in a narwe cotage
Biside a grove, stondynge in a dale.
This widwe, of which I telle yow my tale,
Syn thilke day that she was last a wyf,
In pacience ladde a ful symple lyf.
For litel was hir catel and hir rente.
By housbondrie of swich as God hire sente
She foond hirself and eek hir doghtren two.
Thre large sowes hadde she, and namo,
Three keen, and eek a sheep that highte Malle.
Ful sooty was hire bour and eek her halle,
In which she eet ful many a sklendre meel.
Of poynaunt sauce hir neded never a deel.

(ii) *Sir Gawain and the Green Knight* (fourteenth century (Northern))

Wel gay watȝ þis gome   gered in grene
& þe here of his hed   of his hors swete
Fayre fannand fax   vmbefoldes his schulderes
A much berd as a busk   ouer his brest henges
þat wyth his hiȝlich here   þat of his hed reches
Wat euesed al vmbetorne   abof his elbowes,
þat half his armes þer-vnder   were halched in þe wyse
Of kyngeȝ capados   þat closes his swyre.
þe mane of þat mayn hors   much to hit lyke
Wel cresped & cemmed   wych knottes ful mony
Folden in wyth fildore   aboute þe fayre grene,
Ay a herle of þe here,   an oþer of golde;
þe tayl & his toppyng   twynnen of a sute
& bounden boþe wyth a bande   of a bryȝt grene,
dubbed wyth ful dere stoneȝ,   as þe dok lasted;

Syþen þrawen wyth a þwong,	a þwarle-knot alofte,
þer mony belleȝ ful bryȝt	of brende golde rungen
Such a fole upon folde,	ne freke þat hym rydes,
Watȝ neuer sene in þat sale	wyth syȝt er þat tyme
With yȝe.	

Using a good ME glossary (such as Davis (1979) for Chaucer and that included in Burrow and Turville-Petre (1996) for the *Gawain* extract), answer the following questions:

a. What present participle inflections are used in each text?
b. What present indicative inflections are used in text (ii)?
c. How are plurals marked in each text?
d. What is, or are, the source(s) of loanwords in both texts? Does one text contain more borrowings from one source than the other? If so, why might this be?

4. The following is an excerpt from a ME lyric *Alisoun*. Using Section 4.4, discuss the features that characterize the language at this period (make use of a glossary):

> Bitweene Merch and Averil,
> When spray biginneth to springe,
> The litel fowl hath hire wil
> On hire leod to singe.
> Ich libbe in love-longinge
> For semlokest of alle thinge.
> Heo may me blisse bringe:
> Ich am in hire baundoun.
> An hendy hap ich habbe yhent,
> Ichoot from hevene it is me sent:
> From alle wommen my love is lent,
> And light on Alisoun.

5. The following short excerpts (i) and (ii) are taken from two translations of the Bible (St Matthew's Gospel, Chapter 26, verses 69–71). With reference to Section 3.4 and Section 4.4, compare the two, noting the linguistic changes that have occurred:

(i) Old English (*c*. 1050)

(69) Petrus soðlice sæt ute on þam cafertune. þa com to hym an þeowen ₇ cwæð. ₇ þu wære myd þam galileiscan hælende. (70) ₇ he wyðsoc beforan eallum ₇ cwæð. nat ic hwæt þu segst. (71) þa he ut eode of þære dura. þa geseh hyne oðer þynen. ₇ sæde þam ðe þar wæron. ₇ þes wæs myd þam nazareniscan hælende.
Note: '₇' = 'and'

(ii) Middle English (1375)

(69) And Petir sat with outen in the halle; and a damysel cam to hym, and seide, Thou were with Jhesu of Galilee. (70) And he denyede bifor alle men, and seide, Y woot not what thou seist. (71) And whanne he ȝede out at the ȝate, another damysel say hym, and seide to hem that weren there, And this was with Jhesu of Nazareth.

Notes

1. The label Anglo-Norman is here used to describe the victors of the Conquest who settled in England. Note that it is used, like Anglo-Saxon (see Chapter 3, Section 3.2), as a generic label for the different ethnic groups involved in the Norman invasion.

2. Schendl's (1997) investigation of skilled code-switching between Latin, English and French in sermons, religious prose texts, legal and medical texts, and business accounts, as well as in more literary productions such as macaronic (mixed) poems and drama, is of interest here.

3. Normandy was first taken by Philip Augustus of France in 1204. John tried to reclaim it in 1214 at the Battle of Bouvines but was unsuccessful.

4. Mufwene (2001) notes that Thomason has revised this.

5. See Chaudenson (2001: Chapter 3); Singh (2000: Chapter 2) for more detailed discussion.

6. The original theory of monogenesis postulated that the Atlantic creoles derived from a fifteenth-century proto-pidgin spoken on the West African coast. This West African Pidgin Portuguese (WAPP) allegedly combined 'African syntax' with a Portuguese lexicon. It was assumed that WAPP was learnt by slaves awaiting transportation in West Africa and taken by them to the Atlantic colonies. WAPP was then relexified in accordance with the dominant superstratal language in each environment. Thus, in British territories, the Portuguese lexicon of WAPP was exchanged for English, in French territories for French, and so on.

7. See also DeGraff (2001) for an interesting discussion of morphological processes in Haitian French Creole.

5 | Early Modern English, 1500–1700

5.1 Introduction

In Chapter 4 we mentioned that the Middle English period is often characterized as one of extensive social and linguistic change. As we have seen, this was undoubtedly true, but it was also a period in which many socio-political and very generally sociolinguistic ideologies and frameworks remained relatively untouched. For instance, although the fourteenth century had seen the collapse of the old feudal system and its replacement by one which carried, for certain sectors of the society, more potential for entrepreneurship and economic gain, a stratified class system remained firmly in place. Despite the upheavals and replacements at the upper echelons of the Church and State that had followed the Norman Conquest, as well as the disputes that periodically erupted between the two, these entities remained anchored in a mutually beneficial relationship that had existed for centuries. English had regained its position as an important written language, but was still secondary in status to Latin, which continued to serve as the medium of scholarship and of the all-powerful Catholic Church. Smith (1984: 16) therefore states that a contemporary 'perceptive observer' would very likely have assumed that the new, sixteenth century would simply see a continuation of this status quo.

What Smith's observer could not have foreseen was how, within a relatively short space of time, the medieval fabric of England would begin to be ripped apart and reshaped into a more modern form. The years approximately between 1500 and 1700 (Early Modern) in particular would see significant social, political, religious and indeed linguistic change as a result of various factors; the most important of which included increasing hostility to the established church, a growing sense of national identity and advances in technology. While some of these elements were not in themselves new or unprecedented, their combined effect was dramatic. The Catholic Church, for example, would continue to face anticlerical feeling but for the first time in its history, would see this grow into a reforming zeal through the widespread, and therefore damaging, dissemination of printed heretical literature to an increasingly literate populace. It would also engage in a dispute with the crown – again, not an unprecedented event in its history – but one which, this time, would not end in 'compromise and conciliation' but instead in a 'clear rejection of papal authority and the creation of an English nation state' (ibid.: 17). In addition, part of the tensions between English Protestantism and Roman Catholicism, as well as between the English monarchy and Roman papacy, would be reflected in debates about language use. Although Latin would maintain its classical prestige for many Renaissance scholars, it would also come to be derided by some as a 'popish' tongue that had little or no place as the language of the new English nation and English Church. Overall, this Early Modern period would be characterized by the operation of 'forces of centripetalization' in state, religion and print which when combined, not only 'tied the [English] language firmly to the nation', but was also 'victorious in establishing recognisable forms of the English language as central and stable' (Crowley, 1996: 55). By the beginning of the eighteenth century, the ideology of a 'monolithic' English language would begin to take hold (leading to the standardization efforts of that century and beyond) – not just within England but also within the nascent British Empire.

Although the Early Modern period spans only about two centuries, it would be impossible to do justice to all its events and developments. We will therefore focus on those landmark events which would be of consequence for English in Section 5.2.

5.2 Social History

As Crowley (1996) implies, political, religious and technological developments were not only centripetal in nature, but *central* to the shape of the EMod period and, most importantly for us, to the use of English. The discussion in this section is therefore shaped around consideration of such developments and of their linguistic impact.

One of the social changes most focused on in this period is the decline in the power of the Catholic Church in England and the related emergence of an English Bible. Since Pope Gregory's sixth-century missionaries had set foot on Anglo-Saxon soil, the Church had gone from strength to strength. It had become the spiritual heart of English life, much as the actual bricks and mortar of its churches had become centres of daily activity. Schama (2000: 280–2), for example, quoting a sixteenth-century account of the Holy Trinity church at Long Melford, Suffolk, writes that it was the core of a 'wrap-around world which spilled over from the church porch into the streets'; a world in which there was 'no hard-and-fast border between the secular and the spiritual'. The institution of the Church had come to serve as 'school and theatre, moral tutor and local government' and even as the repository of 'magic and medicine'.

Pivotal in this world was the priest; the sanctioned and only intercessor between the people and their God. This authority, however, had begun to be undermined in the fourteenth century, partly through the devastation caused by bubonic plague (see Chapter 4). The decimation of the priesthood through the Black Death (since many of the clergy came into contact with the sick and dying) had led in 1349 to a decision that the last rites could be received from the laity if no priest was available. Initially envisaged as a temporary measure, this 'DIY' approach in fact facilitated the influence of radical thinkers such as John Wycliffe, who held that the priest was dispensable in matters of salvation and that each true Christian, with the guidance of the scriptures, could therefore be responsible for their individual spiritual well-being. This principle would later become primary in the teachings of Martin Luther (1482–1546), whose followers would find the role of the priesthood in determining salvation an offensive, even blasphemous symbol of ecclesiastical power (Schama, 2000: 282).

The 'new Christians', or *evangelicals*, as they called themselves, held instead that all that was needed for salvation was faith and easy access to the Word, and with this in mind, sought to 'replace the monopoly of wisdom claimed by the Church of Rome with the gospel truth available in their own [English] tongue', as opposed to Latin (ibid.: 282). Their effect was far-reaching: from the early 1500s, it was possible to hear 'heresies' in the mouths of the English as they rejected some of the long-established customs of the Church. Schama (2000) and Smith (1984), cite as an example the case of the London tailor Richard Hume, who refused to pay the mortuary due to the Church when his infant child was buried in 1514. Hume was taken to task by the Church court but overthrew their expectations of meek submission by deciding instead to launch a countersuit in the King's court. He was arrested by the Bishop of London, who also ordered that his house be searched for heretical literature. Hume was found hanged in his cell two days after his imprisonment – according to the coroner, the victim of a murder. Hume was publicly branded a heretic by the Church but the case continued to provoke a great deal of criticism and debate in Parliament. For the first time, the power of the Church began to be thought of 'as infringing the equity of the common law' (Schama, 2000: 284).

This episode, and in particular, the search for heretical literature, neatly illustrates the Church's anxieties about losing control over a once-dependent flock. Of what use was an ecclesiastical guide if people could read their own signposts to salvation? The limited literacy and limited (hand-written) textual production of earlier centuries had meant that this had never been a significant worry, but the late fifteenth–sixteenth century had seen a steady increase in the reading population, as well as the introduction of a new machine that made multiple text production relatively quick and cheap: the printing press, brought to London in 1476 by William Caxton. It took no great leap of imagination for Church officials and the new evangelicals to see, with respective horror and hope, the potential of the press in producing and disseminating English translations of the Bible.

One of the best-known advocates of an English Bible, William Tyndale, who felt that the scriptures should be 'plainly laid before [the people's] eyes in their mother tongue', had a great deal of faith in the potential of print. He requested funds from the Bishop of London for the printing of his translation which were, unsurprisingly, refused. Tyndale eventually managed to have copies of his translation of the New Testament printed in Germany (3,000 were produced in 1526), and smuggled into England in casks of wax or grain (Schama, 2000: 285).

The Church's reactions to such perceived 'rebellions' were nothing short of horrific. Men such as Cardinal Wolsey and later, Thomas More and John Fisher, sought to quell 'the noise of the new Bible' with royal backing (ibid.: 285). In 1521, Henry VIII, Defender of the (Catholic) Faith and husband of the Catholic

Catherine of Aragon, had sanctioned a treatise which labelled Lutheranism 'an abominable heresy'. With his king's endorsement, Wolsey attempted to purge England, often consigning heretics and their books to the flames. Tyndale himself was burnt at the stake in 1536.

Interestingly, the 'concatenation of state, religion and print' (cf. Crowley, 1996: 55) that would favour English began its consolidation at almost the same time. In 1532, Henry VIII severed his loyalties to the papal authority in Rome (partly because of his dissatisfaction with the pope's refusal to annul his marriage to Catherine of Aragon) through his (orchestrated) recognition as the supreme head of the church in England. As befitting the head of the English Church and English State, Henry sanctioned a translation of the Bible into English – a decision wholly endorsed, and indeed perhaps even encouraged, by his new Archbishop Cranmer. It was no doubt obvious that an authorized translation would work effectively on a number of levels: it would satisfy the evangelical precept of making the word of God directly available to the people (a perspective that Cranmer subscribed to); it would clearly symbolize the independence of the English Church (governed by an English king for English people) from that run by Rome; and it would re-establish some control over the Word once on the street. In 1539, the Great Bible was published, with the illustration on its frontispiece clearly encapsulating the idealized marriage of Church and State. Henry sits in the top centre of the page, receiving the Word directly from God. He passes this on (in the form of the Bible) to Cranmer, who as Archbishop, oversees the spiritual welfare of the realm, and also to Cromwell, who looks after secular matters. Each in turn ministers it to smiling and grateful clergy and laity.

Henry had little more to do with the Great Bible, apart from in 1546 when he forbade women and members of the lower classes from reading it themselves, since they were prone to misinterpret it and be led astray. He died in 1547 and was succeeded for a short time by his son Edward (by Jane Seymour), who lived only until 1553. Even in his short reign, however, Edward's strong Protestant leanings made themselves felt. With Cranmer and Edward Seymour, the Duke of Somerset and Lord Protector, he began a reformation of the English Church which stripped it of many of the Catholic traditions which had survived under his father and sanctioned the publication of the *Book of Common Prayer* and of biblical translations in English. Such 'centripetalizing' developments in Church, State and print were curtailed with the ascension of Henry and Catherine of Aragon's Catholic daughter Mary (1553–1558) to the throne but gathered momentum again under Elizabeth I (1558–1603), later becoming explicitly realized with the publication of the Authorized Version, or King James Bible, in 1611 (see Crowley, 1996: 55).

The authorized translations, plus their dissemination through the printing press, undoubtedly gave written English a dimension of status and acceptability that had previously been reserved for languages such as Latin. But the printed Bible was as much a reason for the 'success' of English in the written medium as a symptom of it: as stated earlier, from the sixteenth century onwards, there was simply a significant sector of the population which was literate, and which desired reading material in the language. The sixteenth and seventeenth centuries saw a significant expansion of educational facilities, a process initially begun in the fifteenth century, at the level of both the school and institutions of higher education. In terms of the former, there were increases in the number of 'petty' schools (which taught basic literacy), apprenticeship facilities (which also included mathematical and accountancy training) and grammar schools (which continued to be dominated by a classical, Latin-based curriculum). At the level of higher education, new colleges were founded at Oxford and Cambridge, and enrolment at these two institutions, as well as at the Inns of Court, increased substantially in the 1500–1600s (Smith, 1984: 195). This scholastic growth was greatly encouraged by the effects of the Reformation as well as by the influence of certain Renaissance scholars. For example, in pre-Reformation society, many high offices of state had been held by members of the clergy. This hold, however, had come to be broken with the establishment of the nation-state, leading to the need for an educated workforce of lay administrators in all ranks of state service (ibid.). Influential humanists and educators such as Colet and Mulcaster also advocated that education was integral not only to shaping a population that would be an asset to the nation but also to the intellectual, and hence social, development of the individual. Education, therefore, came to be seen as a stepping stone to social and material advantage, particularly among the growing, relatively moneyed classes:

> There was a redistribution of national wealth in early modern England with a growing gap between the upper and middling ranks of society on the one hand and the impoverished masses on the other, and this meant that not merely the gentry but many of the 'middling' groups – yeomen and moderately prosperous townsmen – had the means as well as the desire to invest in their children's education.

(ibid.: 197)

Smith (ibid: 185) states that one of the most significant consequences of the growth of educational facilities was the increase in literacy of many of the 'middling sort'. While the grammar schools continued to provide a more traditional, classical education, it would seem that the middling groups received an education in which there was significant focus on literacy in English. Indeed, Görlach (1991: 6) states that this became 'a very important precondition for social upward mobility'. Such education strategies not only necessitated the production of texts and teaching materials in the native language of the pupils, but also produced a market of readers enthusiastic about and interested in areas such as the sciences, literature, rhetoric and language itself. Thus, increase in readership (literacy levels in the EModE period peaked around 1600 for both the upper and lower classes (ibid.: 7)) was accompanied by increases in the authorship of translations and of original works in English. Other socio-cultural developments also played a part in the emergence of the latter: the successful establishment of numerous theatres during the sixteenth century inevitably led to the penning of new material; and the competition for (and shortage of) positions in church and government offices for the growing numbers of university graduates resulted in many trying to earn a living through writing (ibid.: 6).

The expansion of the reading and writing markets was doubtless concomitant with the continuing improvements made to the printing process. Textual production was consistently made quicker, easier and cheaper, inevitably increasing the number of texts and copies in circulation. Between 1476 and 1640, for example, 25,000 English books appear to have been printed; 'more than all the titles produced in the preceding periods of the English language put together' (ibid.: 6). A significant proportion of books in the sixteenth and seventeenth centuries dealt with topics in the natural sciences which, as has happened in subsequent centuries, had captured the public fancy; and many others were aimed at the 'practical men' of the time with little or no Latin: 'there were plenty of Elizabethan treatises on practical subjects like navigational instruments, geometry and warfare, which were written in English for the plain man, and sometimes by him' (Barber, 1993: 177).

In addition, from the seventeenth century onwards, a fair number of texts which provided guidelines for English usage, such as dictionaries, grammars and spelling guides, were also produced. Their general success with the reading populace is a sure indication not only of an increasing confidence in the use of the language in written media but also of an increasing awareness and acceptance of a particular form of written English. In other words, such guides imply, as do dictionaries, grammar drills and spelling bees today, that 'correct' forms and usages in the language exist; and in the EModE period, that ideal of 'correctness' became quickly associated with the increasingly standardized English of the printed word.

But what did this standardization actually entail? Milroy and Milroy (1999: 19) maintain that standardization is in itself an ongoing 'historical process' motivated 'by various social, political and commercial needs' which typically significantly affects written forms, and which also proceeds on both concrete and ideological levels. This does indeed seem to be true of English from the late ME period onwards: its increasing use in various domains as a result of the decline of French in the fourteenth century (see Chapter 4), the later questioning of Latin during the EModE period, plus growing literacy and textual production in English, led to a perception that the language had to be, at least in the written medium, made as adequate as possible for its tasks. This meant the attainment not only, at a practical level, of functional efficiency (it was materially better for authors and publishers if the readership could 'use and understand the language in the same way with the minimum of misunderstanding and the maximum of efficiency' (ibid.: 19)) but also, ideologically, of aesthetic proficiency. The two were not easily separated for EModE scholars comparing the relatively 'untried and untested' written English against centuries of Latin and Greek scholarship:

> Latin, the international language of education, rediscovered in its classical form, was well ordered, prestigious and dominant in many fields of written communication; by contrast, the vernacular was deficient in vocabulary and syntax, imperfect by standards of rhetorical beauty and copiousness, lacking obligatory rules of spelling, pronunciation, morphology and syntax, unsupported by any respectable ancient literary tradition and, finally, subject to continuous change. Indeed, scholars often enough claimed that it was deficient in principle and incapable of attaining the grammatical orderliness and copiousness of Latin.
>
> (Görlach, 1991: 36)

In other words, it was felt that norms of usage, which would not only 'stabilize' written English but also maximize its expressive potential, were imperative. As we will see in this chapter, EModE scholars concentrated on the establishment of such norms in orthographic practice and vocabulary usage. Norms, however, inevitably entail a notion of correctness. It is therefore not surprising that the normalization or standardization of written English gave rise to the perception of 'correct' and 'proper' forms of the language.

Given that we have consistently noted that English has never been a monolithic entity, we could justifiably ask at this point which variety or dialect of the language standardization efforts were centred on. We could also ask if such *selection of form* (cf. Haugen, 1972) was a conscious and deliberate decision by the intellectuals who came to be associated with standardization efforts. It actually seems that this selection occurred, in the late ME period, at a much less cerebral and more practical level: it was largely decided by printers. As indicated earlier, the concomitant increase in literacy and text availability in English necessitated the use of a fixed form for ease of printing. Caxton himself noted that, from the printer's perspective, the variability in English was problematic, stating that 'that comyn englysshe that is spoken in one shyre varyeth from a nother . . . certaynly it is harde to playse euery man by cause of dyuersite & chaunge of langage' (Prologue to *Enydos*, 1490).

His pragmatic solution was to choose a London variety of the South-East Midlands area which 'had already achieved some prominence' politically, commercially and academically (Milroy and Milroy, 1999: 27). In particular, the variety Caxton settled on had been used in the Chancery documents of London scriptoria since about 1430, and had already undergone some standardization in terms of spelling. As we will see in Section 5.4.1, this would serve as the basis of printers' decisions about typesetting and would ultimately influence the codification or fixing of standard spelling – incidentally, the only area in which complete standardization has been achieved.

As mentioned above, the other aspect of written usage which received a great deal of attention in the EModE period concerned vocabulary and its 'eloquent' use. It seemed clear to scholars wishing to use English instead of Latin in various domains that this increasing *elaboration of function* necessitated an elaboration of vocabulary resources as well. The long centuries of Latin use in specialized fields had left it lexically and stylistically well equipped; English, on the other hand, natively lacked much of the necessary terminology and rhetorical devices. Scholars therefore set out to, in the common parlance, 'enrich' the standard's lexicon and increase its capacity for eloquence, with the result that the 'EModE period (especially 1530–1660) exhibits the fastest growth of the vocabulary in the history of the English language' (Görlach, 1991: 135) – largely, as we shall see in Section 5.4.5, through the adoption and adaptation of loanwords, particularly from Latin.

The end of the EModE period would see the growth of an explicitly prescriptive tradition in standardization efforts: a development that is often cited as characteristic of the eighteenth century. The 1700s would see a preoccupation among language scholars with certain aspects of 'correct' usage, and a real desire to inhibit variation and change, which was often viewed as 'corruption' or signs of a language's instability. As we shall see in Chapter 6, the eighteenth-century prescriptivists would succeed in the further codification of certain orthographic, lexical and syntactical norms for written usage, some of which are still in use today. In addition, and very importantly, the eager reception of these codifications both reinforced and reflected a 'much more widespread consciousness of a relatively uniform "correct" English than had been possible before' (Milroy and Milroy, 1999: 29). Indeed, as these authors state, the eighteenth century successfully established 'the *ideology of standardisation*, to which virtually every speaker now subscribes in principle' (ibid.). We return to standardization in Chapter 6.

It might seem at this point that during the EModE period, English rather effortlessly and seamlessly slipped into roles previously played by Latin. It was not, however, as 'bloodless' a usurpation as it might appear. The long and venerable tradition of writing in Latin gave it a level of prestige that was difficult for English to challenge, even with the status and sanction that the latter had gained through use in biblical translation and general print. Although the use of the vernacular tongues in learning and writing was advocated by Reformers and Renaissance scholars alike, their actual use inevitably held these languages up to critical scrutiny. And as in the case of English, they were often found to be lacking, particularly when compared to the poetic and prosodic achievements of the classical Latin and Greek writers, revered in this age of rediscovery. Douglas (1515), for example, expressed a common view in his preface to *Virgil's Æneid* when he wrote that 'Besyde Latyn our langage is imperfite' (in Görlach, 1991: 263). But the *Zeitgeist* increasingly favoured English. There was an increasing confidence in England as a nation to be reckoned with, and the sense that English should serve (in a distant echo of Alfred the Great's hopes for Anglo-Saxon England) as its *nation language*[1] – an ambition that would be more explicitly expressed in the eighteenth century (see Chapter 6). The humanist ideal of linguistic democracy in terms of access to knowledge was also successfully propagated by influential scholars such as Thomas Elyot, Richard Mulcaster, Thomas Wilson and Roger Ascham. Many humanists also believed that the native tongue should be the primary medium of education. Elyot (1531), for example, thought it important that a 'noble mannes sonne' should, from infancy, have someone to teach him Latin, but should also have 'nourises & other women' as well, who would speak only English to him. (Elyot did specify, however, that it should only be English which was 'cleane, polite, perfectly and articulately pronounced'.) Palsgrave (1540) also complained that many teachers could 'wryte an Epistle ryght latyne lyke' but could not 'expresse theyr conceyte in theyr vulgar tongue, ne be not suffycyente, perfectly to open the diuersities of phrases betwene our tonge and the latyn' (cited in Görlach, 1991: 37).

Overall, the influence of such respected scholars, the increase in national pride and the growing confidence of the middle classes in their status as a socially important body who provided a flourishing consumer market for literature in their native tongue, all led to a progressive acceptance of English as a language for all and every purpose. Indeed, the tenor of debates on the comparative worth of English changed throughout the period from 'apologetic self-consciousness to confidence'. Thus, by the end of the period, the language which had earlier been perceived as 'barren . . . [and] barbarous' (Pettie, 1586) had been re-evaluated as the 'plain [and] honest' language of the English nation (in Görlach, 1991: 40).

5.3 Early Modern English Literature

The increasing effectiveness of the printing press in the EModE period meant that for the first time in the history of English, texts could be produced relatively cheaply in bulk. This, in addition to the dynamic effect of so many overlapping socio-political changes and intellectual movements, led to the production of an astonishing range of original works and translations in a variety of fields. For example, the early years of the period saw a significant market for (and therefore increase in) translations of classical scholarship as a result of the Renaissance principle that everyone should have access to the 'rich . . . store of knowledge and experience preserved from the civilizations of Greece and Rome' (Baugh and Cable, 2002: 205). The works of classical historians such as Xenophon, Herodotus, Tacitus and Livy were extremely popular, as were those by philosophers such as Aristotle, Seneca, Cicero and Marcus Aurelius. The translated poetry and drama of Virgil, Ovid and Homer, among others, also found an eager and receptive audience.

Religious and didactic texts were also produced in abundance, partly as a result of the reform of the Catholic Church. The year 1509 produced the English morality play *Everyman*, 1526 Tyndale's translation of the New Testament, 1535 the Great Bible, 1549 and 1552 Archbishop Cranmer's English Common Prayer Book, 1611 the Authorized Version of the Bible and 1678 Bunyan's *Pilgrim's Progress*. The preoccupation with the state of English and its 'proper' usage produced works such as Lily and Colet's *Grammar* in 1549, Wilson's *The Arte of Rhetorique* (1553), Hart's *Orthographie* (1569), Mulcaster's *The First Parte of the Elementarie* (1582) and later in the seventeenth century, a range of dictionaries (see Section 5.4.5) and spelling guides (see Section 5.4.1). There was also a market for historical works such as Hollinshed's *Chronicles of England, Scotland and Ireland* (1577) and Norton's *Plutarch* (1579), as well as for criticism and commentary such as that found in Knox's *History of the Reformation in Scotland* (1586), Hobbes' *Leviathan* (1649–1651) and Locke's *Essay Concerning Human Understanding, Two Treatises of Government, Letter on Toleration* (1690-). Some scientific work was also published in English (such as Robert Boyle's *The Sceptical Chemist* in 1661), although a great deal was originally composed in Latin. William Harvey's now famous essay on the circulation of the blood (1628), for example, appeared first in Latin, as did Gilbert's important work on magnetism (1600; later known as *Treatise on Magnetism*) and Newton's *Principia* (1687). It would seem that Latin remained the *de facto* choice, depending on topic and intended readership, for some English authors (and indeed for others across Europe) for some time. It is only towards the end of the EModE period, when scholars such as Newton chose to write in English (*Opticks*, 1704) that 'Latin can be considered definitely passé as the language of learning' (Görlach, 1991: 39).

Literary production during the EMod period was also substantial (and we therefore consider only a selection here). The sixteenth century saw, for instance, the publication of Nicholas Udall's *Ralph Roister Doister* (c. 1550s), Edmund Spenser's *The Faerie Queene* and *The Shepheardes Calendar* (c. 1575), Christopher Marlowe's *The Jew of Malta, Tamburlaine* and *The Tragical Story of Dr. Faustus* (c. 1587) and the beginning of the production of Shakespeare's sonnets and comedies such as *As You Like It* and *Twelfth Night* (c. 1596). Seventeenth-century writing was equally prolific: witness, for instance, Ben Jonson's *Everyman in his Humor, Volpone or, the Fox* (c. 1605; both in the 1616 portfolio), the metaphysical poetry of Edward Herbert (1582/3–1648) such as *Love's End, To Her Body*, George Herbert's poems of *The Temple* (1633) and the numerous songs, sonnets, meditations, sermons, satires, divine poems and elegies of John Donne. Andrew Marvell's (1621–1678) lyric poems (such as *Young Love* and *To His Coy Mistress*) also emerged in this period, as did the plays and novels of Aphra Behn (*The Rover* (1677) and *Oroonoko* (1688)), Margaret Cavendish's (1623–1673) *The World's Olio, The Soul's Raiment* and *Upon the Theam of Love* (1653), John Ford's *'Tis Pity She's a Whore* (1633) and Shakespeare's tragedies such as *Julius Caesar, Othello, Hamlet, King Lear* and *Macbeth* (1601), and romantic dramas such as *Cymbeline* and *The Tempest* (1608–). John Milton's *Aeropagitica* (1644) and *Paradise Lost* (1667) were also written during this period, as were the Restoration comedies of William Wycherley (c. 1640–1715) (*The Country Wife, The Plain Dealer*) and of William Congreve (*The Double-Dealer* (1693) and *The Way of the World* (1700)). Overall, the list is extensive – the few examples here barely skim the surface of the wealth of literature produced in EModE.

5.4 The Language of Early Modern English

Given the extent of textual production in the EModE era, it would not be unreasonable to assume that discussions of linguistic features (again, as reflected through written usage) give detailed consideration to synchronic variation in, and diachronic change throughout, the period. Yet, just as the limited textual record of the Anglo-Saxon period has shaped discussion of OE around the standardizing conventions of West Saxon (see Chapter 3), so too has the expansion of the printed word some six centuries later focused attention on the standardizing English of the EModE period. While this focus on the emergence of standard English from 1500 onwards may well create the impression that 'the focus of any history of [the language] is necessarily the history of the present-day standard variety' (Trudgill and Watts, 2002: 1), it is difficult to avoid. In terms of linguistic description, for instance, which primarily concerns us here, the regional provenance of a large proportion of English texts is difficult to ascertain from at least the late fifteenth century onwards because of the 'increasing homogeneity' of the printed word (Görlach, 1991:10). Indeed, Fennell (2001: 154) states that 'the underrepresentation of [regional and social varieties of Early Modern English] makes it difficult to talk about them with great certainty'. This (plus constraints of space) necessarily restricts our discussion of features of EModE to a conventional one (cf. Milroy, 2002: 7) – namely, to those evident in standardized texts. We should, however, continue to bear in mind that this represents but one strand in a much larger pattern of English usage that stretched across England as well as the south and east of Scotland and which would, by the end of the period, begin to weave into the social and linguistic fabric of colonial territories.[2]

5.4.1 Features of EModE spelling

As stated in Section 5.2, a major concern at the beginning of the EModE period was the seeming 'instability' of English in comparison with the written conventions of classical Latin and Greek. One of the areas focused on was English spelling, which was deemed to lack 'obligatory rules', and was also 'unsupported by any respectable ancient literary tradition' (cf. Görlach, 1991: 36). This was not completely the case – as we saw in Chapters 3 and 4, OE and ME authors and scribes did in fact make use of certain orthographic frameworks and conventions (although there is more evident variation in the ME corpus). In addition, the London scriptoria of the late fourteenth century had also developed certain consistent orthographic patterns, which would become adopted into the English used in Chancery documents after 1430. Many of these ready-made conventions were adopted by early printers, who also sometimes made and implemented their own practical decisions about spelling and orthographic forms since, as Knowles (1997: 90) points out, one of their major concerns was to allow 'efficient word recognition' for the reader. However, although early printers minimized orthographic variation significantly, they were not always consistent in the spellings that they themselves used; a result of the fact that many of them were foreigners and therefore unfamiliar with contemporary English preferences (Scragg, 1974; quoted in Görlach, 1991: 45). Görlach (ibid.) also points out that even Caxton had worked in Europe for most of his life, and 'when he returned to England he may have lacked insight into recent English spelling conventions'.

Thus, the lack of explicit and shared orthographic norms in English was, for many EModE thinkers, simply not good enough – classical texts reflected not variation of the moment but regularity with an esteemed pedigree. Philologers such as John Cheke (1514–1557), for example, who compared English spelling practices with those in classical Latin texts as well as with contemporary Italian writings, felt that English came off rather badly: authors were inconsistent, and there was not always a transparent relationship between sounds and graphs. In the words of the sixteenth-century phonetician, John Hart, the English spelling system was felt to be a 'hinderance and a confusion' (from *The Orthographie*, 1574). The mid–late sixteenth century therefore saw various attempts at spelling reform, not all of which were successful. Cheke, for example, put together proposals which were based on his ideas about the pronunciation of ancient Greek. The fact that he did not adhere consistently to his own reforms was without doubt a factor in their failure to find a favourable audience. John Hart advocated a more phonetic system for English spelling, proposing among other measures the use of a subscript dot to mark vowel length, as in $ẹ$ (instead of double graphs (as in *ee*, *oo*, *ea*) and final *–e*), and of different graphs for consonant sounds which were ambiguously represented (such as [ð] in *breathe* and [θ] in *thin*) (see Görlach, 1991: 51). William Bullokar (1530–1609) put forward reforms often based on opposition to Hart's proposals, but neither scholar's approaches were ever taken up in earnest. Interestingly, the spelling conventions that ultimately were most influential came from Richard Mulcaster (1530–1611), the author of *The First Parte of the Elementarie* (1582) and not an active spelling reformer. Instead, Mulcaster's intellectual authority (he was headmaster of St Paul's School, London, and a respected educator) made his writing a model. As Görlach (1991: 54) states, 'his importance lies in the impact that the spellings used in his book had on contemporary spelling books: each word was given one spelling, used consistently, and this was usually the one that passed into PrE [present day English]'. Alexander Gil (1564/5–1635), Mulcaster's successor at St Paul's School, made use of a primarily phonemic system of orthography in his grammar of English *Logonomia* (1619), but also included traditional and altered etymological spellings. In the latter type, Gil followed a contemporary trend of changing the spelling of French loans to reflect their ultimately Latin pedigree. Modern spellings such as *throne* (from French *trone*), *theatre* (< *teatre*) and *apothecary* (< *apotecaire*) are some of the results of this process, as are spellings such as *debt* and *doubt*, originally from French *det* and *doute* but altered in accordance with Latin *debitum* and *dubitare*. Interestingly, etymologizing spellers did, however, sometimes get it wrong. Our modern spelling *author*, for example, resulted from a 'correction' of ME *autour* (from French *autor*) along the lines of that undertaken for words such as *throne*, *theatre*. The Latin word, however, was in fact *auctor* (see Pyles and Algeo, 1982: 170, for more examples).

Görlach (1991: 55) states that concerted attempts to institute more phonemically transparent spelling systems for English effectively ended with Gil's proposals. Later seventeenth- and eighteenth-century scholars did make some modifications, but these were quite minor (see ibid.: 55–7). This was very likely because, as Mulcaster had noticed as early as 1582, 'the vse and custom of our cuntrie, hath allredie chosen a kinde of penning'. Indeed, the 'kinde of penning' which had unobtrusively become established throughout all the attempts at spelling reform was in fact based on the increasingly fixed usage of printers. We should reiterate here that orthographic variation in printed texts did not completely disappear (there were, as we shall see, a few instances where final usage was not set until well into the EModE period or after) but it was certainly minimized.

Two of the conventions that appear to have become fixed relatively early concern the use of word-final –*e*. This came to be used to indicate length in the stem vowel, thus altering ME spellings such as *caas/cas* and *liif/lif* to *case* and *life*; and also to indicate certain consonantal qualities: consider *disc*[k] vs *hence* [s] and *rag* [g] vs *rage* [ʤ]. Another widespread printing convention was the use of y to represent [ð] in words such as *the* and *that* (possibly harking back to the much older use of þ which, where it was still used in manuscripts, had evolved to look similar to y (Pyles and Algeo, 1982: 169)). Printed abbreviations of *the* and *that* combined this y with a superimposed *e* or *t*, yielding forms such as yᵉ and yᵗ. While these were presumably not ambiguous to the contemporary reader, subsequent generations of English users have misinterpreted forms such as yᵉ as ye ('you'), hence modern attempts at 'quaint' and antiquated noun phrases such as *Ye Olde Worlde Bookeshoppe*.

Other conventions of note, but which did not become fixed till well into the period, concern consonant representation. Until about 1630–1640, it was possible to use *i* to represent not only a vowel quality, but also consonantal [ʤ], as can be seen in spellings such as *iack* ('Jack') and *iolly* ('jolly'). From about the mid-seventeenth century, however, *j* came to be used in this function, and *i* was reserved for vowels The graphs *u* and *v* continued to be used for both consonant and vowel qualities (see Chapter 4, Section 4.4.1) but by the mid-1600s, English printers were following the Continental practice of using *u* and *v* for vowel and consonant qualities respectively. The upper case letter for both, however, remained V until about 1700 (Görlach, 1991: 48). Finally, there was also variation in the use of *s* and *z*. The latter graph always represented [z], but *s* could symbolize both [s] and [z] (*haste* vs *fees*). This meant that alternative spellings for certain words developed, as can be seen in the pair *criticise~criticize*. Interestingly, the *–ise/–ize* alternatives are often (erroneously) assumed to be geographically differentiated: the former is associated with British spelling and the latter with American.

By about 1650, spelling conventions had largely become fixed and, in particular, the practice of having one spelling per word. Orthographic practice was also successfully disseminated through the education system and spelling books, which reached a wide and captive audience. In the later seventeenth and eighteenth centuries (and indeed even today), great store was put by being able to spell 'correctly' and as a result much of the variation that had characterized earlier periods of writing disappeared, even in texts not meant for public consumption such as private letters and diaries.

5.4.2 Features of EModE pronunciation

The reduction in orthographic variation in EModE texts has added another level of opacity to the process of making plausible hypotheses about pronunciation on the basis of a written corpus. However, certain 'clues' remain evident: the variation that does exist in 'non-standardized' spellings, for instance, very likely reflects contemporary pronunciation, as do more literary devices such as punning, rhyming[3] (note that rhyming dictionaries also exist) and the use of metrical patterns, which can sometimes indicate syllable structure in particular words. In addition, a relatively sizeable corpus of material which includes contemporary linguistic description – compiled largely by spelling reformers and grammarians – is also available, as are language teaching manuals, intended either for English students learning a foreign language or for non-native English speakers (and which therefore necessarily include phonological and phonetic descriptions). However, as Görlach (1991: 61) points out, all such material must be read and interpreted in the context of the author's 'provenance, his attitude (his views of correctness, the influence on him of written English) and the vague terminologies [then] used to describe sounds'.

In addition to providing linguistic information, these sources have also collectively revealed that there was not only a palpable and growing awareness throughout the period of variation in pronunciation, but also a concomitant ideology of 'correctness' in speech. Görlach (ibid.: 64–5) states that a particular sub-system, that of the 'conservative pronunciation of the educated', was described in detail by phoneticians from Hart (1570) to Gil (1619), presumably as a norm of 'correct' speech. This sub-system appears to have had a basis in spelling pronunciation (that is, pronouncing the word as it appeared on the printed page), and was promoted within schools, particularly grammar schools. As a result, pronunciations which did not conform to this system were often denounced as 'vulgar'. Although grammarians may have been concerned to preserve this sub-system as a model of 'correct' pronunciation, it was in fact still susceptible to change. Görlach (1991: 63), for example, explains that change was slow but inevitable, as ' "educated" pronunciations were replaced by more popular ones':

> [P]honetic changes which resulted from 'sloppy' articulation and diverged from the written standard, and which can therefore be assumed to have had their origin in colloquial and proper speech, often took a long time to find general acceptance against the traditions of the schools. This often resulted in delayed adoption of an innovation or . . . in pronunciations that differ from word to word; all this points to the co-existence of various forms in sixteenth century spoken [English].

Let us now turn to a brief description of the main characteristics of EModE pronunciation. We begin with consonants.

5.4.2.1 EModE consonants

Data sources suggest that the consonantal system did not undergo extensive change during the EModE period. There is, however, evidence of variation in pronunciation, and of the fact that some 'common' consonantal articulations were eventually adopted into 'correct' speech. For example, the allophones of /h/ ([ç] next to front vowels, as in *night*, and [x] next to back vowels, as in *bough*; see Chapter 3, Section 3.4.1) were replaced in dialectal and colloquial speech after the fifteenth century: [ç] was lost and replaced by vowel length in words such as *right*, as was [x] in words such as *bough*. In some cases, [x] merged with [f], as in the modern pronunciation of *cough* and *laugh*. Görlach (1991: 75) states that in conservative, educated speech, the older [ç] and [x] articulations continued to be prescribed, and the newer, colloquial pronunciations, especially [f], stigmatized. Nevertheless, from about the middle of the seventeenth century, they had become common even in 'correct' speech.

The reduction of certain word-final clusters also occurred in EModE. The pronunciation [-mb] (in *lamb*) became [-m] and [-nd] became [n] (as in *laun* 'lawn' from ME *laund*). Interestingly, the reverse (that is, adding a consonant to an already present word-final consonant) sometimes happened, possibly through false analogy. Thus, ME *soun* was mistakenly thought to have initially been *sound*, and the latter adjustment to sound and spelling became widespread from about the fifteenth century onwards.

The 'dark l' [ł] which typically occurs before labial and velar consonants in English (such as [f], [v], [m], [k]) became vocalized in EModE, as can be heard in modern 'silent l' pronunciations of words such as *half, psalm, walk, folk* and *yolk*. Pronunciations which retained [ɬ] came to be stigmatized as pedantic: Görlach (1991: 75) cites the caricature of the Pedant in *Love's Labour Lost* (V.I.I.) who, in berating a 'racker of ortagriphie', states that a marker of the latter's ignorance is the fact that he 'clepeth a Calf, a Caufe: halfe, haufe'. Times, however, have changed – it is not uncommon to hear [ɬ] pronunciation in words perhaps typically encountered more often in writing than in speech, and therefore more susceptible to spelling pronunciation. For example, the widely advertised chain of gyms, *Holmes Place*, or literary names such as *Faulkner*, often now have [ɬ] pronunciation.

EModE also gained two new phonemes /ŋ/ and /ʒ/. In ME, [ŋ] had been an allophonic variation of /n/ before velar plosives [g] and [k]. However, in the late sixteenth century, word-final [g] was lost (possibly as a result of the changes to consonant clusters discussed above). The status of the velar nasal therefore became phonemic, since it came to appear in contexts where it served to distinguish meaning (as in the minimal pair *thin–thing*).

In the pronunciation of loanwords such as *leisure*, the medial consonant (represented by *s* but pronounced [z]) was initially followed by a palatal glide [j]. The combination [zj] merged to produce [ʒ] – a pronunciation considered by sixteenth-century grammarians as 'foreign', but widespread by the seventeenth century. It eventually became phonemic, although its occurrence remains relatively rare.

Its voiceless counterpart /ʃ/ was also extended to new contexts of usage in EModE. In words such as *censure*, medial [s] was, as in the examples above, followed by palatal [j]. The same occurred in words such as *temptation* in which the *t* of *-tion*, in accordance with its French provenance, was pronounced [s], as is evident in spellings such as *temtasion* (Hart, 1570; in Görlach, 1991: 51). The [sj] combination in such words became [ʃ], the pronunciation which has survived into modern English. A similar merger of medial consonant and glide also took place in the pronunciation of words such as *Indian*: medial [d] and the following [j] became [dʒ]. This was common in seventeenth-century speech, but became stigmatized in the nineteenth century, when it was largely replaced by the original spelling pronunciation. However, the [dʒ] pronunciation was immortalized by Mark Twain in the name of Tom Sawyer's nemesis, *Injun Joe*.

Other features of note pertain to the pronunciation of word-initial *h-* ([h]), which was variable in the EModE period. However, the phenomenon known as '*h*-dropping' was not widely stigmatized as symptomatic of 'uneducated' speech until the nineteenth century, again on the basis of spelling pronunciation. In addition, there was an early loss of [r] before sibilants in the EModE period. This is reflected in spellings such as *bass* ('fish'; from ME *barse*), *cuss* (*curse*), and *palsy* (*parlesie/paralisie* 'paralysis') which, along with the 'r-less' pronunciations, are still part of modern English (Pyles and Algeo, 1982: 178–9). Finally, orthographic evidence indicates that there was sometimes variable pronunciation of word-medial [d] and [ð] (*–d–* and *–th–* respectively) in EModE, as can be seen in spellings such as *murthering/murdering, burthen, togyder, odur* ('other'), and *althermen* ('aldermen') (Görlach, 1991: 76). This variation in spelling and speech has, as we can see today, disappeared from formal written and spoken usage.

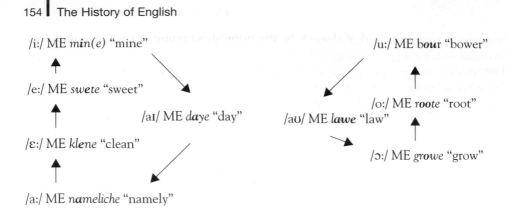

Figure 5.1 The Great Vowel Shift

5.4.2.2 EModE vowels

In the fifteenth century, the pronunciation of the long vowels in the southern Middle English dialects began to undergo changes in articulation, essentially moving upwards in quality and with diphthongization of the highest front and back vowels. A simplified schematic of the movements of this vowel shift (typically termed *Great*) is represented in Figure 5.1.

The motivations for the shift are not completely clear but as Smith (1996: 111) argues, may very well have involved both 'interacting extralinguistic and intralinguistic processes'. Traditional explanations in historical linguistics have tended to concentrate on the internal motivations and processes of the shift, looking, for example, at how such movements may have been catalysed by changes within the vowel system. For instance, Structuralist[4] explanations have focused on the maintenance of symmetry in the long vowel system (in which each vowel occupies a distinct articulatory and acoustic space), positing that a change in equilibrium could trigger subsequent movement. Thus, initial movement which resulted in the appearance of 'gaps' and/or the 'crowding' of more than one vowel in the same phonetic space (the latter of which could result in phonetic merger and the creation of ambiguous homophones) could set off a chain of 'correcting' shifts. On this basis, one Structuralist explanation of the Shift postulates that its initial catalyst was the diphthongization of the high front and back vowels /iː/ and /uː/, which left gaps. This triggered a *drag chain* movement in which the lower long vowels were progressively raised upwards until symmetry was restored. An alternative explanation proposes that the Shift began with low long vowels such as /aː/ which began to encroach on the space of the next highest vowels. This then set a *push chain* into effect, through which the latter vowels moved in the same direction, into the space of the next highest vowels. This process of encroachment and subsequent movement would continue until the system had regained symmetry.

We should note that these explanations are not mutually exclusive – data from some varieties of English indicate that both push and drag mechanisms may interact in such shifts. As an example, the diphthongization of /uː/ has not occurred for all speakers – varieties of Scots, for instance, have preserved pre-Shift /muːs/

mouse and /hu:s/ *house*. It is possible that this is due to fact that ME long /o:/ fronted, leaving a gap in the back vowels. With no /o:/ to 'push' /u:/ towards the diphthong quality, /u:/ pronunciation remained in such words. The fact that movement occurred in other parts of the system, however, indicates the operation of both push and drag mechanisms: 'the vowel to start the whole process may have been /ɔ:/ (and similarly front /ɛ:/) which moved up towards /o:/ where such a vowel existed, and dragged the other vowels along behind' (McMahon, 1994: 31).

While such hypotheses offer plausible explanations for the mechanisms of the Shift, they do not actually address the question of why the initial vowel movements were triggered. Attempts to explain the latter have typically focused on extralinguistic causes such as contact. Le Page (in Samuels, 1972, cited in Görlach, 1991: 67), for instance, suggests that the shifts may have been started by members of the upper classes who, finding their once exclusive rung threatened by the mobile populace climbing up the social ladder, tried to distance themselves through pronunciation. Smith (1996: Chapter 5) is at pains to point out that the reasons triggering the vowel movements may well have differed in various parts of the country, and that those in the south are likely to have begun in the contact between different social groups (with competing vowel systems) in the metropolis of sixteenth-century London. In truth, we may never know exactly what factors lay behind the onset and spread of such change in the long vowels, or indeed whether it really was a 'unitary phenomenon' or instead 'a series of minor individual choices which have interacted diachronically . . . and sociolinguistically, resulting in a set of phonological realignments' (Smith, 1996: 110–11). What we can be sure of, however, is that such changes are not uncommon (see Chapter 1, Section 1.2, for example) and synchronic observations of the contexts in, and processes by which, modern shifts begin and spread may well shed more light on this particular diachronic phenomenon.

Short vowels appear to have remained fairly stable in EModE. Spelling evidence suggests that in contexts where 'correct' short [ɪ] was prescribed, some dialectal pronunciations preferred [ɛ], as evidenced by spellings such as *menysters* ('ministers'), *ennes* ('inns') and *sterope* ('stirrup') (Görlach, 1991: 70). The [ɑ] pronunciation of words such as *God* and *stop* which is often identified as a salient characteristic of modern American English has its roots in the seventeenth-century lowering of short [ɔ] in some dialects. In some instances, lowering continued to [a], resulting in EModE variant spellings such as *Gad/God* (cf. *egads*), *strap/strop*. The unrounded variants were not unfashionable: one of Elizabeth I's letters, for example, contains the phrase *I pray you stap the mouthes* (Wyld, 1936; cited in Pyles and Algeo, 1982: 176). While [ɑ] was taken to America and other parts of the New World, [ɔ] was reinstated in England as the 'correct' variant. Another change of note concerned the lengthening of [æ] and [ɔ] before [s], [f] and [θ] in words such as *staff*, *glass*, *path* and *off* (Görlach, 1991: 72). Finally, some words which had short [ʊ] in ME such as *putt* and *butt* developed schwa. For some speakers a subsequent change to [ʌ] has occurred, unless followed by /l/ as in *pull* and *bull* (Pyles and Algeo, 1982: 176).

In terms of diphthongs (see Chapter 4, Section 4.4.2), ME [ʊɪ] (*oi*), which occurred mostly in French loanwords such as *boil* and *poison*, appears to have

changed in articulation in EModE to [ɔɪ]. Pyles and Algeo (1982: 176) state that this became [aɪ] in the EMod period, a pronunciation that survived for a time in non-standard speech. The more standard [ɔɪ] pronunciation which is used today, however, was promoted as appropriate on the basis of the *oi* spelling.

The ME diphthongs [ɛʊ] and [ɪʊ] (spelt variously as *eu, ew, iu, iw, u*) fell together as [ju] in EModE. This has been retained after labial consonants, as in *pew, mute, feud* and velar consonants, as in *argue* and *cute*. Finally, other ME diphthongs, such as [aʊ] and [ɔʊ] (in the ME pronunciation of words such as *law* and *bow*, respectively) became the monophthongs [ɔ:] and [o:]. In some modern pronunciations, however, that [o] has diphthongized again to [əʊ].

5.4.3 Features of EModE grammar

Although the English of the standardized EModE corpus generally presents no great difficulties to the modern reader, there are a few areas of significant difference, in terms of morphological and syntactic features, from contemporary uses of the language. We begin with EModE nouns.

5.4.3.1 EModE nouns

Nouns in EModE appear to have been very much like their modern descendants, generally marking plurals and possessives through inflection. However, the *–en* plurals of the ME period such as *kine* ('cows'), *eyen* and *hosen* (see Chapter 4) which continued to occur were largely proscribed by EModE grammarians, and have since disappeared apart from a few fossilizations such as *oxen, children* and *brethren*. Historically uninflected plurals such as *deer, sheep* and *swine* also survived intact from OE into EModE and, indeed, are still used in modern English. Some such as *folk*, however, came to be re-interpreted during the EModE period as singular, and acquired the plural form *folks* (still used today). Conversely, and very likely by analogy with nouns like *deer* and *sheep*, other animal-labelling nouns which historically had had plural forms came to acquire an unmarked, collective sense in certain contexts. These too have survived into modern usage: we admire tropical *fish*, and shoot wild *fowl* and wild *boar*.

The possessive inflection descended from OE *a*-stem genitive singular (see Chapter 3, Section 3.4.2) continued to be used in EModE, typically written as *–s* or *–'s* (when affixed to singular nouns). In terms of spelling, the use of the apostrophe in marking the inflection was optional in the sixteenth century but increased in usage until it became fully established in the eighteenth century. Plural nouns were marked for possession by position only (as in *the dogs dishes* vs modern standard *the dogs' dishes*), a textual feature that was sometimes extended to singular nouns that ended in a sibilant, as in *Argus eyes*. Görlach (1991: 81) notes that there is evidence that it could also be used with other nouns, as in *ye quen grace* ('the queen's grace').

In addition to these two processes, EModE also made use of *his*-genitives (Chapter 4, Section 4.4.3), mainly with nouns ending in sibilants (as in *Moses his meekness, Boccacce his Demogorgon*); *of*-phrases, as in *the sins of the father*, and a group genitive, in which the possessive inflection was added to a noun phrase (as

in *the Queen of England's will*). The latter appears to have increased in usage as that of 'split' possessive noun phrases (as in *the Queen's will of England*) declined (Görlach, 1991: 82). The stylistic range and usefulness for rhyme and metre offered by these options were well exploited by EModE authors and poets. Ben Jonson's *Alchemist*, for example, employs practically every type of possessive marking, as can be seen in the extract in Example 5.1 (cited in Görlach, 1991: 81):

Example 5.1 Possessive marking in Ben Jonson's *Alchemist*

The <u>Dragons</u> teeth, *mercury* sublimate,
that keepes the whitenesse, hardnesse, and the biting;
And they are gather'd into <u>iason's</u> helme,
(Th'*alembeke*) and then sow'd in <u>Mars his field</u>,
And, thence, sublim'd so often, till they are fix'd.
Both this, th'*Hesperian* garden, <u>Cadmvs</u> storie,
love's <u>shower</u>, the boone of Midas, <u>argvs eyes</u> . . .

Of all the non-inflectional options, the *his*-genitive received the most condemnation from scholars of the language, and appears to have dropped out of use during the period.

5.4.3.2 EModE adjectives

By the beginning of the EModE period, adjectives carried only comparative and superlative inflections (*–er* and *–est* respectively) but these degrees of comparison were also signalled by the respective use of *more* and *most*. Both options survived into EModE and indeed, were often used simultaneously. Görlach (1991: 83) states that the use of *more* or *most* + *uninflected adjective* was encouraged, and therefore more common, in educated writing, but numerous textual examples of doubly marked forms (such as *most unkindest*), which provided a useful emphatic device, also exist. In the late seventeenth century, however, such forms came to be derided as illogical and were proscribed. In fact, as Görlach (ibid.: 84) notes, they were so stigmatized that they were consistently removed from certain eighteenth-century editions of Shakespeare. By the late 1600s, the use of *–er* and *–est* was largely restricted to monosyllabic and certain disyllabic adjectives (that is, those ending in a vowel sound), and *more* and *most* to polysyllabic – rules which are still observed today.

5.4.3.3 EModE pronouns

Pronouns in EModE continued to be differentiated for person, case, gender and number (and since the forms in the corpus are largely the same in appearance and function as modern English pronouns, they will not be replicated here). There are, however, a few significant developments in this word class of which we should take note.

Perhaps the best known of these concern the use of the second person singular and plural pronouns; namely *thou/thee* and *ye/you*. By the beginning of the EModE period, subject *ye* and object *you* had fallen together in pronunciation as [jə], resulting in what seems to be the indiscriminate use of either pronoun in either function. By 1600, *ye* had largely dropped out of use. In another development, the distinction between *thou/thee* and *ye/you* became increasingly less associated with number and more so with social dynamics of interaction. The use of French in the ME period had introduced what Brown and Gilman (1960) refer to as a 'non-reciprocal power semantic' and a 'solidarity semantic' into the use of the English pronouns. In essence this meant that, as in the T/V (*tu/vous*) distinction of the Romance languages, the *thou/thee* forms came to be used as a term of address to social inferiors and (*ye*)/*you* to social superiors (the non-reciprocal power semantic). At the same time, equals of the upper classes exchanged mutual V and equals of the lower classes exchanged T (Brown and Gilman, 1960: 256). Eventually and, according to the authors, very gradually, a distinction developed between the 'T of intimacy and the V of formality': a manifestation of use on the dimension of solidarity (ibid.: 257). Thus, those who felt socially, emotionally and/or intellectually equal (regardless of class boundaries) would address each other as *thou*, whereas those who did not, but who wanted to maintain a respectful but distant relationship, would use reciprocal *you*. At the same time, however, the older non-reciprocal use of the power semantic was also maintained. Notably, it was also possible to break this code – to express contempt towards a superior or a social equal, for instance, or any number of heightened feelings (Leith, 1983: 107). By the late seventeenth century, the use of *thou* had declined. Brown and Gilman (1960: 267) suggest that this was a consequence of its adoption as a term of address by Quakers, who were perceived as a 'rebellious religious group', and eventually became confined to biblical quotations, prayer and archaic dialectal use.

Another significant change occurred with the use of the possessive pronouns *my/mine* and *thy/thine*. In ME the use of each alternant had been phonologically determined: *my/thy* were used before nouns beginning with a consonant (*my sweet*) and *mine/thine* before those with an initial vowel (*thine apple*). In the EModE period, the distribution became grammatical: *my* and *thy* functioned as possessive pronouns in attributive use (that is, they modified the noun that names the object which is 'possessed') and *mine/thine* as possessives in nominal use. Although *thine* has disappeared from modern English, *my/mine* are still used in this way – we say *that's **my** car* (attributive) but *that's **mine*** (nominal). This distinction also held for the other possessive pronouns in the system apart from *his*, which has always served both attributive and nominal functions. Interestingly, however, analogical '*n*-forms' such as *hisn* and *hern* developed in the EModE period, but because of stigmatization, disappeared from 'correct' usage relatively quickly (Görlach, 1991: 86).

The neuter possessive *his* remained in use until the early seventeenth century (as in: *But value dwells not in particular will/It holds **his** estimate and dignitie* (*Troilus and Cressida* II.II)) but of course was potentially ambiguous in its likeness to the possessive masculine *his*. Attempts to counter this ambiguity included the use of *of it* (as in *Great was the fall of it* (*Matthew* 7.27)) and *thereof* (as in *the leaues **thereof** be long & broade* (Hortop 1591, *The Trauiales of an Englishman*)). The more popular alternative, however, proved to be an EModE creation – *its*, which first surfaced in the late sixteenth century, possibly in analogy with the other possessive '*s*-forms' of the third person singular. Its use spread rapidly throughout the seventeenth century, and by the beginning of the eighteenth had become thoroughly established.

Finally, the sixteenth century also saw the beginning use of *self* compounds to signal reflexivity. Possessive (attributive) pronouns served as the first element of these compounds (as in *myself, yourself, herself, ourselves*), as did object pronouns (as in *himself, themselves*). Notice too that *self* has been marked for number, which means that this is now the only part of the standard pronoun system where a singular–plural distinction holds for the second person pronoun (as in *yourself–yourselves*).

5.4.3.4 EModE verbs

EModE verbs continued to undergo changes begun in the ME period. Table 5.1 compares the present indicative inflections used in ME texts with those in EModE material. (Subjunctive inflections are not apparent in EModE texts, apart from a rare use of third person plural *–en* – a fossilization of older usage. See Chapter 4, Section 4.4.3.) The bolded forms in the EModE columns are those which were used most frequently while those in curly brackets occurred much more rarely, and were 'often regarded as dialectal or archaic' (Görlach, 1991: 88). A blank cell means that no inflection was used.

First person singular *–e* (of both northern and southern ME) seems to have dropped out of use in EModE. The second person singular *–t* was sometimes added to modals (*wilt, schalt*) and sometimes even to past tense forms of the verb *to be*, as in *wast* and *wert*. The second person singular inflection, however, declined in use in the seventeenth century, concomitant with the loss of *thou*.

In the third person singular, the two main EModE inflections were derived from the ME northern and southern forms. Görlach (1991: 88) states that *–eth* appears to have been used in more formal writing, since its frequency of occurrence was very high in official documents and biblical translations (including the Authorized Version), but was noticeably low in private documents and informal writing, where *–es* instead predominated. Both, however, occurred in poetry, where they proved useful in the creation of regular metrical patterns (consider monosyllabic *hates* and disyllabic *hateth*). In the seventeenth century, *–eth* declined in usage and came to be considered archaic and/or typical of biblical usage. The *–es* inflection, of course, has survived into modern standard English as *–s*.

Table 5.1 Present indicative inflections in EModE

	Present indicative		
	ME southern texts	ME northern texts	EModE
I	here	here	
thou	here**st**	here**s**	(e)**st** {es}, {t}
he, she, it	here**ð**	here**s**	**eth**, (e)**s**
we, you, they	here**ð**	here(n), here**s**	{en}, {eth}, {es}

The ME endings for the plural present indicative gave way to zero-marking in the EMod period but–*en*, –*eth* and –*es* were deliberately used by some sixteenth- and seventeenth-century authors. Spenser, for example, used –*en* to give his writing an archaic flavour (as in *they that con of Muses skill/sayne* . . . *that they dwell* (from *The Shepheardes Calendar*, 1579)). The –*es* (spelt –*z*) ending surfaces in one of Elizabeth I's letters (1586) in the line *your commissionars telz me*; and –*th* (from –*eth*) in *wise men* . . . *dothe renew it ons a yere* (from *The Breuiary of Healthe*, 1547).

In talking about changes to the preterite and past participle inflections in EModE, it is still useful to use the strong~weak distinction we first introduced in Chapter 3. The development of weak verb forms for historically strong verbs continued into the EModE period, although grammarians explicitly advocated the use of strong alternatives (Görlach, 1991: 91). However, strong past forms for some verbs did remain common in EModE usage, although the weak alternatives eventually won. Examples include *glide~glode, seethe~sod~sodden* and *wax~wox~waxen*. We should also note that the singular preterite and plural preterite distinction (as in *foond~founden*) appears to have largely collapsed by EModE and rarely occurred in writing.

Verbs which continued to use strong past participle forms appear to have experienced ongoing variation in the use of forms with and without –*en*: a process which had also begun in ME. It is not exactly clear why and how one of these forms for each relevant verb came to be accepted as standard, but Görlach (1991: 92) comments that phonological considerations may have been important: –*en* occurs most frequently after plosive consonants, as in *written, broken*, and no inflection after nasals, as in *run*. Interestingly some –*en* participles that no longer function as verbs, such as *drunken, molten* and *sodden*, have remained in modern English as adjectives.

There are not many changes of note for verbs which historically fall into the weak class. Some of these verbs also had strong preterites which continued to be used in EModE (as in *to snow* > *snowed/snew*). A few weak verbs, however, such as *dig, spit* and *stick*, developed the strong forms *dug, spat* and *stuck* still in use today. Finally, some historically irregular weak verbs (that is, weak verbs which also underwent a vowel change in their preterite and past participle forms) developed regular past forms during the EMod period (*to catch* > *catcht*); and some such as *work* developed irregular weak forms, as in *wrought* (possibly by analogy with *brought*).

The EModE period also saw the further development of auxiliary functions for the verb *do*. In addition to its functions as a main verb, *do* began to be used as a past-marking auxiliary in the ME period, a usage which continued into EModE, as can be seen in *the serpent that did sting* ('stung') *thy Father's life* (*Hamlet*, Act I, Scene V). The choice between this use of *do* and past marking by inflection or ablaut (as in *stung*) was frequently exploited by EModE poets and authors for purposes of rhyme and metre (the line from *Hamlet* may be one such example). Periphrastic *do* was also used to avoid constructions considered clumsy. For instance, many new Latin loan verbs (see Section 5.4.5) were polysyllabic, and the addition of native inflections often resulted in 'awkward' forms, such as *illuminateth*. *Doth illuminate*, however, was seen as a preferable alternative. We should note that in some cases, the auxiliary use of *do* is likely to have been emphatic as well (possibly as in the *Hamlet* example quoted earlier), although this is difficult to consistently discern clearly in a written corpus. It was not, however, until the eighteenth century, when the EModE optional uses discussed here had declined, that its definitive use as an emphatic auxiliary in declarative statements (which is maintained in modern English) became established.

EModE auxiliary *do* also came to be increasingly used in the formation of questions and negative statements when no other auxiliary was present. This may well have occurred through analogy with other structures with auxiliaries. For example, a sentence with an auxiliary could form a question through subject~auxiliary inversion (as in *Is* (Aux) *not the tongue* (S) *geuen* (V)?) but one without would have to invert the subject and main verb (as in *Seest thou these things?*). The use of auxiliary *do*, however, as in *dost* (Aux) *thou* (S) *see* (V) *these things?*, would bring it into line with the more common structure. Similarly, in the negation of sentences already possessing an auxiliary verb, the particle *not* was inserted between the former and the main verb (as in *I* (S) *will* (Aux) *not* (Neg) *force* (V) *any man*). However, if the sentence had no auxiliary, *not* occurred either after the main verb (as in *he seeth not the use*) or after the object if the latter was a personal pronoun (as in *you need them not*). Introducing the *do*-auxiliary therefore allowed originally 'auxiliary-less' sentences such as the latter two to conform to the more common pattern (examples of EModE sentences from Görlach, 1991: 120). *Do* continues to fulfil both auxiliary functions today (as in *he likes chocolate~does he like chocolate?~he does not like chocolate*).

5.4.4 Features of EModE Syntax

EModE texts indicate that word order, in both main and subordinate declarative clauses, generally followed the (S)VO pattern predominant in both OE and ME usage (see Chapters 3 and 4) and typical of present-day English usage. There were, however, instances of subject~verb and (more commonly) subject~auxiliary inversion after adverbials, as can be seen in Example 5.2 (a)–(b), as well as in utterances where the Object had been topicalized, as in Example 5.2 (c). As we have already seen in Section 5.4.3.4, such inversion also occurred in question formation:

Example 5.2 subject~verb/subject~auxiliary inversion

(a) *heere hung*   *those lipps*
           V   **S**

(b) *greeuously*   *hath*   *Caesar*   *answer'd it*
                     Aux   **S**   **V**

(c) *plots*   *have*   *I*   *laide*
     O   **Aux**   **S**   **V**

Smith (1999: 144) also notes the occurrence of what he terms recapitulation in EModE, through which a noun phrase is recapitulated by a pronoun later in an utterance, as in *my two Schoolefellowes*,/*Whom I will trust as I will Adders fang'd,/They beare the mandat*; non-inclusion of subject pronouns in contexts where they are obligatory in modern English, as in *nor do we finde him forward to be sounded,/But with a crafty Madnesse [he] keepes aloofe*; and the placement of one of two or more adjectives after the noun they modify, as in *an honest mind and plaine* (also noted in ME, see Chapter 4). The latter construction, however, is rare in EModE texts, which favour the modern use of adjectives as pre-modifiers (as in *such insociable and poynt deuise companions*).

Finally, we should mention here a stylistic convention of educated writing which affected clause structure. As we will see in Section 5.4.5, authors sometimes introduced new and unfamiliar vocabulary to their readers by pairing them with more well-known words (as in *counterfete and likene*). Such structures had not only a didactic but a stylistic function: they allowed authors to achieve *copiousness*, or *copia verborum*, a highly admired characteristic of Latin prose which essentially required the 'listing' of synonyms, sometimes with the use of conjunctions. Example 5.3 illustrates this, with synonyms italicized:

Example 5.3 *Copia verborum*
What condygne graces and thankes ought men to gyue to the writers of historyes? Who with their great labours/haue done so moche profyte to the humayne lyfe. They *shewe/open/manifest* and declare to the reder/by example of olde antyquite: what we shulde *enquere/desyre/*and *folowe*: And also/what we *shulde eschewe/auoyde/*and *vtterly flye*. For whan we . . . *se/beholde/*and rede the *auncyent actes/gestes/*and *dedes*: Howe/and with what *labours/daungers/*and *paryls* they were *gested* and *done*: They right greatly *admonest/ensigne/*and *teche* vs: howe we maye lede forthe our lyues.

(Froissart and Bouchier, 1523, *The Chronycles*)

5.4.5 Features of EModE Vocabulary

We have seen that many of the intelligentsia who advocated writing in the vernacular in the EModE period also had, for want of a better term, a kind of love-hate relationship with Latin; simultaneously pushing English forward as the 'rightful' medium for the nation with one hand and yet keeping Latin firmly on its pedestal with the other. The continuing veneration of Latin was not only a consequence of its ancient, classical heritage but also an accolade of its practicality – its centuries of use in various disciplines had led to the development of stylistic conventions and in particular, terminology, which English simply did not possess. For many, this seeming inadequacy of their native tongue needed redress if English was to be a worthy usurper of Latin's reign.

Concerns about the shortcomings of English became primarily focused on filling the 'gaps' in its vocabulary and a variety of solutions, encompassing borrowing, coinage and revival, were employed. So productive were these attempts that sources such as the *Chronological English Dictionary*, for example, indicate that the 'fastest growth of the vocabulary in the history of the English language' took place roughly between 1530 and 1600, 'both in absolute figures as well as in proportion to the total' (Görlach, 1991: 136). This rapid expansion, and the processes through which it was achieved, were often commented upon by EModE writers, as can be seen in the following excerpt:

> Since Learning began to flourish in our Nation, there have been more than ordinary Changes introduced in our Language; partly by new artificial Compositions; partly by enfranchising strange forein words, for their elegance and significancy . . . and partly by refining and mollifying old words for the more easie and graceful sound.

> (Wilkins (1668) *An Essay Towards a Real Character, and a Philosophical Language*, quoted in Gorlach, 1991: 138)

Wilkins also commented that the 'forein words' 'now make one third part of our language' and, indeed, the bulk of the new vocabulary items comprised loanwords; with coinages ('artificial Compositions') coming a close second. The majority of these loans were borrowed from Latin, doubtless through both esteem and exigency, and many entered English writing through translations and originals works in areas such as theology, philosophy, law, navigation, biology and anatomy – fields in which Latin had previously held sway. We get a clearer idea of the scale of this borrowing when we consider numbers: between 1610 and 1624, 124 words in the domain of theology were borrowed, 96 in crafts and technology, 125 in biology and 141 in medicine and anatomy. Of the total number of loans in this period, 60 per cent were taken from Latin (Wermser, 1976; cited in Görlach, 1991: 139; 167).

As this percentage indicates, English borrowed from sources other than Latin in the EModE period. French borrowing, for example, remained significant (20 per cent in 1610–1624 (Wermser, 1976 in Görlach, 1991: 167)) and as England's contact with other cultures through trade, travel and colonialism increased, so too did loans from other languages. From Italian came musical terms such as *fugue*, *madrigal*, *violin*, *allegro* and *opera* and architectural constructions such as *balcony*, *piazza* and *portico*. Trade in the New World with the Spanish brought the *alligator* and *mosquito* to English attention, as well as much more pleasant commodities such as *chocolate* and *maize* (borrowed into Spanish from Nahuatl and Taino respectively). Via Portuguese and Spanish came Wolof *banana* while Arabic *alcohol*, *algebra* and *monsoon* entered English through either Italian or French. Many seafaring terms, such as *boom*, *dock* and *yacht*, were borrowed from the Dutch, who were actively involved in navigation and trade, and English settlements in America led to direct contact with indigenous languages such as those of the Alongquian family, which loaned terms such as *racoon*, *opossum*, *moccasin* and *moose*. On the other side of the world, the establishment of the East India company resulted in borrowings such as *bazaar*, *caravan*, *baksheesh*, *shah* and *shawl* ultimately from Persian (and in the case of the first two, via Italian and French respectively), and *bungalow*, *chintz* and *juggernaut* from Hindi, to name but a few.

The spread of cultural and linguistic contact indicated by these examples should not be taken to imply 'depth': the actual number of loans taken from sources other than French and Latin were in fact relatively small. Wermser's 1610–1624 count, for instance, states that just over 2 per cent of loans came from Italian and Spanish respectively, just over 1 per cent from Dutch and about 7 per cent in total from what he terms 'overseas' languages (cited in Görlach, 1991: 167).

As mentioned earlier, English vocabulary was also augmented by the re-fashioning of native and loan material, largely via derivational and compounding processes, into new coinages. Compounding, always a productive process of word-formation in English, was often used in the EModE period not so much as a solution for lexical gaps as as a means of providing native alternatives to loanwords. Thus, Golding, for example, used English creations such as *fleshstring* to replace Latin *muscle*, and Puttenham coined terms such as *misnamer, ouer-reacher* and *dry mock* to explain the respective rhetorical concepts of metonymy, hyperbole and irony to a non-specialist audience. In terms of derivation, authors continued to use productive native English affixes but also began, particularly in the late sixteenth and seventeenth centuries, to employ some which had entered the language through loanwords, such as Latin *–ate* and the negating *dis–*, Greek *–izein* and French *–iser* (> English *–ize*) and the French *en–*. Interestingly, many of the resultant EModE coinages reflected a predilection for combining what was perceived as like with like – 'foreign' bases and 'foreign' affixes went together, as did their native counterparts. Thus, while EModE hybrids such as *womanize* (English *woman* + *–ize* (Greek *–izein*/French *–iser*)) or *bemadam* (English *be–* + French *madame*) did exist, they were in fact comparatively rare. Instead, 'foreignized' coinages along the lines of *disenamour, disinfect, enschedule, endungeon, commemorate, deracinate, championize* and *polygamize* were created, as were 'native' derivations such as *yongth* ('youth'), *bestnesse, forky* (as in *forky lightnings*) and *wordish*.

That some authors preferred using native resources (in both compounding and derivation) is a reflection of the nationalistic feeling that often infused advocacy of writing in English. This was also evident in the attempts to revive and employ archaic English words as gap-fillers. Clearly not suited to the expansion of scientific and technological vocabulary (which remained the domain of loanwords and coinages), however, this device appears to have instead been most popular in poetry, a medium in which it could work as a legitimate, and aesthetic, means of signalling continuity with an esteemed Chaucerian tradition. E.K., for example, stated in the *Epistle Dedicatory to the Shephearde's Calendar* (Spenser, 1579) that the 'olde and obsolete wordes' in the text 'bring great grace and . . . auctoritie to the verse'. This patriotic stance was fed by a 'wave of Teutonism' (Görlach, 1991: 145) in the seventeenth century in which authors such as Camden and Vertsegan extolled the linguistic virtues and distinguished pedigree of the Germanic ancestor of English – a lineage that was on a par with Latin.

On the other hand, many authors felt that the use of loanwords and 'foreign' coinages, particularly those derived from Latin, endowed English with the 'auctoritie' of the classical tradition. This is not to say that there was a clear-cut division between proponents of different solutions – many who advocated the use of English 'vnmixt and unmangeled' (Cheke, 1557, *Letter to Hoby*) with loans and Latinate coinages, for example, also made use of loans when they deemed it necessary. Given the subjectivity that inevitably governed such judgements, many of these 'purists' very often ended up incorporating substantial numbers of loans in their work. With hindsight, it seems appropriate to think of those engaged in EModE lexical augmentation not as operating with polemically opposed processes, but instead on a continuum of 'different degrees of Latinity' (Moore, 1910; in Görlach, 1991: 164).

The idea of 'borrowing where necessary' would also underlie one of the best-known debates over lexical augmentation in the sixteenth and seventeenth centuries – that of *inkhorn terms*. Many scholars and authors were prepared to accept that the use of loanwords and coinages (particularly those derived from Latin) was effective in providing terminology in domains where English had no ready-made equivalent, but the stamp of authority and veneer of polish it brought to texts was inescapable. The use of Latin and Latinate terminology was inevitably viewed as a reflection of intellectual and social sophistication, and a penchant for 'elevated' terminology in non-specialized contexts (such as everyday usage) emerged. This predilection came to be well served by dictionaries such as that of Henry Cockeram, whose 1623 *English Dictionarie*, for example, contained a substantial section on 'the vulgar words, which whensoeuer any desirous of a more curious explanation by a more refined and elegant speech shall looke into, he shall there receiue the exact and ample word to expresse the same'. In other words, Cockeram's dictionary provided sophisticated Latinate alternatives to everyday English words. Examples include the Latinate *latrate* for *to bark*, *carbunculate* for *to burn like a coal*, *adolescenturate* for *to play the boy* and the enduring *phylologie* for *loue of babling*. By all accounts, it was a bestseller.

The success of Cockeram and his like-minded peers points to the existence of a willing and receptive market, despite the fact that such usages had come to be derided as inkhornisms from the mid-sixteenth century onwards. One of the best known contemporary criticisms of such 'peeuish affectation' in writing was Thomas Wilson's mocking inkhorn letter in *The Arte of Rhetorique* (1553), an excerpt of which is quoted in Example 5.4.

Example 5.4 An inkhorn letter

An ynkehorne letter. Ponderyng, expendyng, and reuolutyng with my self your ingent affabilitie, and ingenious capacitee, for mundane affairs: I cannot but celebrate and extolle your magnificall dexteritee, aboue all other . . . What wise man readying this letter, will not take him for a very Caulfe, that made it in good earnest, & thought by his ynkepot termes, to get a good personage.

Wilson's letter may have been fictitious but the sentiment was very real, and shared by contemporary writers and scholars. Day (*The English Secretarie* (1586)), for instance, severely criticized the inkhorn-laden style of Boorde's *The Breuiary of Helthe* (1547) (addressed to 'Egregriouse doctours and maysters of the Eximiouse and Archane Science of Phisicke') by asking 'was there euer seene from a learned man a more preposterous and confused kind of writing, farced with so many and suche odde coyned termes in so litle vttering?' (both in Görlach, 1991; textual data).

Criticisms of inkhornisms among the intelligentsia continued into the 1600s, as did the popular demand for dictionaries which provided them. The seventeenth century produced what have come to be known as *hard-word* dictionaries, starting with Coote's (1596) hard-word list, which comprised new and unfamiliar terminology in the language, and Thomas' Latin~English dictionary (1588), both of which would serve as a basis for the more detailed dictionaries of the 1600s. In 1604, Cawdry published his dictionary of about two thousand 'hard vsuall English wordes, borrowed from the Hebrew, Greeke, Latine or French, etc.'; in 1616, Bullokar's *An English Expositour*, which contained about five thousand entries appeared, and in 1623, one which we have already mentioned – Cockeram's *English Dictionarie*. Later dictionaries came to include encyclopaedic material, dialectal description and etymological information. However, the focus on explaining new terminology generally remained in EModE dictionaries, and the more representative format, including 'all words commonly used in the language' (J.K. *New English Dictionary*, 1702), which modern readers expect from such compilations, would not really begin to take shape until well into the eighteenth century.

The hard-word dictionaries acquainted the public not only with inkhornisms but also generally with the more 'necessary' loanwords and coinages being introduced into English writing. As such, they were vital in the integration of new words into English usage. This was not an unimportant issue – new terminology, whether borrowed, coined or revived, had to be made as transparent as possible to an audience which would have contained members unfamiliar with Latin affixes and obsolete Middle English nouns. Some texts were produced with accompanying glossaries or embedded glosses; and authors sometimes included detailed explanations of new words within the text itself – witness the extract in Example 5.5:

Example 5.5 Explanation of *modestie*

In euery of these thinges and their sembable/is Modestie: which worde nat beinge knowen in the englisshe tonge/ne of al them which vnderstoode latin . . . they improprely named this vertue discretion. And nowe some men do as moche abuse the worde modestie/as the other dyd discretion. For if a man haue a sadde countenance at al times/& yet not beinge meued with wrathe/but pacient/& of moche gentilnesse: they . . . wil say that the man is of a great modestie, where they shulde rather saye/that he were of a great mansuetude.

(Elyot, 1531, *The boke named the Gouernour*)

In addition, as we saw in Section 5.4.4, writers would pair an unfamiliar term with a more recognizable one, as in *foundacion and groundeworke* (Lily and Colet, 1549, *A Short Introduction of Grammar*). Such help, however, was not always consistently available, particularly in the use of English archaisms which, because of their native ancestry, may have been believed to be more familiar to English readers. However, as Ashton (1556) pointed out, such words 'which by reason of antiquitie be almost out of vse' were no more transparent to a sixteenth-century audience than a Latinate inkhornism like *adnichilate* ('reduced to nothing' < Latin *ad* 'from' + *nihil* 'nothing').

By the end of the EModE period, interest in and debate on loanwords and coinages (particularly those from Latin) had waned, and attention became focused instead on the increase in loans from French, a perhaps inevitable consequence of the restoration of a king who had spent many years of exile in France. In an interesting postscript, many of the terms which were derided as inkhornisms during this period have in fact survived into modern usage (see Baugh and Cable, 2002: 217–51).

5.5 Contact and Change: English in Barbados

Until the late 1500s, English 'had no very important role as a foreign or second language anywhere, and was spoken as a native language in a very small area of the globe indeed' (Trudgill, 2002: 29). The technical and navigational advances of the seventeenth century, however, would initiate the language's journey to its modern, global status. With the 1600 chartering of the East India Company, the introduction of English to India began. In the western hemisphere, colonization and settlement took English to Ireland (officially conquered in 1601) and further afield to what is now America, neighbouring isles such as Bermuda, the Bahamas, the Turks and Caicos Islands, and as far up the North American coast as Newfoundland. Plantation settlements also took English into the Caribbean: Anguilla, Antigua, Barbuda, Barbados, the Cayman Islands, Jamaica, Montserrat, St. Kitts and Nevis, the British Virgin Islands, the American Virgin Islands and mainland Guyana and Belize were all claimed and settled in the 1600s. So too were areas of Honduras, Nicaragua and Colombia.

As noted earlier in this chapter, histories of English have tended to concentrate on the standardization of the language in the modern period, consequently paying scant attention to the beginnings of its global life. This section attempts a measure of redress in considering English in the context of one of the earliest landing points for English in the New World, Barbados. We begin with a brief outline of the island's relevant social history.

Barbados, claimed in 1627, was one of the first islands to be settled by England as a permanent, crop-producing colony. Its first settlers, '3 score of Christaynes and forty slaves of Negeres and indeynes' (from a letter of 1627; in Holm, 1989: 446), established the island's first commercial crops of tobacco and cotton. More English settlers soon followed: some moderately wealthy yeomen who had bought or leased land for tobacco plantations, but most indentured workers[5] drawn from the poorer communities of various English counties including East Anglia, Devon, Cornwall, Somerset, Suffolk, Essex, Hertfordshire and Oxfordshire (Watts, 1987: 149–50). The reliance on indentureship continued throughout the 1630s – a period in which the number of plantations (and therefore of English landowners) increased steadily. While African and indigenous Carib and Arawak slaves were retained, they generally remained a minority during Barbados' tobacco-producing years (ibid.: 150–1). Thus, an official population count in 1645 estimated that the island was home to about 24,000 inhabitants, 'among whom were 11,200 landowners, 18,300 white men capable of bearing firearms, and 5,680 slaves, the latter being predominantly African but also including a handful of Arawak and Carib men and women' (Scott, c. 1667; quoted in Watts, 1987: 151).

In the late 1640s to the mid-1650s, the population underwent further increase, mainly as a result of the English Civil War and also because of a change in economic policy. Between 1649 and 1655, approximately 12,000 prisoners-of-war from Cromwell's campaigns in Ireland and Scotland were taken to the island and forced into indentureship. In this, they were joined by others who had been press-ganged (in the language of the time, *barbadosed*), as well as by petty criminals, prostitutes and those whose sentences of death or life imprisonment had been commuted to transportation. Needless to say, these unwilling indentees created, in the eyes of contemporary observers, an unreliable and unimpressive workforce. Whistler (1654), for example, griped that while the colony was 'one of the richest spotes of ground in the wordell' it was also 'the dunghill wharon England doth cast forth its rubidge' (in Watts, 1987: 200).

Between the 1640s and the mid-1650s, the island saw a widespread changeover to sugar-cane cultivation and sugar production – a change that was made more profitable by the importation of slave labour (a cheaper and more efficient alternative to indentureship). Watts (ibid.: 218) points out that population data for slaves prior to about 1650 is lacking, incomplete or unreliable. It is known, however, that the increase after this period was dramatic – for example, about 6,000 slaves worked on estates in 1650, but this figure had risen to about 20,000 in 1653. Contemporary data suggests that from about 1655, the slave population began to outnumber the White and by the mid-1660s, 'black slaves had become numerically dominant over whites by an approximate factor of three to two, women and children being included in both cases' (ibid.: 218). This was also helped by the fact that after 1660 and the restoration of the monarchy, the indentureship scheme underwent a further decline in numbers as the supply of prisoners-of-war dried up and the more stable political and economic conditions in England seduced once potentially willing participants.

The establishment of big sugar plantations forced many small landowners into selling their holdings. Along with ex-indentured workers who could no longer afford to buy land at the end of their contracts, and labourers who could not find work in a slave economy, they began a process of White migration out of Barbados in the latter half of the seventeenth century. Many chose to emigrate to the new English colonies in Suriname, Jamaica and the Leeward Islands. Indeed, Holm (1989: 447) argues that this phase of population movement was significant enough to have 'played a central role in the dispersal of British regional speech in the New World'.

Eighteenth-century Barbados continued to be a population dispersal point in the Caribbean, mainly for slaves brought in from Africa. Sugar production continued its lucrative run in the nineteenth century (slavery was abolished in 1834), and the island's continuing prosperity (conducive to high birth rates and consequently, population increase) led to another significant wave of emigration to Caribbean anglophone territories in the 1830s. The island remained a British colony until 1966, and a census carried out some 40 years later showed a reversal of its earliest population statistics: in 2000, the population comprised 80 per cent Black, 4 per cent White and 16 per cent Other.

It is clear that the colonization of Barbados took place in the context of contact – a phenomenon which, as we have seen in Chapters 3 and 4, can have different linguistic consequences according to its nature. In the case of modern Barbados, English was made the official language of the island but the majority of locals, if not all, also speak Bajan or, as it is sometimes known, Barbadian (Creole) English. The linguistic status of Bajan has been a matter of debate, primarily for two reasons. First, modern Bajan does not conform to an expected 'creole template' (see, for example, Whinnom's list in Chapter 4, Section 4.5) and instead has been analysed as closer in structure to varieties of English. Second, some of the patterns of settlement in the island – specifically long periods of indentureship and small populations living in close proximity – do not accord with a traditional model of creolization in which contact between two socio-politically and numerically unequal groups is necessary, hostile and (sometimes violently) characterized by socio-political oppression and social distance from the outset (as in the context of slave plantations). In this setting, it has been assumed that the language of the socio-politically powerful (superstratal) group becomes the target of the less powerful (substratal) group who, because of the hostile environment, cannot acquire it fluently. Eventually, the interplay between superstratal and substratal languages results in a creole.[6]

The question then of whether Bajan can be considered a creole, or at the very least, a language with creole ancestry (which has become more similar over the years to English through ongoing exposure to the latter), remains unsettled. Hancock (1980), for instance, argues that the sociohistorical dimension of the contact situation does not support the emergence of a creole, and posits that Bajan is essentially a 'local metropolitan, rather than creolized variety of English' (1980: 22). Others such as Cassidy (1980), Rickford and Handler (1994), and Fields (1995) have argued instead that modern Bajan is descended from a creole ancestor which has undergone decreolization (that is, in essence, become 'less' creole) at some point in its history. This pro-creole perspective has largely been based on the attestation of certain structural properties in historical texts. Thus, Rickford and Handler (1994) and Fields (1995), for example, have examined textual data from the late seventeenth–nineteenth centuries containing examples of spoken Bajan, and posit a 'full-fledged creole ancestry' for the language (Fields, 1995: 105). Similarly, Cassidy (1980: 14) states that 'present day Barbadian English preserves what can hardly be explained otherwise as a creole residue', and Winford (1993: Chapter 8) concludes that 'there is more creole in its [the speech of Barbados] present and its past than scholars have usually been willing to recognize'.

Arguments for a creole ancestry are not unproblematic. As in all historical perspectives on language use, the necessary reliance on textual material for accurate linguistic description makes analyses somewhat tenuous. As Fields (1995: 93) states in relation to her data:

A note of caution . . . needs to be given concerning the nature of written records of early slave language. In the first place, they are all second hand, written by white Europeans, who were transcribing what they believe they had heard. Secondly, these transcribers may have had varying degrees of competence in performing this task, some of them being long term residents, others being merely transient visitors. Because of the variable dependability of these texts, one has to be cautious when drawing conclusions about features evidenced by only one author.

A second issue lies in the assumption of distinctive creole structural properties in earlier stages of Bajan (and in a comparative perspective, in modern Bajan as well). As we have already seen (Chapter 4, Section 4.5), creoles do not appear to form a unique typological class but instead share many features and processes with other non-creole languages. A good illustration of this can be seen in the list of 'significant creole features' used in Fields's (1995) analysis. Many of these, such as 'absence of plural marking on nouns, absence of case marking on pronouns . . . unmarked past tense' and multiple negation (ibid.: 98), are not specific to creoles but can also be found in languages such as English and indeed, are cross-linguistically common. As Mufwene (1986: 131; in Chaudenson, 2001: 144–5) states, 'the features which hitherto have been associated with creoles cannot distinguish these languages from non-creole languages. There are many of the latter which have not only the same features but also almost the same combinations thereof.'

A further issue concerns the reconciliation of a Bajan creole ancestor with Barbados' settlement patterns. As stated earlier, Barbados does not wholly conform to what we might call the established template for creole emergence: Fields (1995: 89) states that 'the sociohistorical situation in Barbados . . . was not as straightforward and as clear-cut as in most other English-speaking Caribbean islands'. This is because the first 30 or so years of settlement, and of contact between groups, were not conducive to creolization: English speakers were in the majority, and populations were small enough to allow for its acquisition by non-native speakers with relative ease. Thus, arguments for a Bajan creole ancestor typically place its emergence sometime after 1655, when the number of Africans began to consistently outnumber Europeans (see above) and social, and linguistic, distance between the two groups significantly increased. This is not in itself a problematic stance; indeed, it is extremely plausible. What is perhaps a bit more awkward, however, is the fact that the posited early phase of English acquisition and use is treated as separate and distinct from the later phase of creolization. In other words, the early phase of non-creole use is deemed somewhat unimportant to the later creole development of Bajan, and the two may be made to seem discrete periods of language history. This is not unjustifiable: pre-1655 data for linguistic and social interaction are sparse and as intimated earlier, a substantial phase of superstratal and substratal interaction has not typically been assumed to precede the emergence of a creole. However, as we have consistently noted throughout these chapters in relation to English, language use cannot so easily be compartmentalized – there is evident continuity between the Anglo-Saxon period and OE, on the one hand, and the ME period and ME, on the other, for instance. To postulate continuity between the early and later phases of Barbados' linguistic history therefore would not seem unreasonable.

One such approach is that of Mufwene (2001), whose theory of creolization posits a line of development from early non-creole to later creole use. Mufwene (ibid.: 9–10) argues that creoles developed in settlement colonies, or colonies where contact was, in the first instance, intimate and regular between European colonists (many of whom were indentured servants) and other ethnic groups (such as those comprised of slaves). In the homestead phase of these settlements, non-Europeans were in the minority and although subject to socio-political discrimination, were relatively well integrated. Mufwene (2001: 9–10) maintains that this less powerful group 'had full access to European languages . . . which they acquired through regular interactions with their native or fluent speakers'. Importantly, the European languages being acquired in these contexts were not standard forms but colonial koinés of the non-standard regional and social lects of the majority of Europeans sent out to the colonies; Europeans who comprised 'large proportions of indentured servants and other low-class employees of colonial companies' (ibid.: 28).

Once settlements moved into bigger plantation economies, the dynamics of the contact situation changed. The extensive importation of labour (such as African slaves) onto such holdings, and European migration out of them, would not only shift population ratios of European to non-European (with the latter becoming the majority) but also make contact between these two groups (and therefore, fluent acquisition of the European language) increasingly difficult. Mufwene (ibid.: 9–10) therefore hypothesizes that creolization occurred through the attempts of new, non-European labour arrivals in the plantation period to acquire the colonial vernaculars being spoken around them. However, given the difficulty in interacting with native and fluent speakers, these attempts ended up being 'imperfect replications' (Lass, 1997: 112); a process 'intensified . . . by the decreasing disproportion of native and fluent speakers (creole and seasoned slaves) relative to nonproficient speakers' (Mufwene, 2001: 9–10).

This approach certainly seems to fit the social and linguistic situation outlined for Barbados (see social history above). Importantly, it also plausibly links the two phases of non-creole use and creolization. In addition, Mufwene's approach also offers an explanation (alternative to decreolization) for the structural parallels that have been observed between Bajan and English. Mufwene (ibid., 20–9) argues that 'structural features of creoles have been predetermined to a large extent (though not exclusively) by characteristics of the vernaculars spoken by the populations that founded the colonies in which they developed'. In essence, those vernaculars would have been heavily based on the European colonial koinés, carrying features already native to a substantial number of their (European) speakers and therefore linguistically 'dominant'. Through inter-generational transmission, such features would have become 'deeply entrenched as predicted by Wimsatt's (1999, 2000) principle of *generative entrenchment*', meaning simply that older features have a better chance of survival than newer ones because 'they have acquired more and more carriers, hence more transmitters, with each additional generation of speakers' (Mufwene, 2001: 28–9). Many would therefore eventually pass into creoles once they began to emerge.

In this perspective, structural similarities between Bajan and English varieties can be accounted for diachronically. A particular study of interest here is that of Niles (1980), who has highlighted similarities in patterns and features between Bajan and non-standard EModE varieties, particularly those of the south-western regions of England, from which the majority of English settlers came. Niles also argues that early Bajan (1627–1655) was ultimately a variety of English, properties of which eventually became part of a Bajan creole (which she hypothesizes emerged in the eighteenth century at the height of the plantation era) and which have survived into modern speech. For example, Niles posits that modern Bajan gender compounds such as *head-piece* 'head', *nose-hole* 'nostril', *before-time* 'before, formerly' (as in *I was a great fighter beforetime, and I is still a great fighter now*), *dusk-time* 'dusk' and *lower-side* 'below' (ibid.: 101, 103) have a south-western dialectal English (SWDE) source. In terms of pronouns, modern Bajan makes use of pronouns designated as subject in standard English usage in object position (as in *he like she* 'he likes <u>her</u>'), and vice versa (as in <u>*me*</u> *eh going dere* 'I am not going there'). According to Wright (1905: 270–1), one of Niles' main sources for SWDE, similar usages existed in the latter: *I opes <u>us</u> chell do the same* ('I hope <u>we</u> shall do the same' (Somerset)) and *<u>Er</u> dresses erzel' uncommon fine* ('she dresses extremely well' (Devon) (Wright, 1905: 270–1)). Niles (1980: 115) found instances such as *she did glare at <u>we</u>* ('she glared at us' (Essex)), *he do starve <u>I</u> at nights w' the cold* ('he starves <u>me</u> [of heat] on cold nights' (Wiltshire)) and *I will bring <u>she</u> in, so that you may see <u>she</u> on Vriday* ('I'll bring <u>her</u> in, so that you may see <u>her</u> on Friday' (Devon)). Some modern Bajan speakers also make use of *um* as a third person pronoun. Fields (1995) states that it is specifically used with singular, neuter reference (that is, the equivalent of *it*) although textual citations from the nineteenth century indicate that it could at one time have plural reference (as in *Then you have stolen them said I? No misses, me no tief <u>um</u>, me take <u>um</u>, was the reply '. . . no mistress, I did not steal <u>them</u>, I took <u>them</u>'* (Bayley, 1833; quoted in Fields, 1995: 96). Niles (1980: 116) found evidence of parallel usages in SWDE: *urn in an git tha kay a tha zeller, an let Jack car <u>um</u> up tu barn* ('run in and get the keys to the cellar, and let Jack carry them up to the barn' (Devon)), *Bant <u>um</u> purty little craychers?* ('Aren't <u>they</u> pretty little creatures?' (Devon)).

In terms of verbs, modern Bajan speakers make use of uninflected forms in the expression of past temporal reference. Elworthy (1877; cited in Niles, 1980) noted this in SWDE usage, as in *uur kaech dhu dwuuyz* ('I caught the boys' (Somerset)) and *aaay waive tain yeard u-voaur braksus* ('I wove ten yards before breakfast' (Somerset)). Finally, Niles notes that the use of multiple negative markers occurs in both modern Bajan and SWDE. Examples from the latter include *I never did'n zee no jis bwoys, nor vor mischy, not in all my born days* ('I have never seen such boys, nor such mischief, in all my days' (Somerset)), *you can't never make no sense of women folks of a Saturday* ('you can't ever make sense of women on a Saturday' (Sussex)) and *er idden no better than nobody else* ('she isn't better than anyone else' (Devon)) (Elworthy, 1886: 38; in Niles, 1980: 130).

Theories of creolization such as that of Mufwene, then, offer a plausible framework for reading the changing dynamics of contact situations such as that which obtained in colonies such as Barbados, and for our purposes, for understanding at least one dimension of change that English began to undergo in the EModE period. What is particularly interesting in the context of the latter is the fact that at the same time that norms and ideologies of 'correctness' in language use were explicitly beginning to take shape and to be perceived as important in the evolution of an intellectually progressive and increasingly powerful nation (see Section 5.2), the non-standard everyday use of socially ordinary English speakers was taking root in the colonies; and indeed, laying the foundations for the new directions of change the language would follow. We will look more closely at the development of these ideas of language and nation in the modern period in Chapter 6.

5.6 Study Questions

1. In light of our earlier observation that *thou* and *you* not only marked relationships of status and solidarity but also had the potential to express a range of feeling and emotion, consider the movement between *thou* and *you* forms in *Hamlet*, Act III, Scene IV. How do the switches between *thou* and *you* contribute to the effect of the exchanges between speakers? Useful reading: Brown and Gilman (1960), Barber (1981), Mulholland (1967).

2. *Thou* and *you* have disappeared from everyday English use as indicators of status and solidarity. Have we substituted them with other markers? If so, do the same levels of multi-dimensional usage hold for these new indicators? (You might want to consider here, for example, the use of address terms.)

3. The following excerpt is a translation from the Authorized Version (1611) of the passage in Chapter 4, question (5).

(69) Now Peter sate without in the palace: and a damosell came vnto him, saying, Thou also wast with Iesus of Galilee. (70) But hee denied before them all, saying, I know not what thou seist. (71) And when he was gone out into the porch, another maide saw him, and saide vnto them that were there, This fellow was also with Iesus of Nazareth.

a. What characteristic EModE features are displayed here?

b. Compare the passage to the Middle English version in Chapter 4, question 5. What changes have taken place?

Notes

1. Edward Brathwaite coined this term in relation to creole languages as a positive expression of their role as linguistically and socio-politically native tongues for their speech communities.

2. For discussion of regional and social lects in the EModE period, see Görlach (1991) and Barber (1997).

3. The use of rhymes as evidence for pronunciation needs to be considered in the context of the poet's general practice. For example, if the poet is one who frequently used features such as 'eye rhymes' (that is, words which correspond visually but not phonetically, such as *heard–beard*), then conclusions about pronunciation can be undermined.

4. A school of linguistics based on the theories of Ferdinand de Saussure. See McMahon (1994) for an accessible discussion of Structuralist principles.

5. In indentureship schemes, participants are contracted to work for landowners or leaseholders for a stated period, following which they became entitled to a land grant themselves.

6. See Singh (2000), Sebba (1997), Holm (1988), Mufwene (2001), Chaudenson (2001) for details on creolization.

6 | Modern English, 1700 Onwards

6.1 Introduction

In this final chapter, we look at some of the major phenomena surrounding English usage from the eighteenth century onwards. The developments of the eighteenth century which typically, and justifiably, receive the most attention in histories of English are those which contributed to the standardization of the language. We will pursue this ourselves in Section 6.2, but it is notable that one of the other major developments of this period (and indeed, in some ways, a contributory factor to calls for standardization) was the establishment of English as a significant language throughout the Empire. This global expansion continued throughout the nineteenth century: in the 1800s, for example, English was referred to as the 'language of administration' for a staggering one-third of the world's population (Graddol, 1997: 11), and as a result of the Industrial Revolution (which ultimately triggered a 'global restructuring of work and leisure' (ibid.: 7)), would become established internationally as the language of advertising and consumerism.

By the end of the nineteenth century, the pre-conditions for the rise of English as a global language had been established, with communities of speakers around the world linked by trade and communications technology. Interestingly, this would come to fruition not through the continuation of the British Empire but instead, the rise of America as a world superpower. The impact of Anglo-American culture, as well as of American economic resources, was significantly felt after the Second World War when global financial institutions, such as the International Monetary Fund (IMF) and the World Bank, were established with substantial American involvement. Through such corporations, America became closely involved in post-war reconstruction programmes in Europe, Japan and Asia, inevitably creating in these areas 'cultural, economic and technological dependency' (ibid.: 9). In addition, institutions such as the IMF and World Bank have continued to oversee international economic relations, one dimension of which has been the replacement of centralized markets by free markets in certain countries. This has opened them to the international flow not only of goods but also of culture, including the influence of English.

Other post-war international organizations, such as the United Nations, have also had a significant impact on the spread and use of English, since the majority have adopted it as their primary language. Some 85 per cent of such institutions are estimated to use English in such a manner (Crystal, 1997), and it is very likely that even those who officially list other languages, such as French or German, as their main working language in fact engage in a *de facto* use of English (see Graddol, 1997; Crystal, 1997).

In addition, English is the major language of the global publishing industry. Over 60 countries publish in this language, and Britain (which publishes almost exclusively in English) is far ahead of other countries in the sheer number of titles per year. America, of course, also contributes significantly to the volume of publishing in English, and the long print runs of American publishers, plus the fact that some of their British counterparts adopt their house styles, means that books published in American English receive a wide global circulation. English has also become the international language of scientific and technological publishing, again largely because America has been at the forefront of such research since the First World War. After the Second World War, many countries began publishing such journals exclusively in English, rather than in one of their national languages. Thus, the Mexican medical journal *Archivos de Investigación Médica* eventually became the all-English *Archives of Medical Research*, just as German *Zeitschrift für Tierpsychologie* changed to *Ethology*. Overall, as Graddol (1997: 9) states, publishing statistics clearly show that an enormous amount of intellectual property is being produced in English, a factor which doubtless aids in reinforcing the language's dominant position world-wide.

By the beginning of the twenty-first century, therefore, English is seen by many as a language which is extremely economically and intellectually viable. This seems to be reflected in the growing numbers of people across the globe who are learning English: current estimates hold that approximately 375 million speakers use English as a first language (L1), roughly the same number speak it as a second language (L2), and 750 million are learning it as a foreign language (EFL). These three groups, however, are in a state of continuous flux – many areas which are today classified as primarily having EFL speakers are likely to eventually shift to L2 status and by extension, L2 areas will generate communities of speakers where English is an L1.[1] It is not surprising therefore that linguists such as Graddol (1997) and Jenkins (2003) predict that the future of English will be decided by multi-lingual speakers of the language, an issue that we will return to in Section 6.4.

One of the interesting results of English becoming an important L2 in many areas is the development of new, local varieties influenced by co-existing indigenous languages. This is distinct from the adoption of a standard form for formal and public (typically written) usage (we will return to the question of standard English on a global scale in Section 6.4). As far as the new 'hybrid' varieties go, many are now recognized by their speakers as distinctive forms which reflect a particular national and cultural identity. We will address this in more detail in Section 6.3, which considers the development and characteristics of Singapore Colloquial English.

The global appropriation of English has also raised or highlighted questions to do with national and cultural identity. The language's high global profile, as well as 'its close association with social and economic changes in developing countries' (Graddol, 1997: 39), has led to an assumption of a causative link between its spread and the endangerment and loss of other tongues, as can be seen in the quotations cited below.

(a) Linguistic capital, like all other forms of capital, is unequally distributed in society. The higher the profit to be achieved through knowledge of a particular language, the more it will be viewed as worthy of acquisition. The language of the global village (or McWorld, as some have called it) is English: not to use it is to risk ostracization from the benefits of the global economy.

(Nettle and Romaine, 2000: 30–1)

(b) 'Globalisation is the wave of the future', more than one recent newspaper headline (not to mention the popular received wisdom) has announced, and, to some extent, this is so . . . In our day and age, it is definitely the globalisation of pan-Western culture . . . that is the motor of language shift. And since America-dominated globalisation has become the major economic, technological and cultural thrust of worldwide modernisation and Westernisation, efforts to safeguard threatened languages (and, thorofore, contoxtually weaker languages) must oppose the very strongest processes and powers that the world knows today.

(Fishman, 2001: 6)

Graddol (1997: 39), however, cautiously observes that since English is increasingly becoming *one* of the languages in multilingual settings across the world, it actually functions *within* (and therefore does not necessarily dominate) individual language hierarchies.[2] In India, for example, English co-exists with approximately two hundred other languages (with differing levels of status) and shares the position of official language with Hindi. Other languages such as Telugu, Bengali, Marathi, Tamil, Urdu and Gujrati (to name but a few) are also nationally important in their use in primary education, local government and the media. Thus, while English is invariably a language high up or at the top of such hierarchies, it is not necessarily the only important one. Furthermore, when languages do undergo obsolescence (typically those at the lower levels of the relevant hierarchy), English is not inevitably the direct cause or benefactor. Indeed, in many such cases,

> there will be a shift towards languages higher in the hierarchy. One of the concomitant trends will be increased diversity in the beneficiary languages: regional languages will become more diverse and 'richer' as they acquire more diverse speakers and extend the range of their functions.

(ibid.: 58)

If Graddol is right, then the relationship between English and language endangerment may not be as ubiquitously direct as many of us have assumed. However, we must not forget that in many individual cases, overt governmental policies and grass-roots ideologies which favour the promotion of English have played a significant role in the historical and contemporary decline of some languages – witness, for example, the decline of the Celtic languages in Britain, of Native American languages in North America and of Aboriginal languages in Australia, to name but a few.[3] Constraints of space prevent us from exploring this particular facet of English language history in detail here, but the following sections attempt to exemplify other important developments and issues which have arisen from the use of English in the modern era. Section 6.2 addresses the growth of the prescriptive tradition, beginning with the concerns of eighteenth-century scholars such as Swift, who voiced complaints and suggestions for usage which are still being echoed by modern 'guardians' of the language. Section 6.3 considers the development of Singapore Colloquial English, providing an example of the spread and adoption of English through the continuing expansion of the British Empire in the nineteenth century. Finally, Section 6.4 addresses a twentieth–twenty-first-century concern by outlining some of the main questions which have been asked about the future of English as a world language.

We turn now to the eighteenth century and the rise of prescriptivism.

6.2 The Eighteenth Century and the Rise of the Prescriptive Tradition

On 17 February 2004, Mike Tomlinson, former Chief Inspector of Schools, talked in a radio interview about the possibility of secondary school students taking 'less examinations' in the future (the *Today Programme*, BBC Radio Four). The result was a number of e-mails to the station pointing out that Mr Tomlinson should have known better: the 'correct' adjective in this context, correspondents stated, should have been *fewer*. Some used Mr Tomlinson's 'slip' as a springboard for expressing other concerns about 'incorrect' usage. One complainant, for example, whose 'eyebrows were raised by the grammatical error of Mike Tomlinson', stated that she had been similarly shocked by an earlier assertion by her son, and his English teacher, that the phrase *more fitter* was not wrong, but non-standard English. She concluded that the assessment of such usage as not 'incorrect linguistically but perhaps incorrect socially' was 'codswallop': it was 'incorrect full stop' (posted 17 February 2004).

A week later (21 February 2004), the *Today Programme* spoke to Lynn Truss, author of *Eats, Shoots and Leaves* (2003) and self-confessed stickler for punctuation, about whether their listeners as a body were right to worry about 'bad grammar'. She replied that they were indeed, and that listeners justifiably looked to Radio Four to uphold standards.

Such (sometimes heated) exchanges about language use and upholding standards of correctness are today quite common. The *Today Programme* website, for example, has a message board devoted to the topic 'Language Change' which attracts hundreds of posts, many of them complaints based on the unquestioned assumption that usage *must* follow certain patterns, since to do otherwise is to jeopardize clear and unambiguous communication. This does not necessarily stand up to scrutiny – in the case of Mike Tomlinson, for instance, critics of his use of *less* doubtless understood his meaning, and understood him well enough to suggest the use of *fewer*! Indeed, the fact that many such complaints also either explicitly associate or imply a link between linguistic variation and change, on the one hand, and perceived socio-cultural changes on the other (such as the rise of 'politically correct' methods of teaching, the apparent abandonment of standards of behaviour among certain sectors of society, and so on) suggests a much deeper concern about the threat that change potentially holds for upsetting established ideals of order (see Cameron (1995: Chapter 3) for a detailed discussion of this point).

Such anxieties can be traced back to the eighteenth century, when 'complaints about specific aspects of usage' (Milroy and Milroy, 1999: 27) first began to be aired publicly. The previous century had seen rapid and unsettling socio-political change in which 'England had swung from near absolutism to parliamentary moderation to parliamentary dictatorship to military dictatorship to cautious monarchy to incautious monarchy to limited, constitutional monarchy' (Claiborne, 1990: 167). In addition, by the end of the 1600s, England was no longer just a relatively small, autonomous region but an emerging colonial power that would soon, through the 1707 Act of Union, spearhead the British Empire. Given that territorial acquisition was not always matched with acquiescence from other involved parties, war, economic hostility and political revolt were ever-present threats. It is therefore not surprising that two of the most commonly expressed anxieties in eighteenth-century English writing are about stability and identity: how was the often 'uneasy amalgam' (Crowley, 1996: 68) of disparate peoples to be unified into a stable and glorious empire whose place in history would be assured?

One of the most obvious solutions appears to have presented itself through language. Sheridan (1756: 213; quoted in Crowley, 1996: 68), for example, stated that nothing could bring about union more effectively than the 'universality of one common language' and conversely, nothing could preserve 'odious distinctions between subjects of the same King' like linguistic differences (1762: 206; in ibid.: 69). Given the balance of political power within Britain, the 'common language' was inevitably English; in particular, the standard form which had begun to emerge in the previous century (see Chapter 5). The job of the eighteenth-century intelligentsia concerned with language, then, was to perfect this standard form, fix it in guides for usage (for example, dictionaries, spelling guides and grammars) and overall, create a valued linguistic commodity that would represent (and perhaps even help achieve) a unified empire and a civilization as worthy of admiration as those of ancient Rome and Greece.

The eighteenth century, therefore, was 'fascinated by language' and as a result:

> The English language, as perhaps never before, became subject to various kinds of scrutiny . . . One pamphlet purporting to tell the truth about the history of the English language was followed by another denouncing it as nonsense . . . Academies of the language were suggested and rejected. Grammar books describing themselves as comprehensive were ridiculed for their limited scope . . . elocution texts . . . attacked each other viciously on grounds which ranged from a tendency to undermine the political unity of the kingdom, to deliberate attempts to corrupt the morality of women. It was, in all its various ways, a great feast upon language.

(ibid.: 54)

And the skeleton at the feast was a very real anxiety about linguistic mutability, and what it could signal or catalyse socially.

One of the best-known texts putting forward the case for continuing standardization in the eighteenth century is Jonathan Swift's *Proposal for*

Correcting, Improving and Ascertaining the English Tongue (1712), composed in letter form to the Earl of Oxford and Mortimer (also then Prime Minister). It provides an excellent guide to understanding the individual points of concern which underlay the general contemporary worry about the perceived instability of English, and therefore serves as a useful illustration of the issues which dominated arguments for standardization.

It would seem that for Swift, the state of English was a matter of extreme importance: as Crowley (1996: 59) points out, it is the only piece of prose writing he ever put his name to. He also put 'correcting, improving' and fixing English on a par with other undertakings that would bring profit and glory to the empire. For example, Swift states in his opening paragraph that if the Earl were to support attempts to address the 'Grievance' outlined in the *Proposal*, then it would constitute

> [hls] own Work as much as that of paying the *Nation's Debts*, or opening a Trade into the *South Sea*; and though not of such immediate Benefit as either of these, or any other of Your glorious Actions, yet perhaps, in future Ages, not less to Your Honour.

> (Swift, 1712· 6–7)

Such a link is interesting in its implication that the state of a language is as much an index of a nation's fortune as is its economic prosperity. Indeed, one of the underlying assumptions of the *Proposal* appears to be that language and nation are inextricably tied together, so that the 'historical vicissitudes of a language' can be used 'as a way of reading the [shifting] moral and political fortunes of its speakers' (Crowley, 1996: 63). Thus, Swift appears to have accepted that concomitant social and linguistic change was inevitable, but believed that perfecting and fixing one form of English (namely that already in widespread written use) as well as regulating any change it would undergo, was a very real and significant possibility.

Swift established these ideas for English, and gave them authority, by framing his argument in relation to the examples provided by ancient civilizations, in particular that of Rome. The textual record for Latin, he stated, showed that the language had 'suffered perpetual Changes' during the centuries of its everyday use, so much so that the language 'Three hundred years before *Tully*, was as unintelligible in his Time, as the *English* and *French* of the same Period are now' (Swift, 1712: 11–12). Such change occurred for a number of reasons, the most notable (and perhaps inevitable) of which were seeded in social and moral decline. This, he hypothesized, had been the main cause of the 'corruption' of Latin, which occurred because of socio-political changes such as 'the Change of their [Romans'] Government into a Tyranny, which ruined the Study of Eloquence', the migration of workers from Gaul, Spain, Germany and Asia into Rome, the 'Introduction of forein Luxury, with forein Terms to express it', and invasions from hostile tribes (ibid.: 12).

Yet the Romans had managed to refine and fix a 'perfect' form of Latin before such 'decline' took hold and as such, had managed to preserve records of a glorious time in a medium fit to carry them. As Swift (ibid.: 13) wrote, 'The *Roman* Language arrived at great Perfection before it began to decay' (see Schleicher's assumption re morphological typological change; Chapter 1, Section 1.5), which was fortuitous not only for Roman historians themselves, but also for chroniclers in other territories such as England, who had adopted this standardized Latin as a language of record:

> As barbarous and ignorant as we were in former Centuries, there was more effectual Care taken by our Ancestors, to preserve the Memory of Times and Persons, than we find in this Age of Learning and Politeness, as we are please to call it. The . . . *Latin* of the *Monks* is still very intelligible; whereas, had their Records been delivered only in the vulgar Tongue [English], so barren and so barbarous, so subject to continual succeeding Changes, they could not now be understood, unless by Antiquarians who made it their Study to expound them.

> (Swift, 1712: 39)

Overall, Swift narrated a history of Latin in which the ideologies and socio-political fate of its speakers were simultaneously and implicitly constructed (Crowley, 1996: 63–4). It is therefore unsurprising that when Swift turned 'his attention to the English language his reading of its history [became] automatically a construction of the history of the English nation and people' (ibid.: 64). It is also unsurprising that the history of Latin in the *Proposal* reads as a salutary warning to the emerging British Empire: as Rome and Latin had fallen, so too could Britain and English. A corrected, improved and ascertained English was therefore imperative, not only as a contemporary marker of an admirable civilization but also as a medium that would preserve it for posterity.

Swift's 'Grievance' about English is stated early in the *Proposal:*

> our Language is extremely imperfect; . . . its daily Improvements are by no means in proportion to its daily Corruptions; and the Pretenders to polish and refine it, have chiefly multiplied Abuses and Absurdities; and, that in many Instances, it offends against every Part of Grammar.

> (Swift, 1712: 8)

In addition, it is 'less refined' than the contemporary tongues 'of *Italy*, *Spain*, or *France*' (ibid.). For Swift, its unpolished nature was due to factors which subsumed both biological and cultural predisposition. In terms of the former, Swift used a horticultural analogy to argue that just as the 'ill Climate' of Britain made it difficult to produce the 'nobler kinds of Fruit', so too did 'the same Defect of Heat [give] a Fierceness to our Natures, [and] may contribute to that Roughness of our Language, which bears some Analogy to the harsh Fruit of colder Countries' (ibid.: 26). Thus, despite 'all the real good Qualities of our Country', Swift felt that 'we are naturally not very Polite'[4] (ibid.: 24) and that certain changes or 'corruptions' in English were symptomatic of an innate 'tendency to lapse into the Barbarity of those *Northern* Nations from whom we are descended' and whose languages inevitably 'labour all under the same defect' (ibid.: 25). However, the difference between barbarity and civilization was the determination to struggle against such 'natural Disadvantages' (ibid.: 26). England and English may have been born of 'northern savagery', but they were certainly no longer confined by it, or at least, should not have been. England had grown beyond its humble, 'unrefined' beginnings and come to play a significant role in a new, potentially vast and profitable empire. As society moved from primitive to polished, it was only fitting that its language also do the same, and not be allowed to 'relapse'.

Interestingly, Swift argued that many of those who were in a position to influence the 'civilizing' of English in fact often did the very opposite, usually as a result of blindly following fashionable, but in his eyes tasteless, trends. This 'corrupting' of English by 'false Refinements', Swift believed, had begun in earnest after the rebellion of 1642, which had brought the golden age of Elizabethan English civilization, and of course of the English language, to an end. The conservative Swift associated anti-royalist feeling and the later, more permissive atmosphere of Restoration England with moral, and of course linguistic, decline:

> From that Great Rebellion to this present Time, I am apt to doubt whether the Corruptions in our Language have not, at least, equalled the Refinements of it . . . During the usurpation, such an Infusion of Enthusiastick jargon prevailed in every writing, as was not shaken off in many years after. To this succeeded that Licentiousness which entered with the *Restoration*, and from infecting our Religion and Morals, fell to corrupt our Language.

> (ibid.: 16–17)

Products of the tarnished years of the Restoration received the brunt of complaint in the *Proposal*; Swift (ibid.: 27) railed against the cultural and linguistic influence of 'illiterate Court-fops, half-witted Poets, and University Boys'; the 'Pretenders' to the language's polishing but in reality the architects of its 'Absurdities'. The 'Court-fops' were supporters of Charles the Second 'who had followed Him in His Banishment . . . or young men who had been educated in the same company' and who displayed affectation in both their general behaviour and language, so much so that 'the *Court*, which used to be the Standard of Propriety and Correctness of Speech, was then, and, I think, hath ever since continued the worst School in *England* for that Accomplishment' (ibid.: 18). The effect of their influence, Swift said, could be seen in contemporary plays and literary writing, which were riddled with 'affected Phrases, and new, conceited Words' – the 'Produce only of Ignorance and Caprice' (ibid.: 19).

Restoration poets had also contributed significantly to 'the spoiling of the *English* Tongue' (ibid.: 20) because they

> introduced that barbarous Custom of abbreviating Words, to fit them to the Measure of their Verses; and this they have frequently done, so very injudiciously, as to form such harsh unharmonious Sounds, that none but a Northern ear could endure: They have joined the most obdurate Consonants without one intervening Vowel, only to shorten a Syllable . . . [as in] *Drudg'd, Disturb'd, Rebuk't, Fledg'd*, and a thousand others.

> (ibid.: 20–1)

Eventually this custom, which started life under the guise of 'Poetical License', became a 'Choice' – such poets alleged that 'Words pronounced at length, sounded faint and languid'. It also surfaced in prose, where such 'Manglings and Abbreviations' became commonplace.

'University-boys', who 'read Trash' but believed that because of their position and status they 'know the World', shared in the blame as well, since they 'reckon all their Errors for Accomplishments, borrow the newest Sett of Phrases, and if they take a Pen into their Hands, all the odd Words they have picked up in a Coffee-House, or a Gaming Ordinary, are produced as Flowers of Style' (ibid.: 23). Other followers of fashion included 'Dunces of Figure' 'who had Credit enough to give Rise to some new Word, and propagate it in most Conversations, though it had neither Humor, nor Significancy' (ibid.: 19). If the new usage 'struck the present Taste':

> it was soon transferred into the Plays and current Scribbles of the Week, and became an Addition to our Language; while the Men of Wit and Learning, instead of early obviating such Corruptions, were too often seduced to imitate and comply with them.

> (ibid.: 19–20)

Swift (ibid.: 30–1) argued that all such misguided attempts at refinement had also influenced Latin, when 'the Romans . . . began to quit their *Simplicity* of Style for affected Refinements . . . which ended by degrees in many Barbarities, even before the *Goths* had invaded *Italy*'. However, Rome's example in 'perfecting' Latin before it was too late had not been followed for English – for Swift, a matter that necessitated speedy redress, even if 'decay' did not seem imminent. Nearly all of Swift's examples and analogies in the *Proposal* centre around the inevitability of change and transience: the tensions between relapses into barbarity and progress into civilization are in constant flux, people take to heart fashions of the moment and abandon them the next day, empires grow and then fall away into distant memory. The only chance of immortality therefore lay in the record that could be left, and the success of that depended hugely on the medium in which it was written.

The need for fixity, and desire for posterity, in a sea of change was a point Swift made repeatedly in the *Proposal*, and appears to have been his strongest argument for standardization. Thus he postulated that if English

> were once refined to a certain Standard, perhaps there might be Ways found out to fix it for ever; or at least till we are invaded and made a Conquest by some other State; and even then our best Writings might probably be preserved with Care, and grow into Esteem, and the Authors have a Chance of Immortality.

> (ibid.: 13–14)

The desirability of immortality for authors is re-stated later in the *Proposal* in the suggestion that 'The Fame of our Writers is usually confined to these two Islands, and it is hard it should be limited in *Time*, as much as *Place*' (ibid.: 31).[5] However, it was not just authors who would benefit from a fixed standard but also the historical record of the 'great and good'. Swift (ibid.: 37) cunningly argued that unless a form of English was polished and fixed, there would be no suitable medium for accurately chronicling the achievements of the current sovereign, Queen Anne. It was the duty of the Prime Minister therefore 'to give order for inspecting our Language' and ensure that it was fit to record the 'Glory' of 'so great and good a Princess' in 'Words more durable than Brass', so that 'our Posterity may read a thousand Years hence, with Pleasure as well as Admiration' (ibid.: 36–7). To ensure that his point struck home, Swift pointed out too that the Earl's reputation to future generations was also in danger if a standard was not fixed:

> about two hundred Years hence, some painful Compiler, who will be at the trouble of studying the Old Language, may inform the World, that in the Reign of QUEEN ANNE, Robert Earl of Oxford, a very wise and excellent Man, was made *High Treasurer*, and saved his Country, which in those Days was almost ruined by a *Foreign War*, and a *Domestick Faction*. Thus much he may be able to pick out, and willingly transfer into his new History, but the rest of Your

Character . . . and the particular Account of the great Things done under Your Ministry, for which You are already so celebrated in most Parts of *Europe*, will probably be dropt, on account of the antiquated Style and Manner they are delivered in.

(ibid.: 38–9, 40)

In addition, the lack of a standard did not only affect the historical chronicle, but would also limit the chronicler himself. What could prove more of a disincentive to a historian than the fact that his very vocation would come to naught? As Swift (ibid.: 41) wrote:

How then shall any Man who hath a Genius for History, equal to the best of the Ancients, be able to undertake such a Work with Spirit and Cheerfulness, when he considers, that he will be read with Pleasure but a very few Years, and in an Age or two shall hardly be understood without an Interpreter?

Complete standardization, therefore, was a must: what he had 'most at Heart' was 'that some Method should be thought on for *ascertaining* and *fixing* our Language for ever, after such Alterations are made in it as shall be thought requisite' (ibid.: 30). Such an aim was not an impossibility: the Romans, Greeks and Chinese had created stable written forms of their respective languages,[6] and the Italians and French (the latter of whom Swift explicitly mentions) had set up Academies towards this end. Swift therefore proposed the setting up of a regulatory body 'in order to reform our Language'; a 'Society' in which 'a free judicious Choice be made of such Persons, as are generally allowed to be qualified for such a Work, without any regard to Quality, Party or Profession' (ibid.: 28).

This Society, Swift (ibid.: 29) hypothesized, could take as their model the work of the French Academy, 'to imitate where these have proceeded right, and to avoid their Mistakes'. In particular, there were a few areas which Swift (ibid.: 29–30) felt they should turn their attention to.

Besides the grammar-part, wherein we are allowed to be very defective, they will observe many gross Improprieties, which however authorised by Practice, and grown familiar, ought to be discarded. They will find many Words that deserve to be utterly thrown out of our Language, many more to be corrected; and perhaps not a few, long since antiquated, which ought to be restored, on account of their Energy and Sound.

It is worth noting that although Swift saw a standard as a means of uniting English users through time and space, he did not assume that it would remain unchanged. He stated:

but where I say, that I would have our Language, after it is duly correct, always to last; I do not mean that it should never be enlarged: Provided, that no Word which a Society shall give a Sanction to, be afterwards antiquated and exploded, that they may have liberty to receive whatever new ones they shall find occasion for.

(ibid.: 33)

Even Latin and Greek, he argued, had undergone 'enlargements' as they came to be used in different domains. Thus, his disapproving statements about change ('I see no absolute Necessity why any Language would be perpetually changing' (ibid.: 15) and 'I am of the Opinion, that it is better a Language should not be wholly perfect, than it should be perpetually changing' (ibid.: 30)) seem to be about *unregulated* change, such as the unchecked 'false refinements' of fops and pedants and the natural 'barbarities' of the everyday English user which brought 'corruption'. Once a standard had been fixed, however, members of the Society, with their authority on language matters, could halt any potential 'backsliding' into 'absurdities' and 'imperfections'. Swift (ibid.: 42–3) concluded his proposal to the Earl with words of 'Caution, Advice or Reproach': 'if Genius and Learning be not encouraged under Your Lordship's Administration, you are the most inexcusable person alive. All Your other Virtues, My Lord, will be defective without this.'

Baugh and Cable (2002: 268) state that the publication of Swift's *Proposal* was in fact not the beginning but 'the culmination of the movement for an English Academy'. Scholars and authors such as Dryden, Evelyn and Defoe had been proponents of the idea in the late seventeenth century and by the time Swift's *Proposal* was made public, it was unlikely to have been seen as an unusual one. The impact of the *Proposal*, however, was that 'it came from one whose judgement carried more weight than that of anyone else at the beginning of the eighteenth century who might have brought it forward' (ibid.: 268). Where it failed, perhaps, was in the fact that it was viewed by many as a divisive political document which if carried out could represent a threat to British autonomy. As Crowley (1996: 61) points out, Swift made his Tory political leanings clear: he addressed the *Proposal* to the Tory Prime Minister and directly attacked the opposing Whigs in his desultory comment about the Earl saving the country from ruin by the impact of a 'domestic faction' (see above). Swift's suggestion that the Académie Française serve as a model also caused outrage amongst the Protestant Whigs – the French Academy had been instituted by the aristocratic Catholic Cardinal Richlieu. Oldmixon, Swift's fiercest Whig critic, wrote that the Tory agenda in this regard was highly suspect:

> [they would] not only force their principles upon us, but their language, wherein they endeavour to ape their good friends the French, who . . . have been attempting to make their Tongue as Imperious as their Power . . . imposed upon us already [is] the Court Stile of France, and their Politicks would soon come after it.

> (Oldmixon, 1712: 2, 30; quoted in Crowley, 1996: 61)

The call for an academy would resurface later in the 1750s, sometimes with much more explicitly authoritarian overtones. The author George Harris, for instance, believed that a successful academy should be backed by legislation and severe penalties for those who did not comply with its regulations. It seems, however, that proposals such as Swift's and Harris' alike, despite the difference in approach, simply did not accord with the dominant, contemporary ideology that the English were 'free-thinking, independent, able to engage in rational discussion in order to produce a consensus, and by dint of the fact that they consented, able to obey laws in good faith' (Crowley, 1996: 62). To be subject to the absolutist regulations of an academy, therefore, was anathema.

Despite the failed attempts at an academy, the perceived need and reasons for the standardization of English remained. Sheridan, for example, reiterated Swift's concerns about transience, the potential inaccuracy of the historical record, and the problem of an unfixed medium for historians:

> How many British heroes and worthies have been lost to us; how have their minds perished like their bodies . . . England has never wanted proper subjects, but historians; and historians will not be found 'till our language be brought to a fixed state and some prospect of duration be given to their works.

> (Sheridan, 1756: ix; in Crowley, 1996: 66)

He also voiced these concerns for authors: 'Suffer not our Shakespeare, and our Milton, to become two or three centuries hence what Chaucer is at present' (ibid.).

A major anxiety in the later eighteenth century which Sheridan also addressed in his support for standardization (both written and spoken) was the need for a unified identity within the British empire. It was clear, for example, that the recently united nation actually comprised a potentially volatile mix of peoples with different cultures, languages and world-views. Sheridan expressed concern that the Scots, Welsh and Irish 'spoke in tongues different from the English' and were 'far from being firmly united with them in inclination'. In addition, this linguistic problem was compounded by the fact that English speakers themselves were also divided by usage: 'persons born and bred in different and distant shires, could scarcely any more understand each others speech than they could that of a foreigner' (Sheridan, 1756: 214; in Crowley, 1996: 68). Successful integration, therefore, could be achieved through the propagation of an accepted standard which would create linguistic uniformity 'throughout Scotland, Wales and Ireland, as well as through the several counties of England' (Sheridan, 1762: 206; in Crowley, 1996: 68–9).

How, though, was the standardization effort to be furthered, especially without the focused authority and direction of an academy? The answer lay in the influence of the 'Learned and Polite' individuals on whose behalf Swift had written his proposal. These members of the gentry, it was believed, were the repositories of the 'proper language', and so pronouncements on language use with their stamp of authority would therefore have been extremely influential.[7]

The main efforts from influential individuals were concentrated on producing a dictionary and grammar for the standard. Samuel Johnson produced A Dictionary of the English Language in 1755 – an immensely popular work at the time and in many ways the template for later lexicographical publication in its inclusion of a relatively wide range of vocabulary (as opposed to the limited hard-word dictionaries of the Early Modern period), the prescription of a standard, fixed spelling and pronunciation for each word, plus the citation of a range of meanings as well as illustrations of use. The Dictionary was therefore both descriptive and prescriptive: it described English usage, but only that which was deemed acceptable by the lexicographer. The regulating role of an academy therefore became appropriated by Johnson, who stated in the Dictionary's Preface that his task was not only one of recording, but also of ascertaining and correcting:

> Every language has its anomalies, which, though inconvenient, and in themselves unnecessary, must be tolerated among the imperfections of human things, and which require only to be

registred, that they may not be increased, and ascertained, that they may not be confounded: but every language has likewise its improprieties and absurdities, which it is the duty of every lexicographer to correct or proscribe.

(Baugh and Cable, 2002: 272)

In the same vein and in an echo of the language of Swift's *Proposal*, he had earlier written in a paper published in the *Rambler* that in the *Dictionary* he had 'laboured to refine our language to grammatical purity, and to clear it from colloquial barbarisms, licentious idioms, and irregular combinations' (quoted in Baugh and Cable, 2002: 272–3). Indeed, it seems that many of Johnson's contemporaries believed that he had achieved one of the defining jobs of the English academy that never was: Chesterfield stated that he had supplied a 'lawful standard . . . for those who might choose to speak and write it grammatically and correctly'; Sheridan declared that the *Dictionary* should be considered the 'corner stone' of standard English and Boswell opined that Johnson had 'conferred stability on the language of his country' (quoted in Baugh and Cable, 2002: 273–4).

The production of guidelines for standardized grammatical usage was also a concern for eighteenth-century scholars and authors such as Dryden, Priestley, Campbell, Lowth and of course, Johnson. This was an area in which English was felt, in the words of Swift, to be extremely 'defective' and 'imperfect'. The aims of these and other eighteenth-century grammarians, therefore, were to 'correct' perceived errors, regulate on matters of usage (especially in situations where alternatives existed) and codify their decisions in rule form: a job, in effect, of prescription and proscription. This was achieved primarily through reference to 'reason, etymology, and the example of Latin and Greek' (ibid.: 280). Reason typically meant the invocation of analogical principle. Thus, Campbell (1776), for example, stated that if the forms *backwards* and *forwards* were 'preferable to backward* and *forward*, then by analogy, *afterwards* and *homewards* should be preferred to *afterward* and *homeward*' (quoted in Baugh and Cable, 2002: 281). Etymology often played a part in settling usage when it 'plainly [pointed] to a signification different from that which the word commonly bears'. In such cases, it was felt that 'propriety and simplicity both require its dismission' (Campbell, 1776; quoted in ibid.: 281). An example of this could be seen in the verb *to unloose*, which meant, as it does now among those who still use it, 'to loosen'. However, etymology suggests that its literal meaning should be 'to not loose', in other words 'to tighten', just as *to untie* means 'to not tie' or 'to loosen'. The 'unetymological use' of *unloose*, then, was an unnecessary 'imperfection': 'To what purpose', Campbell demanded, was it to 'retain a term, without any necessity, in a signification the reverse of which its etymology manifestly suggests?' (quoted in Baugh and Cable, 2002: 282).

Finally, the example of classical languages such as Latin was sometimes cited as an authority for English usage. This led to the formation of prescriptive rules such as not splitting the infinitive verb from its preposition (as in the proscribed *why are we told to never split infinitives?* or *to boldly go where no man has been before*). However, it seems that this was not a frequent recourse for the grammarians, who came to generally agree that 'there were more disadvantages than advantages in trying to fit English into the pattern of Latin grammar' (Baugh and Cable, 2002: 282).

The above discussion doubtless implies that the grammarians made objective, rational decisions in correcting and improving various aspects of usage. What we must not lose sight of, however, is the fact that judgements on what constituted 'imperfection' and 'corruption' were subjective and often based on negative perceptions of certain groups of users: note, for example, that Swift complained explicitly about the adverse effect of 'illiterate Court-fops and half-witted poets' and less about usages which may have been problematic for communication (it is very unlikely that the use of *rebuk't* rather than *rebukéd*, for instance, caused intelligibility issues for speakers). The same subjectivity and social appraisal applied to the decisions made by the later grammarians. Webster, for example, thought that the verb *was* should be used with the second person singular pronoun (as in *you was*) but Lowth and Priestley argued for *were*, which has survived into the modern standard. Similarly, Webster argued for constructions such as *I don't like his doing that*, while Harris and Lowth advocated *I don't like him doing that*. On the whole, such points of dispute revolved around usages which were in fact all perfectly serviceable in linguistic terms. The final decisions on correctness, Milroy and Milroy (1999: 14–15) point out, were based less on considerations of 'logic, effectiveness, elegance or anything else' than on 'the observed usage of the "best people" at that time. The choice of [forms] was probably *socially* motivated.'

Interestingly, the subjective and at times arbitrary nature of the decisions of the eighteenth-century grammarians has been largely erased from the dominant, public narrative of standard English. Instead, what have survived are a number of prescriptions and proscriptions primarily for written usage, such as the preference for *different from*, rather than *different to* or *different than*; the proscription of nominative pronouns in phrases such as *between you and I* and their prescription in subject complements, as in *It is I* (versus *it is me*); the use of adjectives in the comparative degree for only two things (as in *she is the prettier of the two sisters*); and the condemnation of more than one negative marker in an utterance. These were successfully propagated in the eighteenth century by texts such as Lowth's *Short Introduction to English Grammar* (1762) and James Buchanan's *The British Grammar* (1762); [8] and many continue to be used in the written medium today, and to serve as markers of 'correct' and 'proper' usage.

The standardization efforts of the eighteenth century appear to have been largely successful in codifying a set of conventions for written usage. Milroy and Milroy (1999: 29) argue, however, that the real success of the prescriptive grammarians lay in their propagation of the ideology of standardization, which still has currency today. In other words, since the eighteenth century, people have come to believe that a perfect and immutable form of the language exists; reflected in the 'best' writing and the 'best' speech of the 'best' of English users (whoever they may be at any one point), and embodied in guides such as dictionaries and teaching materials. Like the e-mail complainant cited at the beginning of this section, many of us believe that there are ways in which English 'has to be', and others in which its usage is simply 'incorrect full stop'. Yet that perfect entity is more of an abstraction than a tangible linguistic form: 'What Standard English actually is thought to be depends on acceptance (mainly by the most influential people) of a common core of [written] linguistic conventions, and a good deal of fuzziness remains around the edges' (Milroy and Milroy, 1999: 22). Interestingly, this fuzziness may well be on the increase as the mechanisms which once maintained these conventions are replaced by ones which favour 'destandardization'. Graddol (1997: 56) argues for example that a significant measure of the stability once conferred by print has now been lost by the increase in electronic, in particular computer-mediated, communication which is continuously blurring the distinction between spoken and written forms of the language. Broadcasting, which became an important 'gatekeeper' of standard forms in the twentieth century, has also since lost a great deal of its influence, as 'the patterns of fragmentation and localisation, which are significant trends in satellite broadcasting, means that television is no longer able to serve such a function'. In addition, cultural trends which encourage 'the use of informal and more conversational style, a greater tolerance of diversity and individual style, and a lessening deference to authority' are also taking hold (ibid.). Such developments suggest that in native English-speaking areas like Britain, the influence of the institutions that supported both the ideology of a standard form as well as the use of the conventions typically held as markers of a standard form, is weakening. At the same time, however, new standard forms of the language are emerging elsewhere, in countries where English has become an important L2. We will return to this point in Section 6.4.

Although 'destandardization' may be occurring, it is not likely that (British) standard English will disappear overnight. Its construction as a valuable and tangible commodity has been well entrenched since the eighteenth century, when its projected worth lay in its potential to guarantee historical immortality, to act as an 'agent of unification for the nation' and also as a form in which the nation's superiority was made manifest. In the twentieth century, standard English has been promoted as a guarantor of social and economic success (see, for example, the arguments of Honey, 1997). Thus, although Swift's dream of a fixed, 'perfect' and immortal form of English has never truly been realized, his ideology seems alive and well. And his *Proposal*, he might be pleased to know, has survived for over two centuries in that most imperfect of tongues.

6.3 Nineteenth-Century Contact and Change: The Case of Singlish

As stated in Section 6.1, the nineteenth century saw the continued expansion of the British Empire. English speakers settled in Hawai'i and in southern hemisphere territories such as Australia, New Zealand and South Africa, as well as South Atlantic Islands such as St Helena, Tristan de Cunha and the Falklands. Pitcairn Island and Norfolk Island in the Pacific also became home to anglophone colonies, as did areas of Panama and Costa Rica in the Atlantic. In the Caribbean, many islands which had initially been colonized by the French (such as St Lucia, Trinidad and Dominica) gave way to British settlement and began a 'slow process of becoming anglophone to different degrees' (Trudgill, 2002: 30). Namibia, Botswana, Zimbabwe and Kenya also saw the establishment of British English-speaking colonies.

Although the patterns of British colonization in the nineteenth century varied from territory to territory, they were in general characterized by ideologies somewhat different from those which had governed earlier stages of expansion. Kandiah (1998: 27) maintains for example that the War of American Independence (1775–1783) taught Britain some harsh lessons about the 'follies of the mercantilist imperialism which had created America'; in particular, the notion that colonies existed for the sole purpose of enriching the mother country. The nineteenth-century wave of expansion, on the other hand, 'gave expression to what was called the New Imperialism':

> The Agrarian and Industrial Revolutions had taken place in Britain in the late eighteenth century and the concern now was to service the rapidly growing industries of the burgeoning capitalist economy. There was a need to find new sources of raw materials, markets for the goods that the factories were producing in increasing quantities and places for profitable ventures in which surplus capital could be invested.

> (ibid.)

In this perspective, displacement of indigenous peoples and settlement by colonists were not primary concerns. The main aim instead was to either create new, or infiltrate already extant and lucrative, trading routes and control them. When these territories became part of the British empire, therefore, they became home not to waves of British migrants but instead to relatively small numbers of British (English-speaking) administrators. In most cases, this group generally did not learn the native languages of the populace (although some may well have done on an individual basis), but importantly, were also not interested in linguistic genocide: Kandiah (ibid.: 28) states that given the primary aims of the 'second British empire', the multi-lingual and multi-cultural character of these territories was generally left alone. The resultant linguistic gap between administrators and the general populace, however, was filled by 'go-betweens': indigenous 'intermediate-level administrators' who learnt enough English to be able to 'maintain records, to help effectuate directives, implement decisions and so on' (ibid.: 29). Native recruits for these 'intermediate' positions typically came from the higher native social echelons (for example, from families of native chieftains, or from relatively wealthy families). Eventually, the empire would see this stratum as a useful basis for creating an 'influential, western-oriented intelligentsia as an aid to stabilizing colonial rule' (de Souza, 1960; quoted in Kandiah, 1998: 29) as expressed in Macaulay's (1835) famous Minute on education in India: the need was to form a 'class of interpreters between us and the millions we govern – a class of persons, Indian in blood and colour, but English in taste, in opinions, in morals and in intellect'.

The education system in these territories therefore came to play a crucial role in the acquisition of English. The nineteenth century saw the establishment of English-medium and British curriculum schools, at both primary and secondary (and sometimes tertiary) levels, in many territories. On the whole, these schools provided 'an emerging élite with ready access to the language . . . [and] kept [standard British English] consistently in the forefront of its use and development' (Kandiah, 1998: 30). Given that the acquisition of English was initially achieved through the formal medium of the school, and with specific purposes in mind, it is not surprising that it at first entered each territory's language hierarchy specifically as one for official and formal use. However, given the fact that the language was taught in the context of a curriculum which emphasized British economic, intellectual and cultural superiority, it is equally unsurprising that elite native bilinguals would eventually extend the functions of English to other domains, including the home. Thus, in general:

> Many members of the élite began to acquire the language, often alongside another language, from their parents and, also, through everyday exchanges with people in important spheres of their daily lives. There were, of course, others who belonged to non-English-using homes and came, therefore, to acquire it outside of their homes. But they, too, tended to 'pick it up', not just in the classroom but, in addition, in normal, everyday transactions. These included those which took place in school outside the classroom.
>
> (ibid.: 32)

Once English was extended out of its original domains and restrictions of use, and 'picked up' by non-native speakers, it also inevitably began to be influenced by the wider multi-linguistic setting. As we will see in the following discussion, these are the patterns that governed the arrival of English to Singapore and its adaptation in this new environment.

Singapore is a small island nation at the tip of the Malay Peninsula – a strategic location which historically made it an important trading point and a coveted acquisition by various powers, including India and Siam (modern Thailand). In the fifteenth century, Iskandar Shah, a prince of Palembang (Indonesia), created the Malacca Sultanate – a dynasty which incorporated Singapore – and encouraged settlement from China. By the time European colonization began in the sixteenth century (Malacca was taken in 1511 by the Portuguese), the Peninsula and Singapore were already multicultural and of course, multilingual.

The Portuguese foothold in Malacca was prised away in 1641 by the Dutch, who managed to hold on to it until 1795, when it was captured in turn by the British. The latter were interested not only in the area's economic importance but also in its location, which made it a useful pit stop and haven for the East India Company merchant fleet. In 1818, Lord Hastings, Governor General of India, authorized Sir Stamford Raffles, Lieutenant-Governor of Bencoolen, to establish a trading post at the southern tip of the Malay peninsula. In 1819, Raffles settled on doing just that in Singapore. A formal treaty was effected in that year between the East India Company and Sultan Hussein of Johor, the ruler of Singapore (with the approval of the Temenggong – the highest stratum of officials).

Migration from British colonies such as India and Sri Lanka began almost immediately, accompanied by a further influx from southern parts of China. By 1820, Singapore had become an extremely lucrative settlement and trading post; and the British sought to quickly formalize its status as a colony. In 1824, a treaty with Sultan Hussein ceded the island to the British in return for financial recompense and in 1826, Singapore, Malacca and another British-established and controlled trading post, Penang, were grouped together for the purposes of administration as the Straits Settlements.

In addition to the indigenous languages that Indian, Sri Lankan and Chinese migrants took to Singapore during this period, certain settlers such as Eurasians (primarily from India and Sri Lanka) sometimes also spoke English. Added to this linguistic mix were the Portuguese creole used by Eurasian migrants from Malacca, the variety of Malay used by the Straits Chinese, (descendants of earlier Chinese settlers in Malacca), as well as the native English of migrants from Britain and America (many of whom arrived as part of Methodist missions). Gupta (1998b: 108) maintains that Singapore also received numbers of Armenians and Jews, who had 'operated in British territories for generations' and had come from Baghdad via India. Many were therefore familiar with English and took on roles as teachers, translators and clerical staff in Singapore. As such, they were the initial 'brokers' (Gupta's term) in the contact between non-English-speaking subjects and English-speaking administrators, and may therefore have had significant influence on the development of English in Singapore. Overall, by the 1950s (the last years of the colonial era) 33 mother tongue groups were settled in Singapore, 20 of which had over a thousand native speakers (Bokhorst-Heng, 1998: 288).

During the early years of British colonization, education in the Straits Settlements had been carried out mainly through missions and charitable organizations. After 1867 (when Singapore was made a Crown Colony), the British government allowed each ethnic community to establish their own schools. English-medium schools (with British-centric curricula) were therefore set up for European children, as well as 'for the sons of those few natives willing and able to afford it' (Gupta, 1998b: 110). These schools, which attracted children from Straits Chinese as well as English-speaking Eurasian, Armenian and Jewish homes, received a high proportion of government funding and were the only ones which led to higher education opportunities and jobs in the public sector. As Bokhorst-Heng (1998: 289) states, 'English education very quickly developed into élite education' and the separatist policies of the schools inevitably created a class of Asian-language educated whose job prospects outside of unskilled labour were limited, and another of 'the English-educated who formed the aristocratic élite and middle class'.

True to their form and purpose, the English-medium schools officially propagated standard forms of the language in the classroom, although Gupta (1998b: 111) reminds us that since staff were drawn from a mixed pool of *Europeans* (meaning 'White'; hence referring to teachers from Britain, the USA and Australia) and *natives* ('non-European'/'non-White'; typically referring to teachers from Ceylon and India, many of whom were Eurasian), children would have been exposed to the various 'Englishes' not only of their peers but also of their instructors. However, the schools did not provide a meeting point just for different forms and varieties of English. Many of the staff and students also made use of a contact variety of Malay known as *Bazaar Malay*, which 'Eurasians, Europeans, Indians, Jews and Straits Chinese all would to some extent be able to speak' (ibid.: 109). In addition, Straits Chinese also made use of another contact Malay: *Baba Malay*, which carried influences from Hokkien as well as from Bazaar Malay. It is therefore very likely that the beginnings of Colloquial Singapore English (CSE) or Singlish, which displays features and usages very similar to those in these two contact varieties of Malay, are rooted in the informal contact situations of the nineteenth-century English-medium playground and school.

Gupta (1998b: 114–16) argues, however, that CSE really began to take hold in the first decade of the twentieth century, when large numbers of native Hokkien- and Cantonese-speaking children began to attend English-medium schools. She suggests that while these new pupils learnt (with varying levels of proficiency) standard models of English in the schoolroom, they would also have picked up the CSE of their peers in the playground and begun a second phase of change influenced by their native Hokkien and Cantonese. This CSE was of course not limited to the school compound, and was taken into other domains of interaction, including the home. These patterns of (standard) English and CSE acquisition were repeated throughout the first few decades of the twentieth century, which also saw an increase in the number of Chinese and Indian female students at English-medium schools and consequently, according to Gupta (ibid.: 115), the beginnings of the transmission of English contact varieties such as SCE natively in the home.

English-medium education became increasingly popular in the post-war and pre-independence years. After independence in 1965, English-medium education became the norm and in 1987 became an official requirement for all government-controlled schools. As Gupta (ibid.: 115–16) states, 'in every generation, a higher proportion of students would be second-generation English-educated, which would often mean that they spoke some English on arrival'. The continued English-medium education of women was 'crucial for this step', as it continued to allow the emergence of CSE as a native variety. By the end of the twentieth and the beginning of the twenty-first centuries, therefore, a significant proportion of children will have begun schooling already with some native competence in a variety of Singaporean English, including CSE.

Singaporean English ranges from a local standard, Standard Singapore English (SSE) to the most informal usages of CSE. In terms of standard conventions, SSE is very similar to British, American and Australian standard forms but also incorporates (like many, if not all standards), vocabulary and terminology which is peculiar to the native environment and which is sometimes drawn from the other languages present. CSE, on the other hand, appears to make use of a higher proportion of non-English words and structures that are quite different from those of SSE. The following examples of the same passage in SSE and CSE (Examples 6.1 and 6.2) neatly illustrate the difference between the two:

Example 6.1 SSE

You had better do this properly. If you don't, you may get told off. And since you are always asking her for favours, you should at least do this properly for her. You should! You cannot do it like this. Do it again. Come, let me help you.

Example 6.2 CSE

Eh, better do properly, lah. Anyhow do, wait kena scolding. And then, you always ask her for favour, and still don't want to do properly. Must lah. Like that do cannot. Do again. Come, I help you.

(after Alsagoff and Lick, 1998: 129)

In terms of vocabulary, all varieties of Singapore English, from the standard to CSE, make use of three main categories: (1) English words which are used in ways identical to other English varieties; (2) English words which are used differently from other English varieties; and (3) loanwords from other languages present in the Singapore context (Wee, 1998: 175). Unsurprisingly, the latter two groups have attracted the most attention from linguists. In terms of group (2), Wee (ibid.: 181–5) cites the use of words such as *batch* for human reference, as in *we have a batch of girls promoting this product*; *fellow* for both male and female reference (*she's a nice fellow*) and *send* with the meaning that the sender accompanies the sendee, as in *I'll send you home* ('I'll give you a lift home'). In terms of group (3), CSE makes use of Chinese loans such as *kiasu* (used to describe someone afraid of losing out), *samseng* ('ruffian/gangster'), *ang moh* ('a Caucasian') and *cheem* ('deep'/'profound' (somewhat ironic)). From Malay, Singaporean English has borrowed words such as *hantam* ('to make a wild guess'), *bedek* ('to bluff') and *tahan* ('to endure') (ibid.: 181). Many of these loans are adapted into English patterns (see Chapter 1, Section 1.3). *Cheem*, for instance, is used like English adjectives in the sense that it can be pre-modified by an adverb such as *very* and can itself pre-modify a noun (as in *some very cheem books (can be) found there*) and occur in an adjectival complement (as in *aiyah, lecturer very cheem, what*). It also takes English affixation: comparative *cheemer* and superlative *cheemest* exist, as does the derived noun *cheemness*. There are, however, certain distinctive Singaporean English usages: the English adjective > adverb derivation through suffixation of *–ly* is not possible for *cheem*, for example, making **cheemly* ungrammatical. In addition, the meaning of *cheem* in Singaporean English is strictly metaphorical, whereas its source Hokkien also uses it to refer to physical depth. In Singapore English, **the drain is very cheem* is therefore ungrammatical (Kandiah, 1998: 85–6).

Wee (1998: 191–5) also looks at the use of some of the 'exclamations and particles . . . [which] convey attitudes and emotions, and are often seen as lexical items which are most uniquely Singaporean'. These particles, it is worth noting, tend to have a higher rate of occurrence in CSE than SSE. Wee (1998: 192) looks, for example, at the use of *what* in exchanges such as that in Example 6.3:

Example 6.3 CSE *what*

A: Can I have some pins, ah?
B: Notice board got pins, *what*.

Wong (1994; cited in Wee, 1998: 192–3) states that B's use of *what* signals a contradiction to a belief that Speaker A has. Thus, B interprets A's request for pins as being predicated on the latter's belief that no pins are available. However, B knows that pins are on the noticeboard, and *what* signals that A is wrong in her original assumption.

An example of another common particle is *ma*, which is used in exchanges such as Example 6.4:

Example 6.4 CSE *ma*
A: How come you call me?
B: You page for me *ma*.

Ma is agreed to be a borrowing from the Chinese dialects, possibly either Hokkien or Cantonese, and in Singapore English, is typically 'attached to a proposition to indicate that the proposition serves as a justification' (Wong, 1994; paraphrased in Wee, 1998: 193). Thus, in this example, A's question makes it necessary for B to provide justification for calling. B's use of *ma* signals to A that that is precisely what he is doing in his answer that he was paged. Overall, Singaporean English, CSE in particular, makes use of approximately 11 different particles, mostly drawn from Hokkien and Cantonese. In addition to the two mentioned here, *ah* is commonly used to signal that the speaker expects agreement (as in *otherwise, how can be considered Singapore, ah?*) and *lah* to signal a strong assertion (as in *there's something here for everyone, lah*).

While SSE and CSE in general share the same lexicon (although the use of group (2) and group (3) words is higher in the latter), the two differ most significantly in terms of grammatical features. For example, Alsagoff and Lick (1998: 136–51) note the use of adverbials instead of verb inflection in CSE to indicate past reference (as in *she eat here yesterday*) as well as perfect aspect (as in *my baby speak already* 'my baby has started to speak'). *Already* is the most common adverbial for the latter function, and has been argued to have been influenced by the use of *liau* in Hokkien to mark completed action.[9] Alsagoff and Lick (ibid.: 139) note that some CSE users may make use of *inflected verb form + already* in expressing perfect aspect (as in *my father passed away already*) but the use of *auxiliary + inflected verb form* (as in *my father has passed away*) remains in the domain of SSE.

Progressive aspect in CSE is always signalled by verb-*ing* forms and sometimes the use of *still*. Hence, a CSE speaker could say *don't disturb them, they studying* or *don't disturb them, they still studying*. Whereas *still* is optional, verb-*ing* is not: hence **don't disturb them, they still study* would be considered ungrammatical. Present habitual aspect is signalled through use of *always*, as in *my brother always jog every morning*. Finally, the verb *to be* is not always used to link subjects and complements: CSE users can say *this coffee house very cheap, my sister in the garden, John my teacher*.

In terms of the noun phrase, certain English non-count nouns which have been inherited by CSE are treated as count, hence forms such as *furnitures* and *luggages*. In addition, some nouns can function as both count and non-count. Thus, when a noun is preceded by a quantifier, it carries a plural inflection (as in *her brother very rich – got four cars*) but when used in a generic sense, it remains uninflected: *she queue up very long to buy ticket for us*. Alsagoff and Lick (1998: 144) state that this pattern can also be found in Chinese languages such as Mandarin, as well as in Malay.

In terms of sentence structure, one of the most discussed features of CSE is the use of clauses where the subject and/or object is not explicitly expressed but is clear to participants in the interaction. Thus, a CSE sentence such as *every year must buy for Chinese New Year* might contextually translate as 'every year we must buy pussy-willow for Chinese New Year' (ibid.: 147). OSV word order is also quite common in CSE, as in *certain medicine we don't stock in our dispensary*. Yes/no questions are typically signalled by a 'tag' *or not*, which is added to a declarative statement, as in *you can eat pork or not?* A common idiomatic question is *Can or not?* which essentially asks for the addressee's opinion about, or approval for, whatever is being asked. The set answer is either a positive *can* or a negative *cannot*. Finally, CSE also makes use of the tags *is it?* or *isn't it?* The former is used when the questioner is genuinely soliciting information and the latter when she assumes that there may be some disagreement about a proposition. Thus, utterances such as *they give him a medal, is it?* and *they never give him a medal, is it?* are asking whether someone has or has not received a medal. *They give him a medal, isn't it?*, on the other hand, signals that the questioner believes that a medal has been given but that there may be some disagreement over this. It can therefore be roughly translated into 'Am I not correct in assuming that they gave him a medal?' (ibid.: 150–1).

These examples of grammatical and lexical usage should clearly illustrate that CSE is a systematic, rule-governed and dynamic native tongue for its users. None of the features highlighted, from lexical borrowing and change in meaning to the use of OSV structure and tag questions, are in any way unusual or typologically distinct. Yet, CSE has carried, for many Singaporeans, heavy social stigma as 'bad' or 'broken' English, largely because it is inevitably compared to standard forms such as SSE (as well as those of Britain and America) which are perceived as 'correct'. CSE has been viewed as a local corruption of a language which is important internationally for trade, science and technology, for fostering a sense of a shared national identity, as well as for individual economic and social advancement (Professor Jayakumar, the Minister of State, in *The Straits Times*, 19 August 1982; cited in Bokhorst-Heng, 1998: 290).[10] Since the 1970s, the government has shown concern about CSE, stating that it was of paramount importance that the English used by Singaporeans was 'internationally intelligible' (*The Straits Times*, 18 August 1977; cited in Bokhorst-Heng, 1998: 303). Bokhorst-Heng states that this concern led to increased recruitment of native English-speaking teachers (who, presumably, were thought to have the best grip on standard forms of English), and to the organization of seminars and courses to 'improve' the level of English in companies and the civil service. However, CSE is acquired and used in informal contexts. Emphasizing the importance of standard forms and conventions may go some way to increasing proficiency in their use in certain domains but certainly will not eradicate the everyday use of CSE which, as we have seen, now has native speaker status. Thus, even in 1994, the former Prime Minister Lee Kuan Yew was speaking publicly against CSE, equating it with 'losers':

> I think it's important that you know the English language because it is the international language, and you speak it in the standard form. Do not speak Singlish! If you do, you are the loser. Only foreign academics like to write about it. You have to live with it. And your

interlocutors, when they hear you, their ears go askew. You detract from the message that you're sending.

(Speech to National University of Singapore students, 29 July 1994; cited in Gupta 1998a)

This perspective was also adopted by Lee Kuan Yew's successor, Prime Minister Goh Chok Tong, who in his 1999 National Day Rally Speech (*Speaking Good English*, 22 August 1999) implied that CSE was in effect a collection of linguistic 'bad habits' which could seriously impede the acquisition of a standard and so, personal development. It was difficult enough, he argued, for pupils to learn just 'one version' of English; and the challenge of having to 'unlearn' Singlish, 'or learn proper English on top of Singlish' would mean that they might 'end up unable to speak any language properly'. The Prime Minister also justified the use of standard English by arguing that its use would bring individual and (inter-)national economic advantage: 'to become an engineer, a technician, an accountant or a nurse,' he stated, 'you must have standard English, not Singlish'. Furthermore, did it not make economic sense to undertake any enterprise – 'publishing a newspaper, writing a company report, or composing a song' – in the language of the 'hundreds of millions who speak English around the world?' Such realities, the Prime Minister concluded, clearly showed that Singapore could not be 'a first-world economy or go global with Singlish'.

Goh Chok Tong drove his point home by comparing CSE to other forms also often stigmatized as corruptions of 'proper' languages: pidgins and creoles. He warned that if Singlish remained unchecked, then 'the final logical outcome is that we too will develop our own type of pidgin English, spoken only by three million Singaporeans, which the rest of the world will find quaint but incomprehensible'.

For Goh Chok Tong, CSE has been the result of limited access to 'proper' English through education and the home: 'many of us', he states, 'studied in Chinese, Malay or Tamil schools, or came from non-English-speaking homes even though we went to English schools.' It is therefore a regrettable mistake ('we cannot help it and it is nothing to be ashamed of') which fortunately can be rectified by 'discouraging the use of Singlish'.

Discouragement, the Prime Minister stated, would take place through the education system. Many schools had already implemented Speak English campaigns, which not only included speech and drama programmes to 'promote good English' but also fined students caught speaking CSE. The Ministry of Education also began revising its English Language syllabus in line with promoting the use of 'good' English and Goh Chok Tong announced that they would also provide English proficiency courses for the eight thousand teachers of English language in primary and secondary schools (eventually leading to the Singapore Cambridge Certificate in the Teaching of English Grammar).

As testimony to the power of 'proper' schooling, Phua Chu Kang, a national television actor who used CSE on television, acknowledged that he had made the 'teaching of proper English more difficult' by making Singlish 'attractive and fashionable'. He agreed, said the Prime Minister, to enrol himself in English-improvement classes, since he had forgotten 'what he had learnt in school and his English [had therefore gone] from bad to worse.' Goh Chok Tong concluded that 'if Phua Chu Kang can improve himself, surely so can the rest of us.'

The Speak Good English Movement emerged soon after as a formal body whose objective was to 'promote good English among Singaporeans'. 'Good English' is defined as 'grammatically correct English . . . where rules for constructing sentences are strictly adhered to and avoiding words and phrases from local dialects'. In addition, pronunciation is 'not an issue but should be accurate'.[11] The specification of 'grammatical correctness' and 'accuracy', plus the non-specification of what features they actually refer to, indicate that the campaigners have some standards, or conventions of usage, in mind. The Movement's on-line lessons (60 in all) in how to use 'good English' in interactions ranging from buying cutlery or making a date to getting on with work colleagues show that a clear objective is to discourage Singlish as inappropriate in most contexts, since it impedes clear communication as well as positive self-presentation.[12] Each lesson takes the form of a conversation between two fictional characters and incorporates commentary and 'correction' from a narrator. Example 6.5 illustrates the typical format of the lessons:

Example 6.5 Lesson 23 (Conversation between a sales assistant (SA) and a customer (Simon))

Simon:	I'd like to get some cutlery.
SA:	Don't have, lor.
Simon:	Cutlery? Knives? Forks? Spoons?
SA:	Oh, yes, yes. Over here. Like or not? How many you want?
Simon:	Umm, let me see. I'll need some spoons . . .
SA:	Teaspoons, is it?
Simon:	Well . . .

The narrator comments that 'the shop assistant certainly confused Simon', and states that the sales assistant's questions such as *teaspoons, is it?* sound rude (although perfectly appropriate in Singlish; see above). 'Good' English forms (which are also 'polite') such as *would you like teaspoons?* and *would you like some of these?* are therefore recommended instead.

Lessons such as these are aimed at young Singaporeans (given that they are on-line, can be accessed by phone and are centred around a fictional group of 'young, dynamic whiz kids at *HotDotCom*'). Their potential success, however, in 'turning' their target audience is uncertain, given that they are in some ways out of step with the linguistic realities of Singapore. Take, for instance, the construction of CSE as a medium which fosters miscommunication *within* its speech community and in settings where it is normally used (as here, in an interaction with a local shopkeeper). The premise that Simon, as a native Singaporean, would be fazed by CSE seems somewhat unrealistic. Though not quite in the same context, a similar point had been made in 1983, when the *Straits Times* ran an article in which a CSE conversation between two nurses was criticized. One reader wrote in their defence that 'given the context and presumably, the tacit understanding between the nurses, any other way of saying the same thing would sound most affected and ridiculous' (cited in Bokhorst-Heng, 1998: 304). The *Business Times* (25 June 1992) also noted that CSE was becoming increasingly used in the workplace between young professionals, to express both solidarity and identity (cited in Bokhorst-Heng, 1998: 304). However, they did not use CSE when a foreigner was in the group, making it clear that it serves certain functions for its users in such a context, and also that they are very much aware of when it is appropriate. Overall, if young CSE speakers have such awareness of the appropriateness of CSE and standard English in different domains and confidence in their ability to control both, then it may be very difficult to convince them that there is anything truly wrong with CSE interactions such as that in Example 6.6.

It is also worth noting in this context that a strong link exists not only between CSE and everyday life, but also between CSE and local identity. The young professionals mentioned in the *Business Times* above clearly have such a sense, and the reader of the *Straits Times* who wrote in defence of the CSE conversation between the nurses went on to state that CSE was 'distinctively and delightfully Singaporean. We don't have to apologise for it and we should be free to use it – unblushingly – when the occasion arises' (Bokhorst-Heng, 1998: 304). Catherine Lim, a native novelist, was quoted in the *New York Times* (1 July 2001) as saying 'I need Singlish to express a Singaporean feeling', and a local taxi-driver, Neo Lolaine, as stating that Singlish belonged to all Singaporeans. This is not to say that all Singaporeans look as favourably on CSE: there are a significant number who agree with the government that it is simply a corruption of English, or who have branded it the result of 'mongrel-lingualism' (the *Straits Times*, 24 January 1985; quoted in Bokhorst-Heng, 1998: 304).

From Swift to Goh Chok Tong, it can be seen that the language through which a nation presents itself to the rest of the world is of primary importance: it needs to embody and express success and potential. However, from eighteenth-century everyday users of English to twenty-first-century users of Singlish, language is not something that they necessarily want controlled or legislated. Academies and 'good' language campaigns may well have a long and difficult fight on their hands.

6.4 The Twenty-First Century and Beyond: Where Will English Boldly Go?

Throughout this book, we have seen English change from a collection of Germanic dialects used by a relatively small population into a language that has had, and is continuing to have, global effect. At this point, the global importance of English seems truly unquestionable. But is this secure position likely to continue? Crystal (1997: 139) points out that it is difficult to predict what will happen to English, especially since there are no precedents for understanding the potential fate (or fates) of a language 'when it achieves genuine world status'. In *The Future of English?* Graddol (1997) agrees that accurate prediction is unlikely but also maintains that the fortunes of the language will be linked to economic, demographic and political changes across the world, and the often competing trends that will emerge as the 'new world order' of the twenty-first century becomes established. Thus, for example, the economic dominance of the OECD countries – which has helped circulate English in the new market economies of the world – is being eroded as Asian economies grow and become the source, rather than the recipient, of cultural and economic flows. Population statistics suggest that the populations of the rich countries are ageing and that in the coming decades young adults with disposable income will be found in Asia and Latin America rather than in the US and Europe. Educational trends in many countries suggest that languages other than English are already providing significant competition in school curricula . . . As the world is in transition, so the English language is itself taking new forms . . . on the one hand, the use of English as a global lingua franca requires intelligibility and the setting and maintenance of standards. On the other hand, the increasing adoption of English as a second language, where it takes on local forms, is leading to fragmentation and diversity.

(Graddol, 1997: 2–3)

Its future is therefore unlikely to be one of unchallenged, monolingual supremacy. In the rest of this section, we will look at some of Graddol's (ibid.: 56–61) predictions for the use of and 'desire' for English across the globe as the twenty-first century progresses.[13]

One of the major issues Graddol (ibid.: 56) addresses is whether a single world-wide standard English is likely to emerge. Will British or American standard English, for example, become a form which everyone looks to as a model of correctness and which will serve as a global lingua franca; or will those roles be filled by some 'new world standard . . . which supersedes national models for the purposes of international communication and teaching'? At the moment, the fact that English is increasingly serving as a lingua franca means that some measure of global uniformity in usage (cf. Milroy and Milroy's set of 'linguistic conventions') will be – if this process has not already begun – established. At the same time, however, as the language is appropriated as an important L2 in various communities, it also increasingly becomes, as we saw in Section 6.3, involved in the construction of local cultural identities. The effects of this are twofold: not only are 'hybrid' varieties such as CSE developing but also local, standard forms of the language (such as SSE). While various standard forms are likely to maintain a high level of mutual intelligibility across regions, they will certainly each contain distinctive usages and structures.

The English Language Teaching (ELT) industry currently serves as one of the main disseminators of standardized conventions across the globe. As Strevens (1992: 39; cited in Graddol, 1997: 56) states, 'throughout the world . . . two components of English are taught and learned without variation: these are its grammar and its core vocabulary'. At the moment, these conventions of grammar and vocabulary are predominantly based on models of American and British English, but there is no reason why L2 English countries could not promote their own respective standards through ELT publishing, thus creating diverse successful markets. As Graddol (1997: 56) states, 'there is no reason why, say, an Asian standard English may not gain currency' as a model in other areas. However, such new standards will not replace older ones easily. As Graddol (ibid.: 57) points out, the British standard, for instance, still carries a great deal of currency:

Most territories in which English is spoken as a second language still have an (ambiguous) orientation to British English; British publishers have a major share of the global ELT market and there are signs that even US companies are using the British variety to gain greater acceptance in some world markets. Microsoft, for example, produces two English versions of intellectual property on CD-ROM, such as the *Encarta Encyclopaedia*: a domestic (US English) edition and a 'World English' edition based on British English.

Graddol (ibid.: 57) concludes that, given the importance of the ELT industry, it would seem that it is 'non-native speakers who [will] decide whether a US model, a British one, or one based on a second language variety will be taught, learned and used' in different areas (ELT publishers already provide materials in several standard Englishes). Thus, the development of a single world standard English seems unlikely, and a more viable prediction is for 'a continued "polycentrism" for English', in which a number of standards, including older ones such as those of Britain and America, will compete across the global market.

Another question raised in *The Future of English?* concerns which languages are likely to join English as languages of global importance. Such predictions, however, and the basis on which to make them, are not easily determined. Crystal (1997: 7), for example, has suggested that political (particularly military) might is a significant factor for language use – something which may have been true once, but which does not seem as viable a force today, given 'changes in the nature of national power . . . the way that cultural values are projected and . . . the way markets are opened for the circulation of goods and services' (Graddol, 1997: 59). Graddol (ibid.) therefore proposes, as an alternative, that economic and demographic factors might be more useful for shedding light on how languages acquire importance. The *engco* (English Company) model used for projections in *The Future of English?* considers economic factors 'such as openness to world trade', demographic statistics such as numbers of young speakers of a language, and the human development index (HDI) for different countries. The HDI, produced by the UN, indicates the proportion of literate native speakers of a language 'capable of generating intellectual resources' in it. Together, these factors are put together to calculate a linguistic index of 'global influence'; in other words, to provide an indication of which languages belong to native speakers who have the means and wherewithal to promote themselves, their cultures and of course their languages in the wider world. While Graddol does not claim that the *engco* model is the most accurate and satisfactory way of generating indications of linguistic 'global influence', he maintains that 'it does seem to capture something of the relative relations between world languages which other indices, based crudely on economic factors or numbers of native speakers, do not convey'. Thus, an *engco* generation for the top six languages in 1995 demonstrated that English was way ahead, in terms of global influence, of Chinese – a language whose importance is sometimes predicated on the sheer number of speakers.

Projections on the *engco* model, taking once more into account economic and demographic changes, as well as the possibility of language shift to tongues that become increasingly attractive to speakers, predict that the 'big six' languages in 2050 are likely to be English, Spanish, Arabic, Chinese and Hindi/Urdu, and that languages currently perceived as globally significant, such as German, French and Japanese, may concomitantly decline in status. In a hypothetical world-language hierarchy, these six would occupy the top stratum, followed by the regional language of major trade blocs (including Russian and Malay), the national languages of nation states and finally, the local languages of the world, which will carry varying degrees of official recognition. This projected hierarchy therefore sees increased linguistic pluralism at the apex – in part a result, as Graddol (1997: 59) reminds us, of shifts from less prestigious languages at the lower levels. Many of the latter, perhaps several thousand, will be lost. The shift to oligopoly, then, will bring 'pluralism in one sense, but huge loss of diversity in another' (ibid.: 59), partly offset by an increase in the number of new hybrid varieties, many of which will result from contact with English.

Finally for our purposes, Graddol (ibid.: 60–1) looks at the potential influence of technology, including satellite television and the Internet, on the use of English. The relationship between the language and leading-edge technology, particularly in the domain of computers and information systems, has traditionally been a close one. A great deal of research and developmental work takes place in America (albeit in collaboration with Japanese transnational companies), and the dissemination of the results of such work, through journals and conferences for example, tends to occur in English. Inevitably, this has meant that a great deal of the technology – from keyboards and software to support systems – has been developed around English. However, this interdependence between (English) tongue and technology may not last, since as the field continues to advance, increasing amounts of technological support for other languages will be made. Indeed, this process has already begun: desktop publishing and laser printers can now handle a significant number of other languages and a variety of writing systems. In addition, computer systems and software can now also operate in many other languages, and in many cases, 'the user can further customise the product, allowing even very small languages, unknown to the manufacturer, to be accommodated' (ibid.: 61). Thus, whereas the technological world seemed once to be geared solely to the benefit of the English speaker, it is no longer necessarily the case that this exclusive relationship will last.

In terms of satellite television culture, Graddol (ibid.: 60) believes that here too, English will lose some ground. It has played a significant role in the promotion of English across the globe – Star TV in Asia, for example, used English in its start-up phase since this was guaranteed to reach large audiences, as did MTV in its early years. However, the development of satellite technology has made a larger number of channels available, and increasing numbers of operators from around the world have been able, and will continue, to enter the market. Thus, the potential for non-English medium programming, for 'local and niche audiences', is growing, and in fact, such programming has already begun. National networks in English-speaking countries are establishing operations in other areas of the world, but are making use of local languages. MTV in certain areas of Switzerland, for example, makes almost complete use of German or at the very least, of German subtitles. Graddol (ibid.: 60) states that at the time of writing, the American network CBS was intending to launch a news and entertainment channel in Brazil which broadcast in Portuguese; and that CNN International was seeking to establish Spanish and Hindi services – an aim which has since been realized.

In addition, non-English medium national networks are also entering the world of satellite technology. Doordashan, the Indian state-television company, for example, is looking to provide satellite broadcasting to audiences from South-East Asia to Europe. In a similar vein, 'Spanish television networks in Mexico are . . . establishing a global presence, producing programming for Europe as well as for Spanish speakers elsewhere in the Americas' (ibid.: 60). Thus, such trends indicate that English will, as in other areas, come to share its satellite space with other languages. A 'more crowded and linguistically plural audio-visual landscape in the twenty-first century' (ibid.) is likely to result.

Finally, it seems that English dominance on the Internet may also decrease. Currently, it appears to be the dominant language on-line, largely because 90 per cent of Internet hosts are based in English-speaking countries. It is therefore unsurprising that the majority of web-sites, and of web-based communications, are in English. However, the Internet appears to have become an important support mechanism for 'minority and diasporic affinity' groups. There is therefore an increasing use of languages other than English on-line (and remember that the technology to support this is growing concomitantly) and, interestingly, to debate the perceived hegemony of the latter language (ibid.: 61).

Graddol (ibid.) believes that the quantity of Internet materials in languages other than English will expand significantly in the next decade or so and will be supported by the increasing use of local languages for informal social and family email communication. Again, this is not to say that English will be marginalized: instead, as in other media and domains, it will become one of many options, and will probably remain dominant in certain areas, such as 'international forums, the dissemination of scientific and technical knowledge, [and] advertising'. Overall, the 80 per cent monopoly that English has had on computer-based communication is expected to fall to 40 per cent by about 2010.

6.5 Conclusion

The last section has outlined some of the predicted socio-political directions that English may follow in its global journey, but they are just that – predictions. They are, of course, reasoned and plausible, but we can no more make complete and accurate forecasts for the next few centuries and beyond than PIE speakers could a few thousand years ago about the divergences and developments of their own language. We simply cannot know if entities such as Space Crew English (see Chapter 2) will ever exist, or if English will become a mother-node on a linguistic family tree, or a dead branch. Similarly, we cannot predict exactly what linguistic changes English will experience as it moves into new domains of usage and is adopted by new communities of speakers: what sound changes will occur, what new meanings will emerge, what auxiliaries will grammaticalize; overall what will be adopted and rejected by myriad speech communities around the world remains a matter for conjecture.

This is not to say that our story of English has ended. What we can be sure of is that, as long as English continues to be a living language functioning in both native speaker communities and multi-lingual situations of contact, it will continue to undergo linguistic change of the nature described in Chapter 1, which in some cases will ultimately play a role in 'bigger' changes such as creolization (see Chapter 5, Section 5.5), or the emergence of contact varieties of the language (see Section 6.3) and perhaps eventually, in the distant future, new daughter languages. We can also be fairly certain that various patterns and features of English usage will continue to attract both complaint and approbation, and possibly even further attempts at standardization as it becomes used in new media. On a larger scale, it also seems likely that, as in past and current times, the abstract notion of *the English language* will be intertwined with ideas of individual and national identity, both embraced as a language which ensures and reflects socio-economic success, and reviled as a language of imperialism which spreads the influence of one culture at the linguistic expense of others. Overall, what we can be completely certain of is that its ultimate history, like that of every living language, is far from over; and our current moment as users of the language is simply another chapter in its story.

6.6 Study Questions

1. Examine two cases of language obsolescence (in different territories) in which shift to English has played, or is playing, a major role. (Useful readings to start with are given in note 3.) Consider the following two questions:

a. Are language shift and language loss proceeding in exactly the same way in both cases? What similarities and differences obtain between the two?

b. Are revival attempts being made for the obsolescing languages in your case studies? If so, what form do they take? Assess how successful they currently are, and/or are likely to be. Useful additional reading: Dorian (1989), Fishman (1991), Gal (1979), Schmidt (1985).

2. In light of the discussion in Section 6.2, consider the following questions:

a. Do any or all of Swift's arguments for maintaining standard forms still have currency today (perhaps in more modern guises)?

b. Swift (1712) targeted certain groups as being responsible for language change and corruption. What groups are blamed for the alleged decline of the language today?

c. In the light of your answers to (a) and (b), do you agree with Cameron's (1995) assertion that anxieties about language standards are in reality a metaphor for deeper socio-political anxieties? Justify your answer.

d. In Section 6.2, we saw that Swift believed that only the 'learned and polite' (typically those at the high upper end of the social ladder) could arbitrate successfully on matters of language use. Who are the modern setters of standards?

e. Is it possible to regulate a spoken standard? Give reasons for your answer.

Useful readings: Cameron (1995: Chapter 3 for (a)–(c)), Watts (2002: Chapter 8 for (d)), Millar (2002: Chapter 9 for (e)), Milroy and Milroy (1999), Crowley (1996: Chapter 5).

3. Examine the establishment of English in a nineteenth-century colony, and compare its situation in that new environment with the account of Singaporean English in Section 6.3 (try to choose one that will offer a good contrast). What parallels (if any) obtain between the two?

Notes

1. English speakers are typically divided into three groups, and one of the best-known models is that of Kachru, which uses the categories of *inner circle*, *outer circle* and *expanding circle*. Each circle represents 'the types of spread, patterns of acquisition, and the functional allocation of English in diverse cultural contexts' (Kachru, 1992: 356). Colonial settlements of substantial numbers of L1 English speakers (as occurred in America, Canada, Australia, New Zealand, Wales, Scotland and Ireland) established English as a distinctive, native language (ENL) in these countries. These comprise the *inner circle*. The second diaspora, which affected areas such as India, West and East Africa and the Philippines) established English as an elite second language (ESL) and created the *outer circle*. The *expanding circle* comprises EFL areas, such as China, Indonesia and Saudi Arabia. The English spoken in the *inner circle* is classified as 'norm-providing', that of the *outer circle* as 'norm-developing' and that of the *expanding circle* as 'norm-dependent'. Although the model is still widely used, it has also been criticized (see for example, Jenkins, 2003: 17–18, and Kandiah, 1998: Chapter 1, for an incisive discussion). One of its main criticisms is that it places ENL areas at the heart of the spread of English globally. As Graddol (1997) and Jenkins (2003) point out, however, this is no longer a straightforward issue, and ESL and EFL areas appear to be becoming increasingly influential in this question.

2. See Graddol (1997: 12–14) for a more detailed discussion of this point.

3. See, for example, Jones (1998) on Welsh, Dorian (1981) on Scots Gaelic, Hindley (1990) on Irish Gaelic, Schiffman (1996) on language policy in America.

4. Watts (2002: 162) states that 'the eighteenth century ideal of politeness was composed of the following values: decorum, grace, beauty, symmetry and order'.

5. This was a fairly common complaint in the early eighteenth century. Oldmixon, for example, writing in 1712 quotes Edmund Waller's lines: 'Poets that lasting Marble seek/Must Write in Latin or in Greek;/We write in Sand' (in Crowley, 1996: 65).

6. Swift wrote of the Greeks that 'from *Homer* to *Plutarch* are above a Thousand years; so long at least the purity of the *Greek* Tongue may be allow'd to last, and we know not how far before', and that the Chinese 'have Books in their Language above Two Thousand Years old, neither have the frequent Conquests of the *Tartars* been able to alter it' (1712: 15–16).

7. See here Watts (2002: 155–72) for a full and interesting discussion of ideals of *polite language* in eighteenth-century England.

8. See Baugh and Cable (2002: 274–6) for an overview of other influential publications.

9. See Bao (1995) for a detailed analysis of this use and its proposed derivation from Hokkien.

10. English is one of the four official languages of Singapore. The others are Malay (the national language), Mandarin and Tamil.

11. From the Speak Good English Movement website at http://www.goodenglish.org.sg/SGEM, which also offers excerpts of Goh Chok Tong's speech.

12. The lessons were developed jointly by the Speak Good English Campaign and the British Council in 2001–02.

13. For an in-depth discussion of the trends outlined here, see Graddol (1997), and the *Global English Newsletter* available online at http://www.engcool.com/GEN.

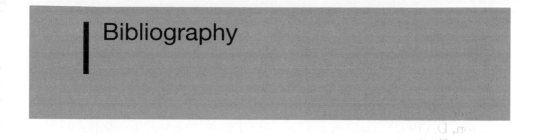

Bibliography

Alsagoff, L. and Lick, H.C. (1998) 'The grammar of Singapore English', in J.A. Foley *English in New Cultural Contexts*, Oxford: Oxford University Press, pp. 125–51.

Asher, R.E. (ed.) (1994) *The Encyclopaedia of Language and Linguistics*, Oxford: Pergamon Press.

Bailey, C-J.N. and Maroldt, K. (1977) 'The French lineage of English', in J.M. Meisel (ed.) *Langues en Contact*, Tübingen: TBL Verlag Narr, pp. 21–53.

Baker, P.S. (ed.) *The Beowulf Reader*, New York: Garland Publishing, Inc.

Barber, C. (1981) '*You* and *thou* in Shakespeare's *Richard III*', in V. Salmon and E. Burness (eds) *A Reader in the Language of Shakespearean Drama*, Amsterdam: John Benjamins, pp. 163–79.

Barber, C. (1993) *The English Language: A Historical Introduction*, Cambridge: Cambridge University Press.

Barber, C. (1997) *Early Modern English*, Edinburgh: Edinburgh University Press.

Bao, Z.M. (1995) '*Already* in Singapore English', *World Englishes*, 14, 2: 181–8.

Baugh, T. and Cable, A. (2002) *A History of the English Language*, 5th edn, London: Routledge.

Beal, J. (1996) 'Modals on Tyneside', in D. Graddol *et al.* (eds) *English*, London: Routledge, pp. 252–3.

Bickerton, D. (1986) 'The sociohistorical matrix of creolization', *Journal of Pidgin and Creole Languages*, 7, 2: 307–18.

Bokhorst-Heng, W. (1998) 'Language planning and management in Singapore', in J.A. Foley *et al. English in New Cultural Contexts*, Oxford: Oxford University Press, pp. 287–309.

Bradley, S.A.J. (1982) *Anglo-Saxon Poetry: An Anthology of Old English*, London: Dent.

Bright, W. (ed.) (1992) *International Encyclopaedia of Linguistics*, Oxford: Oxford University Press.

Brown, K. (1991) 'Double modals in Hawick Scots', in P. Trudgill and J.K. Chambers (eds) *Dialects of English: Studies in Grammatical Variation*, London: Longman, pp. 74–103.

Brown, R. and Gilman, A. (1960) 'The pronouns of power and solidarity', in P.P. Giglioli (ed.) *Language and Social Context*, London: Penguin, pp. 252–82.

Bucholtz, M. (1996) 'Geek the girl: language, femininity and female nerds', in J. Ahlers *et al.* (eds) *Gender and Belief Systems*, Berkeley, CA: Berkeley Women and Language Group, pp. 119–32.

Buchstaller, I. (2002) 'He goes and I'm like: the new quotatives re-visited', Internet Proceedings of the University of Edinburgh Postgraduate Conference (http://www.ling.ed.ac.uk/~pgc/archive/2002/pgc02-programme.html).

Burnley, J.D. (1992) The History of the English Language: A Source Book, London: Longman.

Burrow, J.A. and Turville-Petre, T. (1996) A Book of Middle English, 2nd edn, Oxford: Blackwell Publishers Ltd.

Cameron, D. (1992) Feminism and Linguistic Theory, London: Routledge.

Cameron, D. (1995) Verbal Hygiene, London: Routledge.

Cassidy, F.G. (1980) 'The place of Gullah', American Speech, 55: 3–15.

Cavalli-Sforza, L.L. (2000) Genes, Peoples and Languages, New York: North Point Press.

Chance, J. (1991) 'Grendel's mother as epic anti-type of the Virgin and the Queen', in R.D. Fulk (ed.) Interpretations of Beowulf: A Critical Anthology, Bloomington, IN: Indiana University Press, pp. 251–63.

Chaudenson, R. (2001) Creolisation of Language and Culture, rev. edn, London: Routledge.

Cheshire, J. and Trudgill, P. (eds) (1998) The Sociolinguistics Reader: Gender and Discourse, vol. 2. London: Arnold.

Claiborne, R. (1990) English – Its Life and Times, London: Bloomsbury Publishing Ltd.

Cohen, J.J. and the Members of Interscripta (1995), Medieval Masculinities: Heroism, Sanctity and Gender (http://www.georgetown.edu/labyrinth/ e-center/ interscripta/mm.html).

Cohn, C. (1987) 'Slick 'ems, glick 'ems, Christmas trees and cookie cutters: nuclear language and how we learned to pat the bomb', Bulletin of Atomic Scientists, 43: 17–24.

Coupland, N. and Jaworksi, A. (1997) Sociolinguistics: A Reader and Coursebook, London: Macmillan.

Crowley, T. (1996) Language in History: Theories and Texts, London: Routledge.

Crystal, D. (1997) English as a Global Language, Cambridge: Cambridge University Press.

Crystal, D. (2004) The Stories of English, London: Allen Lane.

Dahood, R. (1994) 'Hugh De Morville, William of Canterbury, and anecdotal evidence for English language history', Speculum, 69, 1: 40–56.

Davis, N. (1979) A Chaucer Glossary, Oxford: Oxford University Press.

DeGraff, M. (2001) 'Morphology in creole genesis: linguistics and ideology', in M. Kenstowicz (ed.) Ken Hale: A Life in Language, Cambridge, MA: MIT Press, pp. 53–121.

Dorian, N. (1981) Language Death: The Life Cycle of a Scottish Gaelic Dialect, Philadelphia, PA: University of Pennsylvania Press.

Dorian, N. (1989) Investigating Obsolescence: Studies in Language Contraction and Death, Cambridge: Cambridge University Press.

Dyen, I., Kruskal, J.B. and Black, P. (1992) 'An Indoeuropean classification: a lexicostatistical experiment', Transactions of the American Philosophical Society, 82, Part 5.

Eckert, P. (2002) 'Constructing meaning in social variation', paper presented at the Annual Meeting of the American Anthropological Association, New Orleans.

Eckert, P. (undated) 'California vowels' at http://www.stanford.edu/~eckert/vowels.html).

Eco, U. (1995) *The Search for the Perfect Language*, Oxford: Blackwell Publishers Ltd.

Ekwall, E. (1960) *The Concise Oxford Dictionary of English PlaceNames*, 4th edn, Oxford: Oxford University Press.

Fellows Jensen, G. (1972) *Scandinavian Settlement Names in Yorkshire*, Copenhagen.

Fennell, B.A. (2001) *A History of English: A Sociolinguistic Approach*, Oxford: Blackwell Publishers Ltd.

Fields, L. (1995) 'Early Bajan: creole or non-creole?', in J. Arends (ed.) *The Early Stages of Creolization*, Amsterdam: John Benjamins, pp. 89–112.

Fishman, J. (ed.) (2001) *Can Threatened Languages Be Saved?* Clevedon: Multilingual Matters.

Foley, J.A., Kandiah, T., Zhiming, B., Gupta, A.F., Alsagoff, L., Chee Lick, H., Wee, L., Talib, I.S. and Bokhorst-Heng, W. (1998) *English in New Cultural Contexts: Reflections from Singapore*, Oxford: Oxford University Press.

Frantzen, A.J. (1993) 'When women aren't enough', *Speculum*, 68, 2: 445–71.

Gal, S. (1979) *Language Shift*, New York: Academic Press.

Gamkrelidze, T.V. and Ivanov, V.V. (1990) 'The early history of Indo-European languages', *Scientific American*, March: 110 ff.

Global English Newsletter (2003) 'This year's new words', 25 July http://www.engcool.com/GEN/archive.php.

Görlach, M. (1991) *Introduction to Early Modern English*, Cambridge: Cambridge University Press

Graddol, D. (1997) *The Future of English?* London: The British Council.

Graddol, D., Leith, D. and Swann, J. (1996) *English: History, Diversity and Change*, London: Routledge.

Gupta, A.F. (1998a) 'Singapore Colloquial English? Or deviant standard English?', *Proceedings of the Second International Conference on Oceanic Linguistics*, 1: 43–57.

Gupta, A.F. (1998b) 'The situation of English in Singapore', in J.A. Foley *et al. English in New Cultural Contexts*, Oxford: Oxford University Press, pp. 106–26.

Hala, J. (1997) *The Parturition of Poetry and the Birthing of Culture: The Ides Algoecwif and Beowulf*, London: Pegasus Press.

Halsall, P. (ed.) (2000) 'Bede: ecclesiastical history of the English Nation, Book I', *Medieval Sourcebook*.

Hamer, R. (1970) *A Choice of Anglo-Saxon Verse*, London: Faber and Faber.

Hancock, I. (1980) 'Gullah and Barbadian: origins and relationships', *American Speech*, 55: 17–35.

Hardcastle, V. (ed.) (2000) *Biology Meets Psychology: Constraints, Connections, Conjectures*, Cambridge, MA: MIT Press.

Harris, R. (1988) *Language, Saussure and Wittgenstein*, London: Routledge.

Haugen, E. (1972) 'Dialect, language, nation', in J.B. Pride and J. Holmes (eds) *Sociolinguistics*, Harmondsworth: Penguin.

Heaney, S. (1999) *Beowulf: A New Translation*, London: Faber and Faber.

Highfield, R. (2002) 'Speaking English on the way', *Daily Telegraph*, 16 February.

Hindley, R. (1990) *The Death of the Irish Language: A Qualified Obituary*, London: Routledge.

Hock, H.H. (1986) *Principles of Historical Linguistics*, The Hague: Mouton de Gruyter.

Holm, J. (1988) *Pidgins and Creoles*, Vol. I: *Theory and Structure*, Cambridge: Cambridge University Press.

Holm, J. (1989) *Pidgins and Creoles*, Vol. II: *Reference Survey*, Cambridge: Cambridge University Press.

Honey, J. (1997) *Language is Power: The Story of Standard English and its Enemies*, London: Faber and Faber.

Ickowicz, C. (undated) 'Words: the building blocks of oratory and all other competitive speech events', at http://debate.uvm.edu/NFL/rostrumlib/oratoryickowicz0497.pdf.

Jenkins, J. (2003) *World Englishes*, London: Routledge.

Jones, C. (1988) *Grammatical Gender in English: 950–1250*, London: Croom Helm.

Jones, M.C. (1998) *Language Obsolescence and Revitalization: Linguistic Change in Two Sociolinguistically Contrasting Welsh Communities*, Oxford: Clarendon Press.

Kachru, B.B. (ed.) (1992) *The Other Tongue: English across Cultures*, 2nd edn, Urbana, ILL: University of Illinois Press.

Kandiah, T. (1998) 'The emergence of new Englishes', in J.A. Foley *et al. English in New Cultural Contexts*, Oxford: Oxford University Press, pp. 73–105.

Knowles, G. (1997) *A Cultural History of the English Language*, London: Edward Arnold.

Kortlandt, F. (1990) 'The spread of the Indo-Europeans', *Journal of Indo-European Studies*, 18: 131–40.

Labov, W. (1996) 'The organization of dialect diversity in North America', paper presented at the Fourth International Conference on Spoken Language Processing, Philadelphia.

Lal, P. (ed.) (1964) *Three Sanskrit Plays*, New York: New Directions Books.

Lass, R. (1975) 'Internal reconstruction and generative phonology', *Transactions of the Philological Society*, 1–26.

Lass, R. (1994) *Old English: A Historical Linguistic Companion*, Cambridge: Cambridge University Press.

Lass, R. (1997) *Historical Linguistics and Language Change*, Cambridge: Cambridge University Press.

Lees, C. (1997) 'Engendering religious desire: sex, knowledge and Christian identity in Anglo-Saxon England', *Journal of Medieval and Early Modern Studies*, 27, 1: 17–46.

Lees, C. and Overing, G.O. (2001) *Double Agents: Women and Clerical Culture in Anglo-Saxon England*, Philadelphia, PA: University of Pennsylvania Press.

Lehmann, W.P. (1973) 'A structural principle of language and its implications', *Language*, 49: 47–66.

Lehmann, W.P. and Malkiel, Y. (eds) *Perspectives on Historical Linguistics*, Amsterdam: John Benjamins.

Leith, D. (1983) *A Social History of English*, London: Routledge and Kegan Paul.

Levin, S. (1971) *The Indo-European and Semitic Languages*, Albany, NY: State University of New York.

Lightfoot, D. (1979) *Principles of Diachronic Syntax*, Cambridge: Cambridge University Press.

Lippi-Green, R. (1997) *English with an Accent*, London: Routledge.

Liuzza, R.M. (2000) *Beowulf: A New Verse Translation*, Canada: Broadview Press Ltd.

Mallory, J.P. (1989) *In Search of the Indo-Europeans: Language, Archaeology and Myth*, London: Thames and Hudson.

Marr, A. (2002) 'Notebook', *Guardian*, 16 October.

McMahon, A. (1994) *Understanding Language Change*, Cambridge: Cambridge University Press.

McMahon, A. and McMahon, R. (2003) 'Finding families: quantitative methods in language classification', *Transactions of the Philological Society*, 101, 1: 7–55.

Meillet, A. (1912) *Linguistique historique et linguistique générale*, Paris: Champion.

Meisel, J.M. (ed.) *Langues en Contact – pidgins – créoles – Languages in Contact*, Tübingen: TBL Verlag Narr, pp. 21–53.

Millar, S. (2002) 'Eloquence and elegance: ideals of communicative competence in spoken English', in R. Watts and P. Trudgill (eds) *Alternative Histories of English*, London: Routledge, pp. 173–90.

Mills, A.D. (1991) *A Dictionary of English Placenames*, Oxford: Oxford University Press.

Milroy, J. (2002) 'The legitimate language: giving a history to English', in R. Watts and P. Trudgill (eds) *Alternative Histories of English*, London: Routledge, pp. 7–26.

Milroy, J. and Milroy, L. (1999) *Authority in Language*, 3rd edn, London: Routledge.

Mitchell, B. (1985) *Old English Syntax*, Vol. I, Oxford: Oxford University Press.

Mitchell, B. (1995) *An Invitation to Old English and Anglo-Saxon England*, Oxford: Blackwell Publishers Ltd.

Morrish, J. (2001) *More Frantic Semantics: Further Adventures in Modern English*, Basingstoke: Macmillan Publishers Ltd.

Mufwene, S. (2001) *The Ecology of Language Evolution*, Cambridge: Cambridge University Press.

Mulholland, J. (1967) 'Thou and you in Shakespeare: a study in the second person pronoun', in V. Salmon and E. Burness (eds) *A Reader in the Language of Shakespearean Drama*, Amsterdam: John Benjamins, pp. 153–61.

Nettle, D. and Romaine, S. (2000) *Vanishing Voices*, Oxford: Oxford University Press.

Niles, N. (1980) 'Provincial English Dialects and Barbadian Speech', PhD dissertation, University of Michigan.

Orël, V.E. and Starostin, S. (1990) 'Etruscan as an East Caucasian language', in V. Shevoroshkin *Déné-Sino-Caucasian Languages*, Bochum: Brockmeyer, pp. 60–6.

Overing, G.R. (2000) 'The women of Beowulf: a context for interpretation', in P.S. Baker (ed.) *The Beowulf Reader*, New York: Garland Publishing Co., pp. 219–60.

Peterkin, T. (2002) 'Mowlam comes clean on that four letter word', *Daily Telegraph*, 13 May.

Platzer, H. (2001) 'Grammatical gender in Old English: a case of *No Sex, please, we're Anglo-Saxon?*' *VIEW[z] Vienna English Working Papers*, 10, 1: 34–48.

Pulleyblank, E.G. (1978) 'Sino-Tibetan and Indo-European: the case for a genetic comparison', paper delivered at the Conference on the Origin of Chinese Civilization. Berkeley, California, June.

Pyles, T. and Algeo, J. (1982) *The Origins and Development of the English Language*, New York: Harcourt Brace Jovanovich, Inc.

Renfrew, C. (1987) *Archaeology and Language*, London: Jonathan Cape.

Rickford, J. and Handler, J.S. (1994) 'Textual evidence on the nature of early Barbadian speech, 1676–1835', *Journal of Pidgin and Creole Languages*, 9: 221–55.

Romaine, S. and Lange, D. (1991) 'The use of *like* as a marker of reported speech and thought: a case of grammaticalization in progress', in J. Cheshire and P. Trudgill (eds) *The Sociolinguistics Reader*, London: Arnold, pp. 240–77.

Rothwell, W. (1998) 'Arrivals and departures: the adoption of French terminology into Middle English', *The Anglo-Norman Online Hub*, pp. 1–18. (http://www.anglo-norman.net/).

Salmon, V. and Burness, E. (eds) (1987) *A Reader in the Language of Shakespearean Drama*, Amsterdam: John Benjamins Publishing Co.

Schama, S. (2000) *A History of Britian: At the Edge of the World 3000BC–1603AD*, London: BBC Books Worldwide.

Schendl, H. (1997) '*To London fro Kent / Sunt predia depopulantes*: Code-switching and medieval English macaronic poems', *VIEW[z] Vienna English Working Papers*, 6, 1: 52–66.

Schiffman, H.F. (1996) *Linguistic Culture and Language Policy*, London: Routledge.

Schmidt, A. (1985) *Young People's Dyirbal: An Example of Language Death from Australia*, Cambridge: Cambridge University Press.

Sebba, M. (1997) *Contact Languages: Pidgins and Creoles*, London: Macmillan Press Ltd.

Shevoroshkin, V. (ed.) (1990) *Proto-Languages and Proto-Cultures*, Bochum: Brockmeyer.

Shevoroshkin, V. (ed.) (1991) *Déné-Sino-Caucasian Languages*, Bochum: Brockmeyer.

Singh, I. (1997) 'Superstratal influence on the formation of Trinidad's English-based creole', PhD dissertation, University of Cambridge.

Singh, I. (2000) *Pidgins and Creoles: An Introduction*, London: Arnold.

Smith, A.H.G. (1984) *The Emergence of a Nation State: The Commonwealth of England 1529–1660*, London: Longman.

Smith, J. (1996) *An Historical Study of English*, London: Routledge.

Smith, J.J. (1999) *Essentials of Early English*, London: Routledge.

Starostin, S. (1984) 'On the hypothesis of a genetic connection between the Sino-Tibetan languages and the Yeniseian and North-Caucasian languages', in V. Shevoroshkin *Déné-Sino-Caucasian Languages*, Bochum: Brockmeyer, pp. 12–41.

Strang, B.M.H. (1970) *A History of English*, London: Methuen.

Swift, J. (1712) *A Proposal for Correcting, Improving, and Ascertaining the English Tongue* (at gopher://dept.english.upenn.edu/00/E-text/PEAL/Swift/proposal).

Thomason, S.G. and Kaufman, T. (1988) *Language Contact, Creolization and Genetic Linguistics*, Berkeley, CA: University of California Press.

Trask, L. (1996) *Historical Linguistics*, London: Arnold.

Traugott, E. (1982) 'From propositional to textual and expressive meanings: some semantic-pragmatic aspects of grammaticalization', in W.P. Lehmann and Y. Malkiel (eds) *Perspectives on Historical linguistics*, Amsterdam: John Benjamins.

Treharne, E.M. and Pulsiano, P. (2001) *A Companion to Anglo-Saxon Literature and Culture*, London: Blackwell.

Trudgill, P. (2002) 'The history of the lesser-known varieties of English', in R. Watts and P. Trudgill (eds) *Alternative Histories of English*, London: Routledge, pp. 29–44.

Trudgill, P. and Watts, R. (eds) (2002) *Alternative Histories of English*, London: Routledge.

Ullmann, S. (1962) *Semantics: An Introduction to the Science of Meaning*, Oxford: Blackwell Publishing Ltd.

Voegelin, C.F. and Voegelin, F.M. (1977) *Classification and Index of the World's Languages*, New York: Faber and Faber.

Wales, K. (2002) ' "North of Watford Gap": a cultural history of Northern English (from 1700)', in R. Watts and P. Trudgill (eds) *Alternative Histories of English*, London: Routledge, pp. 45–66.

Wardaugh, R. (1992) *An Introduction to Sociolinguistics*, Oxford: Blackwell Publishing Ltd.

Watts, D. (1987) *The West Indies: Patterns of Development, Culture and Environment Change since 1492*, Cambridge: Cambridge University Press.

Watts, R. (2002) 'From polite language to educated language: the re-emergence of an ideology', in R. Watts and P. Trudgill (eds) *Alternative Histories of English*, London: Routledge, pp. 155–72.

Watts, R. and Trudgill, P. (eds) (2002) *Alternative Histories of English*, London: Routledge.

Wee, L. (1998) 'The lexicon of Singapore English', in J.A. Foley *et al.* (eds) *English in New Cultural Contexts*, Oxford: Oxford University Press, pp. 175–200.

Whinnom, K. (1965) 'Origin of the European-based creoles and pidgins', *Orbis*, 15: 509–27.

Wimsatt, W.C. (1999) 'Genes, memes and cultural heredity', *Biology and Philosophy*, 14: 279–310.

Wimsatt, W.C. (2000) 'Generativity, entrenchment, evolution and innateness', in V. Hardcastle (ed.) *Biology Meets Psychology*, Cambridge, MA: MIT Press, pp. 139–79.

Winford, D. (1993) *Predication in Caribbean English Creoles*, Amsterdam: Benjamins.

Wolfram, W. and Schilling-Estes, N. (1998) *American Speech*, Oxford: Blackwell Publishing Ltd.

Wurm, S. (1982) *Papuan Languages of Oceania*, Tubingen: Gunter Narr.

Index